The Low-Carb Baking and Dessert Cookbook

Ursula Solom

Foreword by Mary Dan Eades, M.D.

John Wiley & Sons, Inc.

Published by John Wiley & Sons, Inc., Hoboken, New Jersey
Published simultaneously in Canada

Design and production by Navta Associates, Inc.

For general information about our other products and services, please contact our Customer Care Department within the United States at (800) 762-2974, outside the United States at (317) 572-3993 or fax (317) 572-4002.

Wiley also publishes its books in a variety of electronic formats. Some content that appears in print may not be available in electronic books. For more information about Wiley products, visit our web site at www.wiley.com.

Library of Congress Cataloging-in-Publication Data:
Solom, Ursula.
The low-carb baking and dessert cookbook / Ursula Solom ; foreword by Mary Dan Eades.
    p.   cm.
Includes index.
ISBN 0-471-67832-5 (cloth)
1. Low-carbohydrate diet—Recipes. 2. Desserts. 3. Baking. I. Title.
RM237.73S637 2005
641.5'6383—dc22   2004014935

Printed in the United States of America

10 9 8 7 6 5 4 3 2 1

I dedicate this book to the few physicians and researchers who, despite condemnation from their peers, have persisted in bringing us this wondrous new way to look at nutrition. It has given us a diet that goes far beyond weight loss, a diet that can improve the health of virtually anyone willing to give it a serious try. My deepest gratitude goes to those among these pioneers who have affected my life directly and personally: Michael R. Eades, M.D., and Mary Dan Eades, M.D., whose informative books explain complex diet issues clearly, and Richard K. Bernstein, M.D., who is selflessly devoting his time to help people with diabetes live healthier and longer lives. His ideas are based on the principles of carbohydrate restriction he discovered on his own as a person with diabetes over thirty years ago; his books also help spread this important message.

CONTENTS

FOREWORD

They say time flies when you're having fun. That sentiment must certainly be true, because it doesn't seem possible that we entered the low-carb arena twenty years ago. But indeed, we began developing and fine-tuning our *Protein Power* diet for our patients and adopted it ourselves in 1984. Those of you who, like us, have been living the low-carb life for years can attest that adhering to its principles took a fair amount of commitment and ingenuity in the olden days.

Today an ever-growing number of low-carb versions of everything, from chips to pasta, jockeys for space on grocers' shelves, although admittedly many of them are not exquisitely tasty. Back then there were no commercially available low-carb snacks or treats, no protein shakes or bars, nothing convenient to make life easier for the struggling low-carb dieter. In fact, as recently as 2002, when along with Ursula Solom we first proposed *The Low-Carb Comfort Food Cookbook* to our publisher, there was but a scant handful of low-carb cookbooks available on the Internet to help dieters cook low-carb meals at home, and none were available in mainstream bookstores. Back then, making low-carb eating work was pretty much a solo project for the committed cook.

It has always been our belief that the pathway to long-term success on a low-carb diet (or for that matter, any diet) must ultimately go through the kitchen. And here's why. Although it's certainly possible to lose weight in what we would call an artificial environment—that is, by using meal replacement supplements or weight-loss shakes instead of everyday food, going to a spa for several weeks, or taking diet pills—these measures are simply tools to make short-term weight loss go faster. Maintaining a healthy weight and keeping a lid on cholesterol, triglycerides, blood sugar, or blood pressure for the long haul demand a sea change in the way a person eats and, more importantly, cooks at home.

Much of low-carb cooking is simple—more a matter of selection of types of foods than inventiveness. For instance: grill a steak, toss a salad, and substitute roasted veggies for potatoes and you're there. Whip up a cheese omelet with a side of sausage and some fruit, hold the toast, and voilà! No problem. Pop a tin of muffins into the oven and . . . uh-oh, now you've got a problem. What, exactly, does one use to replace the 2 cups of flour and the sugar that are the core of a batch of traditional yummy muffins? Or a crusty loaf of bread, flaky pie crust, or chewy cookie? If you're like most people trying to bake low-carb, you're stumped, at least until you learn a few tricks of the low-carb trade.

The task of figuring out how to adapt high-carb recipes—particularly for candies and baked goods—to the low-carb format can be daunting if you have no basis from which to work. Thanks to Ursula Solom, you won't have to undertake that task. As she did in our collaboration, *The Low-Carb Comfort Food Cookbook,* Ursula has worked tirelessly to develop scores of recipes for breads, biscuits, pastries, cookies, pies, cakes, candy, and confections that are not merely low-carb, they're delicious to boot! Her culinary alchemy gives us all a leg up on the learning curve to make luscious low-carb treats that, if we use them wisely, will make it that much easier to stick to the low-carb plan for life.

This comprehensive cookbook contains it all—from breads to coffee cakes, from ice cream to chocolate truffles, from Bavarian cream to blueberry pie. Every delectable sweet treat you've missed on low-carb can now be yours for the making. Just open the book to any page and dive right in; you're sure to find something wonderful. Enjoy.

—Mary Dan Eades, M.D.

ACKNOWLEDGMENTS

What can I say? Writing a book is a lonely undertaking. You need boundless optimism to embark on a project that can take many months or years—with the odds of being published not in your favor. One success by no means assures another. So when it comes to proposal time—when others see what it is you actually have been doing all of these months, even if they originally approved of your idea—suspense rises. While you wait to hear from your agent, a call that is almost akin to receiving a notice from God—after all, your fate is hanging in the balance—you may come to believe, or I did, that it was presumptuous, even a little insane on my part, to expect the answer to be positive.

But the news could not have been better. "I think the proposal is fabulous." The words still ring in my ear and came from my wonderful agent, Channa Taub. Once again, my thanks and appreciation go to her for believing in me, for her expertise in sharpening my proposal, and for her support for the new book. The same gratitude goes to my other great agent, Carol Mann, and for her special skills in placing books and negotiating contracts. But this time, even before that lengthy process could begin in earnest, to my delight Tom Miller, the editor at John Wiley & Sons who bought *The Low-Carb Comfort Food Cookbook*, of which I am a coauthor, bought this book also. He sounded excited and happy about it, as did many on the Wiley staff. It made the project more fun. Tom immediately put the book on a fast track to publication. As before, he has been wonderful to work with, even during many hectic moments. Thanks, Tom. There were other editors on the Wiley staff who had a hand in shaping this book. My thanks go to all of them, especially to Kimberly Monroe-Hill for her hard work and patient, persistent, and thorough efforts to ferret out inconsistencies and other errors—and to do it all with good cheer. I could not have asked for more.

There would be no book had it not been for my husband, Bob, who almost never saw me while I was racing to meet fast-track deadlines, testing and retesting new recipes, or working away at the computer. He took over all the household chores, shopping, and cooking, and was also there with his support and excellent advice. Thanks to my three daughters, Karen, Hilary, and Sandra, for their patience in accepting that "I was busy" and had little time for long conversations for so many months. Thanks also to Paul Botzon (www .computerguruz.com), computer guru, who has become a good friend while being the guardian angel behind my computer for many years, always ready, despite his busy schedule, to attend to any of its little sniffles or big, cranky attitudes that baffled me.

INTRODUCTION

Why make bread, cookies, muffins, desserts, pies, and other delicious sweets—temptations that never used to belong in the low-carb diet—the focus of a low-carb diet cookbook? The answer is simple: many low-carbers do not want to give up these forbidden foods.

A few years ago, pretty much your only choice was going low-carb and avoiding breads and sweets or not going low-carb at all. Today, this is changing. Substitute low-carb baked goods and sweets are finding their way into supermarkets. But this book offers something special. Not only does it give you nearly endless choices from the high-carb world of foods that are normally forbidden, but these goodies are also so delicious they defy the label "low-carb." With help from these recipes, your diet will now become as enjoyable as the one you had to give up.

My own initiation into low-carb dieting took place a number of years ago at a time when one had to put forth herculean efforts to say no, or at least try to, when faced with irresistible high-carb pastries, cookies, chocolates, the aroma of freshly baked bread, and more, for which no replacement was to be had back then. But while the diet was clearly difficult to adhere to, it also surprised me. Virtually from the start, it was a huge success. My weight plummeted and so did my sky-high cholesterol and triglyceride levels; even my blood pressure went down. I dropped to a size 8/10 from a size 16, and that is just some of it.

Clearly, there was no turning back for me. How can you give up the extraordinary health benefits that can be yours, amazingly, merely by changing the way you eat? But it was, of course, easier said than done. The notion that I would have to follow this diet forever made sticking to it unpleasant, even exasperating. Almost as a matter of desperation, my kitchen became a laboratory where—turning myself into an alchemist of sorts—I began to search for ways to create completely new, supremely tasty, low-carb replacements for the foods I longed for but was not allowed to eat. This was the beginning of my first collection of recipes.

Protein Power by Michael R. Eades, M.D., and Mary Dan Eades, M.D., the *New York Times* best-seller, had been my guide to the low-carb diet. The two physicians persuaded me that the diet alone—*without medication*—might solve most of my health problems. They were right. My health changed dramatically for the better and has remained so ever since.

By a lucky coincidence, the Drs. Eades and I shared an excellent literary agent, Channa Taub. When she became interested in my recipes, she suggested a cooperative project and brought us together. My first collection of recipes became part of a collaboration with the Drs. Eades, *The Low-Carb Comfort Food Cookbook* (Wiley, 2002). That book is full of diverse, wonderful everyday meals and snacks. Breakfast begins with low-carb waffles, pancakes, rolls, or crepes. There are some desserts, too, as well as much-loved Italian and Mexican fare like pasta, pizza, tortillas, chips, and dips. Tempting soups, salads, entrées, and appetizers round it all out.

The Low-Carb Baking and Dessert Cookbook features exclusively the foods many of us miss the most. Many of the great-tasting foods you can make from these recipes are also highly nutritious—far more than their high-carb counterparts. Here is an example: a 1.5-ounce muffin you pick up in a store has about 21 grams of carb, on average, and 2 grams of protein. A muffin of the same weight from the many recipes you find here, on average, has about 4 grams of carbohydrate and 11 grams of high-quality protein. You can argue over which tastes better once you have baked a set of them. You may be surprised to find that you prefer the low-carb version. And don't think you won't have time to do it—it takes only minutes to prepare just about anything in this book.

There is even good news for individuals with certain allergies. Many recipes for baked goods, especially quick breads and muffins, are gluten-free. Several recipes are nut-free, and a number are soy-free. They can be found under these headings in the index.

You will find breads and jams and other yummy spreads to put on them. As for cookies, you can make a new type almost every week or pick perennial favorites such as oatmeal cookies, shortbread, pecan sandies, peanut butter cookies, pfeffernüsse, different kinds of chocolate chip cookies, vanilla cookies, and macadamia nut cookies. You can make pies nestled in divine pie crusts, custards, cheesecakes, cream puffs and meringue shells, cakes, frostings, glazes, and frozen desserts.

Chocolate lovers, rejoice! When the sweet urge strikes, you no longer have to transgress. There are recipes for fudges, pecan date chews, truffles, brownies, nutty high-protein candy in several flavors, chocolate-dipped marzipan, macadamia nut candy, and chocolate candy squares, to name a few. All can be created quickly without the need for a candy thermometer.

You may wonder how you can eat all these delicious, low-carb goodies and not overdo it when it comes to carbohydrates. It obviously helps that low-carbohydrate versions of high-carb foods make for impressive carbohydrate savings. The carb count for my recipes drops, on average, to one-third or sometimes one-fourth of the originals. But some carbohydrates are indeed part of these recipes, and they must be added to those you count from salads, vegetables, and fruits. With low counts like these, however, you will be able to manage to fit many formerly forbidden delights into your diet, whatever your personal carbohydrate gram limit.

I allow myself 65 grams of carbohydrate per day, an amount that happens to keep my blood sugar at or near normal low levels. My cravings for certain foods have ceased to be an obsession. Life's back to normal.

Some people may be able to eat limitless amounts of food on low-carb diets without ill effects. I cannot do it, nor have I personally met anyone who can. For most of us it is yes to satisfying meals—and absolutely no to overindulgence. Moderation is the winning password.

Knowing that you can eat the treats you long for may have a profoundly calming effect and may actually reduce your need for some of these indulgences. The anxiety that comes from having to tell yourself *I cannot have this* will almost certainly vanish. And that's a good thing sure to reduce stress-triggered eating.

So whether you try to get by on 50, 60, 70, or if you are lucky, 100 grams of carb a day, this book will help you make it easy and fun. You can forever say good-bye to high-carb cravings and hello to delicious comfort foods!

1

THE LOW-CARB
KITCHEN MANUAL

Grab a cup of coffee and a low-carb cookie or two, and settle down with this chapter, which will make the dos and don'ts of low-carb cooking easy to follow. Come back to it again and again, especially to the section that discusses the sweeteners used in the recipes. Most of what you read here is not repeated elsewhere in the book.

Your goal is to find ways to produce tantalizingly good breads, cookies, muffins, desserts, candy, and more while working around the two big high-carb troublemakers: sugar and flour. Sugar and flour may not seem to be closely related—sugar is sweet, flour is not—but both are cut from the same cloth; they are carbohydrates. Starch—flour is mostly made of it—is sugar in a dormant state and does not show its true colors until digestion begins. Eat it, and the sugar is promptly activated. A single slice of white bread can dump a tablespoon of sugar (glucose) swiftly into your bloodstream; it is no different from eating a small candy bar. What you will find in this book is how to avoid almost all sugar and flour by using foods that when properly combined—the secret is in the combining—will make your new low-carb diet as delightful as your old one. So, what foods will you be using in your low-carb recipes?

NUTS

Although nuts may be sliced and chopped, they are chiefly used as a finely ground meal. Nuts are nutritious and loaded with minerals, vitamins, and healthy oils. Most nuts are widely available, but prices vary; it pays to shop around for the best deal. Check health food stores, the Internet, and vendors listed under Sources at the end of this book. Buying in bulk helps reduce the cost of nuts. Nuts should be kept cool or refrigerated, except for small amounts that you might want to keep handy in the kitchen for instant use. Be careful, though—all of the nuts listed below can be toxic to people who are allergic to them.

Almonds

Almonds, especially almond meal, will become a major food staple in your kitchen. You can grind the nuts yourself in a processor or a blender, but commercial almond meal gives you a finer, more even grind and also saves work. Whole almond meal is ground from whole almonds with the skin on; blanched almond meal is ground from nuts with the skin off.

Hazelnuts

Hazelnuts have a unique, delicious flavor. They are used fairly heavily in the recipes in this book, especially as a meal. Unlike almond meal, which is available from many sources, hazelnut meal is harder to find on the market and is often quite expensive. However, I finally found at least one vendor (Nutty Guys) who sells hazelnut meal in bulk for a reasonable price. You can find the information in the Sources section.

Walnuts, Pecans, and Macadamia Nuts

These appear in recipes, often as a meal but also toasted and coarsely chopped. All three are available as commercial meals. Macadamia nuts are also made into a lightly defatted "flour" (see Sources) that is good but expensive. Occasionally a recipe asks for it, but it is okay to substitute blanched almond meal.

How to Toast Nuts

To toast nuts, preheat the oven to 325°F or 350°F. Put the raw nuts in a shallow baking pan. It takes from 20 to 45 minutes to toast nuts, depending on the oven's temperature and the moisture content of the nuts. Nuts should only change color slightly; they should not get too dark.

Nuts tend to darken unevenly. A handful of nuts that are excessively toasted—even without actually getting burned—can spoil the whole lot with a strong, unpleasant taste. Be extra careful and check on them often. It is practical to keep a large supply of toasted nuts on hand. They keep well if they are stored in the fridge. They can also be frozen.

VITAL WHEAT GLUTEN

This is the protein fraction that remains after the starch (flour) has been removed from wheat kernels. With rare exceptions, vital wheat gluten is used in this book only in recipes for raised breads. It has a high protein count (23 grams in ¼ cup), and the carb count is below 6 grams. Most vendors call this product vital wheat gluten. Red Mill (Bob's Red Mill) calls theirs vital wheat gluten flour, which may lead to confusion. Occasionally you may see a high-carb wheat (white) flour with small amounts of vital wheat gluten added to it that is also labeled "vital wheat gluten flour." This is a product to avoid. Check nutrition labels carefully before buying. Additional information about vital wheat gluten is found in chapter 2.

HIGH-FIBER INGREDIENTS

Inulin

Inulin is a fructooligosaccharide that is harvested from chicory root and many other vegetables and fruits. It is a natural white, tasteless, beneficial, and highly soluble fiber. It is said to increase the activity of good, active cultures in the gut and inhibits those cultures that are hostile. Inulin contains no carbohydrates that need counting. There are claims that inulin may aid in the absorption of calcium by the body. Much is being written about this interesting product; you can look up information about inulin on the Internet. Although it is expensive, prices vary. It is added primarily to recipes meant to have a high fiber load. It is also found in some stevia products (see the section on sweeteners). Four tablespoons of inulin contain 24.2 grams of fiber.

Oat Bran

This is a good source of soluble fiber. I use it only occasionally, chiefly because of its high carb count. Four tablespoons contain 5.3 grams of fiber.

Unprocessed Wheat Bran

This fiber, which is fairly low in carbohydrates, is used in many recipes. Four tablespoons supply 6 grams of fiber, chiefly insoluble. For a little extra zing, toast the bran. Preheat the oven to 325°F. Spread the bran in a shallow baking pan and leave it in the oven for 30 to 35 minutes. Kretchmer's Toasted Wheat Bran is an alternative to toasting it yourself. Untoasted bran also gives excellent results, but if you buy unprocessed bran in bulk, make sure that it has almost no smell. It is best to refrigerate bran or to store it in a cool place.

Whole Psyllium Husks

The psyllium plant is native to Europe and Southern Asia. It contains soluble and insoluble fibers; four tablespoons have 14.8 grams of fiber. Psyllium husks appear in recipes that are specifically intended to provide a high fiber count.

Soy Products

Soy Protein Powder

Also called soy protein isolate or soy isolate, soy protein powder has no carbohydrates and is high in protein. It is part of many commercial soy products, such as vegetarian hamburgers. Some scientists are concerned that toxic substances may be created in the process of extracting the isolate. Although no risk facctors have been established, until more is known, whether to use soy protein powder is a personal decision. I like using soy protein powder, and you will find it in many of my recipes. If you wish, you can substitute equal amounts of either soy powder or soy milk powder in your recipes. There is a relatively small difference in taste and texture, but these ingredients are not carb-free. You will need to adjust the carb counts in the recipes accordingly.

Soy Milk Powder

This is made from lightly toasted, not raw, soybeans. This powder has no smell and no unpleasant taste. You can use soy milk powder in equal amounts as a substitute for soy protein powder. Count 5 grams of carb and 9 grams of protein in ¼ cup.

Soy Powder

This is similar to soy milk powder and created from toasted soybeans, but it does not have as fine a grind. The gram counts are the same. You may find that some stores do not know the difference between soy powder and soy milk powder.

Soy Flour

This is made from raw soybeans, unlike soy powder and soy milk powder. Soy flour has a strong taste and smell that many people dislike. It is not used in this book.

Soy Grits

These are commercially toasted, cracked soybeans that are used in some recipes to achieve a crunchy texture.

Whey Protein Powder

This concentrated powder, extracted from the watery part of milk, is said to be one of the best usable proteins. You will find it in many recipes in small amounts, principally for its high nutritional value. This powder has a beneficial effect on the immune system. It is a great way to get protein, especially for vegetarians or those who do not care to eat much meat. It comes plain and flavored, the latter usually being fairly high in carbohydrates. In this book, whey protein is used in a natural, unflavored form that is carb-free.

Look for natural, unflavored, zero-carb whey protein when you shop. Mix it with a touch of cream to create a good substitute for milk. You can also mix it with fruit for smoothies. Zero-carb whey protein can be found on the Internet, and it is also available from Vitamin Cottage (see Sources). As always, buying in bulk is more economical.

SEEDS

Seeds are concentrated storehouses of healthy nutrition; they provide a big boost to a low-carb diet, adding texture, fiber, protein, and a variety of interesting and often intense flavors.

Flaxseeds

These little seeds contain important precursors to omega-3 fatty acids, which the human body transforms into the omega-3 fatty acids we all need. The direct sources for omega-3 fatty acids are certain cold-water fish, chiefly cod, salmon (not the farm-raised kind), mackerel, and sardines. The oils from either flaxseeds or fish are highly polyunsaturated and, thus, subject to turning rancid in a hurry. This is just as true of flaxseed meal (ground flaxseeds), an item used in many recipes. It must be carefully stored in the refrigerator or freezer.

Most often, when you add a nutrient to a food primarily for its nutritional value, the best you can hope for is that it will blandly meld into the food without becoming a detriment to the food's flavor. But foods made with flaxseeds and flaxseed meal taste terrific. The seeds come in two colors, dark and golden. Golden seeds cost slightly more; you can use either. Flaxseeds are rich in soluble fiber, folic acid, and magnesium.

You can buy flaxseed meal in sealed bags (Bob's Red Mill is one source) or you can grind the seeds yourself. Grinding is ideal for freshness, but it is a noisy affair that takes several minutes. Luckily, Salton has come out with a small mill dedicated to grinding these tough little seeds exclusively. It grinds up to 4 ounces, a handy quantity, in less than a minute. The mill is easy to clean and costs about $30.

Pumpkin Seeds, Sesame Seeds, and Sunflower Seeds

Many of the attributes listed for flaxseeds fit these seeds too. These seeds are always used hulled and are often toasted. Though less sensitive to rancidity than flaxseed meal, hulled seeds still need to be refrigerated in order to maintain their freshness.

How to Toast Seeds

You can toast seeds in the oven or in a skillet on the stove. As with nuts, it may be practical to toast larger batches at a time and then refrigerate or freeze them.

Preheat the oven to 325°F. Spread the seeds in a shallow baking pan and leave them in the oven for 30 to 40 minutes. The seeds will change color unevenly. As with nuts, stop the process before any seeds get too dark.

If you prefer, you can toast small amounts in a skillet. Preheat a heavy skillet over medium heat. Add the seeds and stir constantly until the seeds are lightly toasted. It takes just a few minutes. Remove the seeds instantly from the hot skillet, lest some of them scorch before being transferred to another container.

PEANUTS

Not a true nut, the peanut is a legume. Peanuts and peanut butter are used in several recipes for cookies, pies, and candy. Peanut butter has a relatively high carb count, but because of its concentrated flavor, you do not need to use large amounts. It is also high in protein. Buy only natural peanut butter without added sugar. Natural peanut butter usually has a layer of oil on top and must be stirred well prior to each use.

WHEAT FLOUR, WHOLE WHEAT FLOUR, OAT FLOUR, RYE FLOUR

Small to moderate amounts of some of these holdovers from the high-carb world (usually oat flour, dark rye flour, and whole wheat flour) are included in some recipes in this book. Unbleached white flour, by far the worst of the bunch from a health perspective, appears only in a few recipes where nothing else would do.

SWEETENERS

Most recipes are so good you'd swear they contained sugar. This is great—but it can cause problems. The sweet treats in this book might tempt you to eat more of them than you should. Enjoy the sweets, but remind yourself that they are here principally to enable you to follow a healthy low-carb diet for the rest of your life, since you now can add coveted sweets, albeit with sensible restraint.

Because people's tastes for sweeteners vary, you may find you'll want to use less or more sweeteners than I recommend. Remember to adjust carb counts accordingly. The sweeteners used in this book are considered safe, though it is not known with absolute certainty what the result of steady use for many years or even decades may be. Equal (aspartame), hailed as safe when it first appeared, has been found to cause health problems and is not used in this book.

Splenda (sucralose), a recent and welcome addition to the existing sweeteners that was approved by the Food and Drug Administration in 1998, is used widely in the recipes in this book, but it is coming under increasing scrutiny. We must wait and see about the effects that Splenda has on our health. Another sweetener is stevia, a sweet substance extracted from the leaves of a South American shrub. While all indications show that it is apparently quite benign, its drawback is that it can leave a bitter aftertaste. In recent years, though, the processing of stevia has been greatly improved. Finally, there are sugar alcohols. These are natural substances that are used commercially in sugar-free chocolates and other food products. They are believed to be indigestible. Each of these sweeteners is discussed individually below.

Splenda

Splenda (the generic name is sucralose) is made from real sugar but is chemically altered. In the process, it becomes extremely concentrated and sweet. It contains no carbohydrates. Because of its concentration, Splenda requires a carrier like maltodextrin, which does have carbohydrates. Splenda has a pleasant taste; you can bake with it too. Splenda is available in two forms, one is a granular sugar substitute that can be used, spoon for spoon—according to its manufacturer—in place of cane sugar (sucrose); it has 0.5 gram of carb per teaspoon. That translates to 6 grams of carb in ¼ cup and 24 grams in 1 cup. Splenda also comes in packets. One packet equals 2 teaspoons of sugar at 1 gram of carb. Both can be used for cooking or baking.

Sugar Alcohols

Sugar alcohols (polyols) occur naturally in a variety of fruits and berries, and in birch and other trees. The human body even makes small amounts of them. Sugar alcohols resemble regular cane sugar (sucrose), have the same weight as sugar, and taste and sweeten pretty much the same way too. You can use sugar alcohols just as you would use sugar.

Why the name "sugar alcohol"? Chemically, sugar alcohol is alcohol, but it contains no intoxicants and is derived from real sugar molecules. The main difference is that sugar has six carbon molecules in a chain and sugar alcohol has five. It is this molecular difference that has a huge impact on the body—and by extension, on the low-carb diet. Sugar alcohols are metabolized slowly, trigger little insulin or do so slowly, and cause no sudden rise in blood sugar (as do honey, molasses, and sucrose). Indeed, they are thought to pass through the digestive system pretty much like fiber. They are indigestible and hence are not counted as effective carbohydrates.

Nutrition labels list the carbohydrates in sugar alcohols, which are identical to those of regular sugar, but discount them to zero because they are supposed to be indigestible. This supposition is now being challenged, however. Scientists believe that some sugar alcohols may reach the bloodstream after all, thus becoming *effective carbohydrates* that need counting. There is no clear indication of what that count should be. Individuals seem to respond differently to it too. Since nothing is gained by ignoring these findings, in this book sugar alcohols are treated as if they had an absorption (effective) rate of 15 percent. This may be a tad low and bears watching.

As in *The Low-Carb Comfort Food Cookbook,* the recipes in this book show only the effective carb count, that is, carbohydrates that actually enter the bloodstream, and ignore those that do not, such as fiber. The term ECC (effective carbohydrate count) was originally coined by the Drs. Eades.

Sugar alcohols—with names like mannitol, sorbitol, isomalt, maltitol, and xylitol—are considered to be both safe and even beneficial to your health. Xylitol (which may be the most beneficial) and some others have been shown to prevent tooth decay and also may help improve bone structure and more. Sugar-free chewing gums are often sweetened with xylitol.

In my recipes, I chiefly use xylitol, which is a little coarser than table sugar. I prefer the finer texture of table sugar, which is easy to create by running xylitol through a food processor. Keep the lid on while you do it to prevent the sugar dust from rising. A powdered sugar version of xylitol is also available.

The other sugar alcohol I use is a delicious brown sugar substitute that is sold under the name DiabetiSweet Brown Sugar Substitute. This sugar contains very small amounts of partially hydrogenated vegetable oils. This fat, prevalent in margarines, packaged cookies, and many other food products, contains unhealthy *transfats*. Such fats are not otherwise used in the recipes in this book, but DiabetiSweet Brown Sugar Substitute—used in small quantities—is an exception because a representative of the manufacturer, Health Care Products, assured me that the vegetable oil is in the process of being removed from the sugar. Call the company or check my Web site (LowCarb-BakingandDessertCookbook.com) for updates. Meanwhile, if it concerns you, use xylitol in place of the brown sugar in any recipe.

Sugar alcohols are available in some health food stores, on the Internet, and from certain vendors listed under Sources in this book. Sugar alcohols are expensive; check the prices before you buy them.

Sugar alcohol may come with some unpleasant side effects. If you eat too much of it, its slow passage through the digestive system can generate gas, cramping, and even diarrhea. It usually takes a while before any symptoms show up, and every individual responds differently. A warning about the possible consequences of eating excessive amounts of sugar alcohol is included with all commercial products containing it. So be warned. This may help strengthen your resolve not to overdo sweets.

Stevia

Manufactured from the leaves of the plant *Stevia rebaudiana,* a South American shrub, stevia has been used for eons by indigenous populations. It has not yet received FDA approval as a food additive and is sold as a dietary supplement. Stevia is widely available in health food stores and on the Internet. No adverse effects have been reported. It is intensely sweet; a few grains (¼₂ of a teaspoon) equals about a teaspoon of sugar. It comes in liquid form and as a concentrated powder. There are some types of Stevia that are diluted with small amounts of inulin, the fiber discussed on page 7. One such powder goes by the brand name Stevia Plus, but there are others as well. Many people use stevia to sweeten everything and swear by it. If you are among them, you can continue that practice with most of the recipes in this book.

A ¼ cup of cane sugar has 48 grams of carbohydrates (as does sugar alcohol). The Splenda granular sugar substitute has 6 grams of carb per ¼ cup. Sugar alcohol—at a 15 percent absorption rate—has 7.2 grams of carb per ¼ cup (at least in this book). Stevia is the most difficult to pinpoint; the products vary and manufacturers make different claims. I tested the different sweeteners, using ¼ cup of cane sugar as the default. I used an identical recipe, first with cane sugar, then with the other sweeteners, each alone. (You can do this test yourself.) Sugar alcohol was right up there with cane sugar. Stevia came fairly close but tasted bitter when used by itself. Splenda came in last, sweetening less effectively than the other sweeteners. The Splenda packets fared only mildly better. So a teaspoon-for-teaspoon substitution does not really do it.

Sugar alcohol, though slightly higher in carb count, has greater sweetening power, besides increasing the weight of a recipe.

The results of this test, although approximations at best, are shown in the equivalency table on page 14. It shows the values given to Splenda by the manufacturer in the first column and is followed by the amount that is needed of each of the other sweeteners listed to equal the perceived sweetness of Splenda. Because stevia products are hard to pinpoint, I included only one, Stevia Plus.

How are sweeteners used in this book? Nearly all recipes use three different sweeteners: Splenda, xylitol, and stevia. I do this because Splenda, with its relatively weak power, drives up carb costs if used alone; sugar alcohol, a safe and effective sweetener, is troublesome for possible intestinal disturbances if used in excess; stevia, the best sweetener because it has zero carb and evidently presents no health hazard in the small amounts commonly used, is not a pleasant sweetener by itself for most people. But the three together do a splendid job of sweetening.

This does not mean that you have to stick to the precise combination given in a recipe. If you want to leave out xylitol, double the amount of Splenda called for; reverse this if you wish to leave out Splenda. I recommend that you do not leave out stevia, though, because it is carb-free. If the amount of stevia in a recipe gives you a bitter aftertaste, try reducing it slightly or substituting other stevia products. Such experiments are well worth it. Today many choices are available. The recipes in this book call for Stevia Plus (or equivalent). If stevia works for you, you might even consider increasing it in the recipes beyond the amounts given and cutting back on Splenda and xylitol.

Approximate Sweetener Equivalents

Splenda, loose	CHO (g)	Splenda, packets	CHO (g)	Xylitol	CHO (g)	Stevia Plus	CHO (g)
¼ cup	6.0	5 packets	5.0	2.5 tablespoons	4.5	2 teaspoons	0
½ cup	12.0	10 packets	10.0	5 tablespoons	9.0	4 teaspoons	0
¾ cup	18.0	15 packets	15.0	7.5 tablespoons	13.5	6 teaspoons	0
1 cup	24.0	20 packets	20.0	10 tablespoons	18.0	8 teaspoons	0

Molasses and Honey

Hints of molasses and honey in small amounts are used occasionally for flavor in just a few recipes.

Chocolate

Sugar-free chocolate made with sugar alcohols is wonderful to use for making cookies, desserts, candies, and glazes. It is available from a wide variety of sources on the Internet or from your local candy store. There are many brands of chocolate; experiment to find out which chocolate you like best.

Chocolate is used in many recipes and often needs to be melted. Sometimes different types are combined, such as unsweetened baking chocolate and sugar-free milk or semisweet chocolate. Some chocolate comes in bulk or as bars; some as small disks or even chips. For more uniform melting, you may want to break or chop large pieces into smaller chunks, perhaps ½ an ounce or so. Always melt chocolate over very low heat. If you do it over hot water, keep the water at or below a simmer. In the microwave, choose the briefest period that will do the job. Suggested times are given, but the strengths of microwave ovens vary. To achieve the best flavor and texture, do not allow your chocolate to bubble up.

DAIRY PRODUCTS

Butter

I prefer unsalted butter, but you can certainly use regular butter if you wish. The consequences of using either are not that dramatic, except for the difference in saltiness. Usually, butter needs to be at room temperature. If it is not sitting out, use a microwave to bring it to room temperature. Don't worry if the butter gets a bit runny; no harm will be done to your recipe.

Cream

Heavy cream is called for in all recipes. If you want a lighter cream—to use over fruit or cereal, for instance—dilute the cream with a little water. Heavy cream is included in this book because it gives a little more body to the recipes. However, it is also slightly richer in fat than regular cream. Carb counts are about the same for both. If you prefer to use regular cream instead of heavy cream (heavy whipping cream), you can substitute this in most instances and still get good results.

Cream Cheese

Use full-fat cheese; it has fewer carbohydrates and tastes much better than lower-fat alternatives. You can keep cream cheese refrigerated until you are ready to use it, then soften it in the microwave. When the cream cheese is soft to the touch, it is easier to dispose of the tiny lumps that appear when you whip it.

FATS

In addition to butter, some of my recipes use coconut oil or light olive oil. These are stable oils and should not be refrigerated. I also use small amounts of peanut butter and tahini (sesame butter).

EGGS

Always use large eggs, which I used in developing the recipes. Although the designation "large" is not quite perfect (it applies to a fairly wide range of weights), it will help you select the right size. If you have a microwave, you can use it to bring the eggs to room temperature. You do not want warm eggs, only to remove the chill in a matter of seconds.

FRUITS

I use dates, currants, blueberries, cranberries, and bananas in the recipes in this book. Though they are full of good nutrition, dates, currants, and bananas are very high-carb and must be used sparingly. Currants are preferable to raisins because of their small size. Two tablespoons of currants can really disperse widely—you would not get many raisins in 2 tablespoons.

CARB AND PROTEIN COUNTS

The setup for carb and protein counts in foods is the same in this book as in *The Low-Carb Comfort Food Cookbook*. Standard abbreviations, CHO (cho) for carbohydrate and PRO (pro) for protein, are used as column headers. The counts for individual ingredients are shown to help you understand what is in the foods you are preparing and to provide some flexibility and choice. So if you want to make changes, leave out an ingredient, or add one, simply adjust the carb or protein totals as needed. Also, having the actual counts available (something you generally do not find in other cookbooks) allows you to alter the size of individual portions. For example, if you make your cookies smaller or larger than suggested, you will still know exactly how many carb grams or protein grams are in each cookie if you divide the number of cookies by the total carb and protein counts. Sometimes you will be asked to add gram counts to a recipe. For instance, some pie recipes give you the gram counts for the filling only. You can choose which of several crusts you want to use. You will need to add the counts for the crust you select to those of the filling and use that number to calculate how many grams one piece of pie has—depending on the number of pieces you cut. This holds true for frostings and fillings as well.

As recommended in *The Low-Carb Comfort Food Cookbook,* if you are severely restricted in your intake of carbohydrates, just add 10 percent to the count totals for extra protection. As mentioned earlier, only effective carbohydrate grams (ECC) are listed here; the ones containing fiber have been deducted. Many recipes, as you may notice, contain a good deal of fiber. Fiber is not listed except in instances where a high-fiber product is the intent.

Sources for the counts are *The Complete Book of Food Counts,* 6th edition, by Corinne T. Netzer; *Bowes & Church's Food Values of Portions Commonly Used,* 17th edition, by J. A. Pennington; and the ESHA Nutritional Database Files. Counts do not always agree—they are difficult to pinpoint accurately—but they are close.

UTENSILS AND EQUIPMENT

You probably already have most of what you need, but here is a list of some essential items.

Bread Baking

I prefer heavy-gauge, nonstick metal bake pans. Get a set of four small baking pans (about 3-by-6 inches) and two large ones (about 4-by-8 inches). A perforated French bread pan with a double channel is great for making oblong loaves that resemble French bread.

Cookie Sheets

Use heavy-gauge nonstick metal half sheets. Buy a couple of silicone-coated mats or liners (also called Silpat or Exopat mats). The liners help prevent cookie bottoms from browning prematurely. See Sources for information on where to purchase these items.

Pots and Pans for Cakes, Muffins, and Cupcakes

If possible, get two 8-inch springform pans and one 9-inch springform pan. They are ideal for most cakes, especially cheesecakes. Good quality pans (available at places like Williams-Sonoma), although they can be expensive, will pay for themselves in the long run. Cheap pans tend to lose their enamel finish quickly from repeated scrubbings, causing the batter to leak through the bottom. For making muffins and rolls, you will need 2-inch and 3½-inch muffin pans.

Appliances and More

A food processor (7-cup) is extremely useful, as is a portable electric mixer (get one that is cheap and lightweight if you need to buy it). A stand electric mixer is also nice—it is helpful for some recipes, such as cheesecakes, brownies, and meringues.

A digital scale is a necessity in the low-carb kitchen and a double boiler is also helpful. A microwave is extremely useful to bring ingredients to room temperature and to melt chocolate. Cooling racks are essential. If you don't have an ice cream maker, machines available for under $100 work beautifully. If you find that you are baking many breads, consider investing in a top-notch bread knife. They really do cut as if through butter. A small flaxseed mill will also be useful. For candy-making, a helpful tool is a marble slab. Finally, since you may be shaping not only breads but also many cookies, disposable gloves are a tremendous boon when doing these chores. You can buy them wholesale on the Internet, virtually for pennies.

OVEN TEMPERATURES

Oven temperatures can vary from oven to oven, sometimes considerably. If you find that the baking times given for foods in this cookbook at the suggested temperature settings consistently do not produce the results indicated within the allotted time periods, experiment a bit and adjust times or temperatures up or down as may be needed. Oven thermometers can help, but they are not foolproof, either.

2

MINUTES TO RAISED BREADS

If you have 15 minutes, you can make bread. By that time, your loaves will be rising in the prewarmed oven; all you have to do is reset the temperature when it's time to actually bake the bread. The oven process takes about 1 hour. It's no more trouble making bread this way than using a bread machine—and considerably more flexible. Rather than making one loaf, you can turn out two or four loaves of breads or make rolls as well as other yummy things like breadsticks and pecan buns. The carb count of the various breads per ounce (28 grams) ranges from under 3 grams to over 6 grams; most breads come in between 3.5 and 4.5 grams of carb per ounce. Protein is high in these breads too, thanks to the nut meals, nuts, vital wheat gluten, and other ingredients. You could eat just toast or plain bread for breakfast and get 20 to 30 grams of protein—with very few carbohydrates. Add an egg or two to a serving of bread and you'll have a tasty high-protein meal without a bit of bacon or ham.

In commercial breads, the serving size is usually one slice. On average, these slices weigh 1 ounce (28 grams). The single serving size for bread in this book is listed as 1 ounce (28 grams) as well, but a slice value is not given. Why not? A single slice of your bread is not going to be of uniform weight. The loaves you bake may be large or small, or you may cut the slices thin or thick—in other words, 28 grams could represent one, three, or even four slices. So keep that scale handy.

The process of making these low-carb breads is simple, fairly precise, and varies only occasionally from one bread recipe to the next. Step-by-step instructions, therefore, are given only for the first bread recipe, on page 24. The instructions are detailed, so anyone can follow them. Only steps that differ are given for the bread recipes that follow.

Vital wheat gluten is a major ingredient in all raised breads. It is what causes the breads to rise, since only minuscule amounts of regular flour are used, if any. Though vital wheat gluten works well most of the time, it doesn't work all of the time. If your bread occasionally fails to rise properly, the vital wheat gluten you are using may not have enough punch to deliver the needed bounce. According to one large manufacturer, the geographic region where the gluten was produced, seasonal weather conditions, shelf life, and other circumstances may affect its performance. No matter where you buy the vital wheat gluten, you might occasionally pick up a poor batch. It does not make the gluten bad—it just makes it less useful for the purpose of raising breads, sometimes actually useless. To minimize the potential pitfalls with vital wheat gluten, it is best to buy small amounts of it at a time. You need about 9½ ounces to make one batch of loaves. If it makes great bread, you might want to get more of the same. But if it did not, try another source. Some weeks later, the place that had the poor quality gluten might have a good one again.

In general, depending on things like the density of the dough and its weight, breads will rise from ½ to 2 inches above the rim of the bake pan and about triple in size. Troubleshooting for bread that doesn't rise is further discussed in the section below.

LOW-CARB BREAD: HINTS AND OBSERVATIONS

No sweeteners are needed to make these breads rise or to make them rise better. Most of these recipes contain no sweeteners. But if you like, you may add one or two packets of Splenda to a bread just for the taste. Large amounts of a sweetener, especially sugar alcohol, tend to make breads fall.

The bread recipes yield four small or two large loaves, but the weight of the loaves varies from recipe to recipe. Most recipes produce loaves with a total weight of 22 or 23 ounces; a few go as high as 30 ounces. Variations in ingredients account for most of the differences. Even loaves made from the same recipe may not always weigh precisely the same; this happens chiefly because ingredients are measured by volume, not by weight. So there can also be some variation between the weight given in the book for a recipe and the breads you make from it. For absolute accuracy, you might want to check the weight of your newly baked breads on a scale. Make adjustments to the carb count if needed.

Baking four small loaves is probably preferable to baking two large ones. With smaller loaves on hand you may eat a bit less bread, and you also can keep more of the bread frozen to preserve its freshness.

All of the breads make *superb* toast. This is especially useful if the bread has been in the fridge for a couple of days.

The recipes call for packets of active dry yeast, but you can switch to another type if you wish. Not all yeasts work equally well. It is best, therefore, to first change yeasts in a recipe that has worked well previously before you start using a fresh batch of gluten.

Generally, there is little that can go wrong in making these breads, so if the bread does not rise at all or only to a fraction of what you would expect—especially if it happens on the heels of success or when you begin with a new batch of vital wheat gluten— the vital wheat gluten almost certainly is at fault. If the bread has risen at all, make these changes: the next time you bake with the same gluten, increase it in the recipe by ⅓ cup and reduce another ingredient (except whole wheat or rye flour) by the same amount. The bread may do better. If a problem persists, or if you have any other questions, please contact www.info@ lowcarbbakinganddessertcookbook.com.

Basic White Bread

This light white bread is also great for making French-style bread and dinner rolls.

PREPARATION TIME: 15 minutes. RISING AND BAKING TIME: about 60 minutes.
SERVING SIZE: 1 ounce (28 grams). AMOUNT PER SERVING: 4.2 grams of carb,
9.6 grams of protein. TOTAL YIELD: about 22.0 ounces.

		CHO (g)	PRO (g)
1⅓	cups cold water	0	0
4	tablespoons unsalted butter (½ stick) or coconut oil	0	0
2	packages active dry yeast (or 4 teaspoons)	4.0	8.0
1¾	cups vital wheat gluten	39.2	161.0
½	cup stone-ground whole wheat flour	36.2	5.0
1	cup blanched almond meal	12.0	20.0
¼	cup soy protein powder	0	16.1
	salt to taste (about ½ teaspoon)	0	0
	Total	*91.4*	*210.1*

Preheat the oven to 350°F for about 5 minutes and then *turn it off.* Prepare the baking pans you want to use. No greasing is needed for heavy metal, nonstick pans.

In a medium, microwavable mixing bowl, combine 1 cup of the water and 3 tablespoons of the butter; reserve ⅓ cup of the water and 1 tablespoon of the butter.

Microwave the water and the butter until the butter is mostly melted, about 1 minute. Add the remaining cold water. The temperature of the hot water-butter mix should be between 90 and 110 degrees. This is quite warm to the touch. You may want to check the temperature with an instant-read thermometer until you get a feel for it. Add the yeast, stir, and set aside.

Combine the dry ingredients in a medium mixing bowl and stir well. Warm any ingredients that came directly from the fridge or the freezer for a few seconds in the microwave before adding to the rest of the dry ingredients.

Add the dry mix all at once to the yeast mix. Stir thoroughly with a fork, using about 12 to 14 strokes. The dough will be lumpy. Before mixing the dough, you might want to put on disposable plastic gloves. Mix the dough—it will be squishy at first—into a cohesive ball. This takes only a few seconds. If there are some crumbs left at the bottom of the bowl that will not be absorbed, ignore them. But if there is a fair amount left, you may want to add 2 tablespoons of warm water (not more than that) and work the dough until the crumbs are picked up. Transfer the dough to a cutting board or countertop and knead for about 20 seconds, until well mixed. The dough should be fairly soft yet firm enough to shape. Once you have made a batch or two of loaves, you will get a feel for it. If the dough seems too soft—and this is a judgment call—add a tablespoon or two of soy protein powder to it. (Run hot water promptly into the empty mixing bowl for easy cleanup later.)

Divide the dough in portions, depending on the size of your baking pans. Shape each loaf to fit the pan. Put a portion of the reserved butter in your palms as you shape the loaves; this will help create a smooth loaf and also give the crust some extra shine. For French bread, make two ropes, each about 11 to 12 inches long (the finished loaves will be about 15 inches in length) and place them in a French bread pan. If you want to make rolls, see Rolls to Go (page 43).

Set the bread pans in the prewarmed oven and allow the bread to rise for 30 to 45 minutes. The oven temperature should be between 85°F and 90°F; it should feel just mildly warm to the hand.

When the loaves have risen sufficiently, don't remove them from the oven. Just reset the oven temperature to 350°F and bake the loaves for 25 to 28 minutes or until done. The crust should be light golden brown.

Remove the loaves gently from the pans—most will be soft when they come from the oven and will harden or firm up after a while—and place them on a cooling rack. *Allow the loaves to cool completely before slicing or wrapping or freezing.*

The loaves will keep in the fridge for two or three days. A good way to keep loaves wonderfully fresh is to freeze them; they thaw quickly. It's okay to preslice the bread. If you do that, for extra protection, wrap the sliced loaf in aluminum foil before placing it in a freezer bag. When you thaw frozen bread, remove it from the aluminum foil. Otherwise, moisture accumulated inside the freezer bag may leave the bread a little soggy; however, it will dry out after a few minutes. Store thawed bread in a dry plastic bag.

Variation: Basic White Bread (Soy-Free)

Follow the directions for Basic White Bread above. Make these changes: increase the blanched almond meal by ¼ cup, omit the soy protein powder, and add ⅓ cup of crude wheat bran. This increases the carb count for 1 ounce (28 grams) to 4.4 grams, protein count is 9.0 grams.

Light Almond Bread

A delicious bread, sure to become a staple.

PREPARATION TIME: 15 minutes. RISING AND BAKING TIME: about 60 minutes.
SERVING SIZE: 1 ounce (28 grams). AMOUNT PER SERVING: 3.4 grams of carb,
10.5 grams of protein. TOTAL YIELD: about 22.0 ounces.

		CHO (g)	PRO (g)
1⅓	cups cold water	0	0
4	tablespoons unsalted butter (½ stick) or coconut oil	0	0
2	packages active dry yeast (or 4 teaspoons)	4.0	8.0
1¾	cups vital wheat gluten	39.2	161.0
¼	cup stone-ground whole wheat flour	18.1	4.0
1¼	cups whole almond meal	12.5	25.0
½	cup soy protein powder	0	32.2
	salt to taste (about ½ teaspoon)	0	0
	Total	*73.8*	*230.2*

For bread-making steps, follow the directions for Basic White Bread on page 24.

Oat Bread

This bread, which has all the goodness of rolled oats, has a slightly dense texture.

PREPARATION TIME: 15 minutes. RISING AND BAKING TIME: about 60 minutes.
SERVING SIZE: 1 ounce (28 grams). AMOUNT PER SERVING: 5.2 grams of carb,
   10.3 grams of protein. TOTAL YIELD: about 22.0 ounces.

		CHO (g)	PRO (g)
1⅓	cups cold water	0	0
4	tablespoons unsalted butter (½ stick) or coconut oil	0	0
2	packages active dry yeast (or 4 teaspoons)	4.0	8.0
1¾	cups vital wheat gluten	39.2	161.0
1	cup rolled oats	46.0	6.0
¼	cup stone-ground whole wheat flour	18.1	4.0
¾	cup whole almond meal	7.5	15.0
½	cup soy protein powder	0	32.2
	salt to taste (about ½ teaspoon)	0	0
	Total	*114.8*	*226.2*

For bread-making steps, follow the directions for Basic White Bread on page 24.

Macadamia Nut Bread

Toasted, chopped macadamia nuts, macadamia nut meal, and macadamia nut flour combine to make this bread taste phenomenally good. It is a low-carb treat all by itself—and even better buttered.

PREPARATION TIME: 15 minutes. RISING AND BAKING TIME: about 60 minutes. SERVING SIZE: 1 ounce (28 grams). AMOUNT PER SERVING: 3.0 grams of carb, 7.5 grams of protein. TOTAL YIELD: about 25.0 ounces.

		CHO (g)	PRO (g)
1½	cups cold water	0	0
4	tablespoons unsalted butter (½ stick) or coconut oil	0	0
2	packages active dry yeast (or 4 teaspoons)	4.0	8.0
1¾	cups vital wheat gluten	39.2	161.0
½	cup macadamia nut meal*	2.6	2.0
¼	cup macadamia nut flour (defatted)*	1.7	2.0
1¼	cups toasted macadamia nuts, finely chopped	8.5	11.0
¼	cup stone-ground whole wheat flour	18.1	4.0
	salt to taste (about ½ teaspoon)	0	0
	Total	*74.1*	*188.0*

Please note that this recipe requires 1½ cups of water. Heat 1 cup and 2 tablespoons of the water with the butter. Then add 6 tablespoons of cold water.

For bread-making steps, follow the directions for Basic White Bread on page 24.

Variation: Sweet Macadamia Nut Bread

Follow the recipe for Macadamia Nut Bread above. Add 2 packets of Splenda and 1 teaspoon of Stevia Plus (or equivalent) to the dry mix and 1 teaspoon of vanilla extract to the hot water-butter mix. There is no change in carb grams.

---

*If you do not have macadamia nut flour or macadamia nut meal, replace both with ¾ cup of blanched almond meal. The total increase in carbohydrates is about 6.0 grams.

White Bread with Currants

Currants add a deliciously sweet touch to this yummy bread.

PREPARATION TIME: 15 minutes. RISING AND BAKING TIME: about 60 minutes.
SERVING SIZE: 1 ounce (28 grams). AMOUNT PER SERVING: 4.8 grams of carb,
   10.1 grams of protein. TOTAL YIELD: about 23.0 ounces.

		CHO (g)	PRO (g)
1⅓	cups cold water	0	0
4	tablespoons unsalted butter		
	(½ stick) or coconut oil	0	0
2	packages active dry yeast		
	(or 4 teaspoons)	4.0	8.0
1¾	cups vital wheat gluten	39.2	161.0
⅓	cup stone-ground whole wheat flour	24.1	5.0
1¼	cups blanched almond meal	15.0	25.0
½	cup soy protein powder	0	32.2
1	teaspoon Stevia Plus (or equivalent)	0	0
¼	cup currants	28.0	1.0
	salt to taste (less than ½ teaspoon)	0	0
	Total	*110.3*	*232.2*

Add the currants to the dry mix.

For bread-making steps, follow the directions for Basic White Bread on page 24.

Variation: White Bread with Currants and Walnuts

Follow the directions for White Bread with Currants above. Add 4 ounces of coarsely chopped walnuts to the dry mix. Add 2 more tablespoons of water to the amount you heat with the butter. One ounce (28 grams) contains 4.0 grams of carb and 9.0 grams of protein.

Date Bread

Once you've tried this tasty bread toasted, you'll surely want to make it an occasional treat. Dates pack a high-carb punch, as do all dried fruits. By adding walnuts to this bread (see the variation that follows), the carb count per serving drops a little.

PREPARATION TIME: 15 minutes. RISING AND BAKING TIME: about 60 minutes. SERVING SIZE: 1 ounce (28 grams). AMOUNT PER SERVING: 5.5 grams of carb, 9.2 grams of protein. TOTAL YIELD: about 25.0 ounces.

		CHO (g)	PRO (g)
1⅓	cups cold water	0	0
2	teaspoons vanilla extract	1.2	0
4	tablespoons unsalted butter (½ stick)		
	or coconut oil	0	0
1	teaspoon Stevia Plus (or equivalent)	0	0
2	packages active dry yeast		
	(or 4 teaspoons)	4.0	8.0
10	finely chopped dates (about ½ cup)	50.0	1.0
1¾	cups vital wheat gluten	39.2	161.0
½	cup dark rye flour	30.0	8.0
1	cup blanched almond meal	12.0	20.0
½	cup soy protein powder	0	32.2
	salt to taste (about ¼ teaspoon		
	or less)	0	0
	Total	*136.4*	*230.2*

Add the Stevia Plus to the hot water-butter mix and stir. Chop the dates very fine and mix them with the yeast mix before adding the dry mix.

For bread-making steps, follow the directions for Basic White Bread on page 24.

Variation: Date Bread with Walnuts

Follow the directions for Date Bread above. Add 4 ounces of chopped walnuts (or other nuts) to the dry mix. Add 2 more tablespoons of water to the amount you heat with the butter. The total yield of the bread increases to 29 ounces. One ounce (28 grams) has 4.8 grams of carb. The protein drops to 9.0 grams.

Olive Bread

If you are unfamiliar with olive bread, you will be surprised by its exciting, tangy flavor. This is a great low-carb version.

PREPARATION TIME:15 minutes. RISING AND BAKING TIME: about 60 minutes. SERVING SIZE: 1 ounce (28 grams). AMOUNT PER SERVING: 3.3 grams of carb, 7.3 grams of protein. TOTAL YIELD: about 32.0 ounces.

		CHO (g)	PRO (g)
8	ounces kalamata olives (about 32), chopped	14.4	4.8
1⅓	cups cold water	0	0
4	tablespoons unsalted butter (½ stick) or coconut oil	0	0
2	packages active dry yeast (or 4 teaspoons)	4.0	8.0
1¾	cups vital wheat gluten	39.2	161.0
½	cup stone-ground whole wheat flour	36.2	8.0
1	cup blanched almond meal	12.0	20.0
½	cup soy protein powder	0	32.2
	salt to taste (about ¼ teaspoon— olives are salty)	0	0
	Total	*105.8*	*234.0*

Chop the olives into small pieces; drain and dry them thoroughly on paper towels. Set aside. Add the olives to the hot water-butter mix before adding the dry mix.

For bread-making steps, follow the directions for Basic White Bread on page 24.

Dill and Onion Bread

Just wait till you toast this and spread it with butter. Great as a base for appetizers; there are many suggestions for making them in The Low-Carb Comfort Food Cookbook.

PREPARATION TIME: 15 minutes. RISING AND BAKING TIME: about 60 minutes. SERVING SIZE: 1 ounce (28 grams). AMOUNT PER SERVING: 4.2 grams of carb, 10.6 grams of protein. TOTAL YIELD: about 22.0 ounces.

		CHO (g)	PRO (g)
1⅓	cups cold water	0	0
4	tablespoons unsalted butter (½ stick) or coconut oil	0	0
2	packages active dry yeast (or 4 teaspoons)	4.0	8.0
1¾	cups vital wheat gluten	39.2	161.0
⅓	cup stone-ground whole wheat flour	24.1	5.0
1¼	cups blanched almond meal	15.0	25.0
½	cup soy protein powder	0	32.2
1	tablespoon dried, minced onion flakes	5.1	0
3	tablespoons dill, dried	4.5	2.0
	salt to taste (about ½ teaspoon)	0	0
	Total	*91.9*	*233.2*

Add the onion and the dill to the dry mix.

For bread-making steps, follow the directions for Basic White Bread on page 24.

Variation: Herbed Crouton Bread

You can eat this as bread, but it also makes great croutons. Follow directions for Dill and Onion Bread above. Make these changes: omit the dill and the onion, and add 3 tablespoons of dried basil, 1 tablespoon of dried thyme (or any combination of herbs you like), and ½ teaspoon of garlic powder. There is no change in carb count. When making croutons, it is best to bake four small loaves rather than two large ones.

HOW TO MAKE CROUTONS

Slice each freshly baked, cooled loaf into 8 or 10 slices, and then cube the slices. Toss the cubes in a freezer bag and freeze. When you want to use them, you can quickly thaw and dry them in the oven, set at 350°F. You can also fry the frozen cubes in some heated olive oil and butter in a skillet until golden brown. A loaf has 23.0 grams of carb and 58.3 grams of protein.

Light Walnut Bread

This delicious bread has great flavor, yet is low in carb and high in protein.

PREPARATION TIME: 15 minutes. RISING AND BAKING TIME: about 60 minutes. SERVING SIZE: 1 ounce (28 grams). AMOUNT PER SERVING: 3.2 grams of carb, 11.0 grams of protein. TOTAL YIELD: about 23.0 ounces.

		CHO (g)	PRO (g)
1⅓	cups cold water	0	0
4	tablespoons unsalted butter (½ stick) or coconut oil	0	0
2	packages active dry yeast (or 4 teaspoons)	4.0	8.0
1¾	cups vital wheat gluten	39.2	161.0
⅓	cup stone-ground whole wheat flour	24.1	5.0
½	cup soy protein powder	0	32.2
1¾	cups walnut meal	7.0	47.6
	salt to taste (about ½ teaspoon)	0	0
	Total	*74.3*	*253.8*

For bread-making steps, follow the directions for Basic White Bread on page 24.

Variation: Light Walnut Bread with Chopped Walnuts

Follow the directions for Light Walnut Bread above, but finely chop 4 ounces of walnuts and add to the dry mix. Increase the amount of water by 2 tablespoons. The carb count for 1 ounce (28 grams) drops to 3.0 grams.

Variation: Extra-Low-Carb Light Walnut Bread

It doesn't go lower than this—but remains tasty. Follow the directions for Light Walnut Bread above. Make these changes: omit the whole wheat flour. Increase the walnut meal by ⅓ cup. One ounce (28 grams) has 2.3 grams of carb; the protein change is negligible.

Health Nut Bread

Loaded with healthy ingredients, this bread boasts wonderful flavor.
A dense, coarse, heavy, high-fiber bread—you may like it better than
some of the breads you had to give up.

PREPARATION TIME: 20 minutes. RISING AND BAKING TIME: about 60 minutes.
SERVING SIZE: 1 ounce (28 grams). AMOUNT PER SERVING: 3.3 grams of carb,
   9.2 grams of protein. TOTAL YIELD: about 27.0 ounces.

		CHO (g)	PRO (g)
1⅓	cups cold water	0	0
4	tablespoons unsalted butter		
	(½ stick) or coconut oil	0	0
½	teaspoon Stevia Plus (or equivalent)	0	0
3	dates, finely chopped (optional)	15.0	0
2	packages active dry yeast		
	(or 4 teaspoons)	4.0	8.0
1¾	cups vital wheat gluten	39.2	161.0
¾	cup blanched almond meal	9.0	15.0
½	cup flaxseed meal	3.2	10.0
¼	cup flaxseeds	2.5	7.0
½	cup toasted sunflower seeds	4.6	12.6
½	cup sesame seeds	6.0	14.0
½	cup pumpkin seeds, toasted,		
	coarsely chopped	5.0	20.0
	salt to taste (about ½ teaspoon)	0	0
	Total	*88.5*	*247.6*

   Add Stevia Plus to the hot water-butter mix and stir. Add the finely
chopped dates. Combine all the dry ingredients, including the nuts
and the seeds.

   For bread-making steps, follow the directions for Basic White
Bread on page 24.

Variation: Smooth Health Nut Bread

This is for those who like a bread with a smooth texture yet delicious
flavor. Follow the directions for Health Nut Bread above, but finely
grind the sunflower and pumpkin seeds in a food processor before
adding them to the dry mix.

Brown Bread

A scrumptious brown bread. Try this with butter.

PREPARATION TIME: 15 minutes. RISING AND BAKING TIME: about 60 minutes.
SERVING SIZE: 1 ounce (28 grams). AMOUNT PER SERVING: 3.8 grams of carb,
8.7 grams of protein. TOTAL YIELD: about 25.0 ounces.

		CHO (g)	PRO (g)
1⅓	cup cold water	0	0
4	tablespoons unsalted butter (½ stick) or coconut oil	0	0
2	tablespoons instant coffee (powder)	0	0
1	tablespoon cocoa powder	2.0	2.0
1	tablespoon blackstrap molasses	17.0	0
2	packages active dry yeast (or 4 teaspoons)	4.0	8.0
1¾	cups vital wheat gluten	39.2	161.0
⅓	cup rye flour	20.0	5.0
1¼	cups whole almond meal	12.5	25.0
¼	cup soy protein powder	0	16.1
	salt to taste (½ teaspoon or less)	0	0
	Total	*94.7*	*217.1*

Add the coffee powder and the cocoa powder to the hot water-butter mix; stir well. Add the yeast and stir again.

For bread-making steps, follow the directions for Basic White Bread on page 24.

Variation: Brown Bread with Seeds

Follow the directions for Brown Bread above. Add the following to the dry mix: ¼ cup of sesame seeds and ¼ cup of toasted, chopped sunflower seeds. The change in carb grams is negligible, since there is a slight increase in overall weight.

Variation: Lowest-Carb Brown Bread

Follow the directions for Brown Bread above. Make these changes: omit the rye flour and replace it with ½ cup of crude wheat bran. The carb count for one 28-gram serving drops to 3.0 grams.

Sesame Bread

Go for it, sesame lovers. This is pure sesame satisfaction.

PREPARATION TIME: 15 minutes. RISING AND BAKING TIME: about 60 minutes.
SERVING SIZE: 1 ounce (28 grams). AMOUNT PER SERVING: 3.7 grams of carb,
10.5 grams of protein. TOTAL YIELD: about 22.0 ounces.

		CHO (g)	PRO (g)
1⅓	cup cold water	0	0
1	tablespoon tahini (sesame butter)	2.9	3.0
3	tablespoons unsalted butter (⅜ stick)	0	0
2	packages active dry yeast		
	(or 4 teaspoons)	4.0	8.0
1¾	cups vital wheat gluten	39.2	161.0
⅓	cup oat flour	17.3	5.0
1	cup whole almond meal	10.0	20.0
⅔	cup sesame seeds	8.0	18.7
¼	cup soy protein powder	0	16.0
	salt to taste (about ½ teaspoon)	0	0
	Total	*81.4*	*231.7*

Instead of combining 3 tablespoons of the butter with the hot water, combine the tahini with 2 tablespoons of the butter and the water; reserve 1 tablespoon of the butter.

For bread-making steps, follow the directions for Basic White Bread on page 24.

High-Fiber Bread (Nut-Free)

Wheat bran, flaxseed meal, psyllium husks, inulin, sunflower seeds, and rye flour give this dense, heavy bread a great, hearty taste.

PREPARATION TIME: 20 minutes. RISING AND BAKING TIME: about 60 minutes. SERVING SIZE: 1 ounce (28 grams). AMOUNT PER SERVING: 3.7 grams of carb, 9.3 grams of protein. TOTAL YIELD: about 22.0 ounces.

		CHO (g)	PRO (g)
1⅓	cups cold water	0	0
4	tablespoons unsalted butter (½ stick) or coconut oil	0	0
2	packages active dry yeast (or 4 teaspoons)	4.0	8.0
1¾	cups vital wheat gluten	39.2	161.0
¾	cup flaxseed meal	4.8	15.0
1	cup crude wheat bran	12.0	8.0
¼	cup whole psyllium husks	3.2	0
⅓	cup coarsely ground sunflower seeds	3.0	8.4
¼	cup dark rye flour	15.0	4.0
4	tablespoons inulin fiber	0	0
	salt to taste (less than ½ teaspoon)	0	0
	Total	*81.2*	*204.4*

For bread-making steps, follow the directions for Basic White Bread on page 24.

This bread has a total of a whopping 92 grams of fiber—much of it soluble. Add 4.4 grams of fiber to a 1-ounce (28-gram) serving.

Golden Soy Grit Bread (Nut-Free)

Soy grits (a commercial product made from defatted soybeans), which are high in protein, give this nut-free bread a surprisingly crunchy, nutty flavor.

PREPARATION TIME: 15 minutes. RISING AND BAKING TIME: about 60 minutes.
SERVING SIZE: 1 ounce (28 grams). AMOUNT PER SERVING: 4.0 grams of carb,
9.6 grams of protein. TOTAL YIELD: about 24.0 ounces.

		CHO (g)	PRO (g)
1½	cups cold water	0	0
4	tablespoons unsalted butter		
	(½ stick) or coconut oil	0	0
2	packages active dry yeast		
	(or 4 teaspoons)	4.0	8.0
1¾	cups vital wheat gluten	39.2	161.0
½	cup soy grits	14.0	38.0
½	cup stone-ground whole wheat flour	36.2	8.0
¼	cup soy protein powder	0	16.1
	salt to taste (less than 1 teaspoon)	0	0
	Total	*93.4*	*231.1*

Please note that this dough requires 1½ cups of water. Heat 1 cup and 2 tablespoons with the butter. Add 6 tablespoons of cold water.

For bread-making steps, follow the directions for Basic White Bread on page 24.

Hazelnut Bread

Loaded with delightful hazelnut flavor, this bread is terrific at any meal.

PREPARATION TIME: 15 minutes. RISING AND BAKING TIME: about 60 minutes. SERVING SIZE: 1 ounce (28 grams). AMOUNT PER SERVING: 3.2 grams of carb, 9.8 grams of protein. TOTAL YIELD: about 24.0 ounces.

		CHO (g)	PRO (g)
1⅓	cups cold water	0	0
4	tablespoons unsalted butter		
	(½ stick) or coconut oil	0	0
2	packages active dry yeast		
	(or 4 teaspoons)	4.0	8.0
1¾	cups vital wheat gluten	39.2	161.0
1¼	cups hazelnut meal	9.5	20.0
½	cup whole almond meal	5.0	10.0
¼	cup stone-ground whole wheat flour	18.1	4.0
½	cup soy protein powder	0	32.2
	salt to taste (about ½ teaspoon)	0	0
	Total	75.8	235.2

For bread-making steps, follow the directions for Basic White Bread on page 24.

Variation: Hazelnut Bread with Chopped Hazelnuts

Follow the directions for Hazelnut Bread above. Make these changes: increase the amount of water by 2 tablespoons. Add 4 ounces of finely chopped hazelnuts to the dry mix. The total yield rises to 28.0 ounces. Gram counts do not change significantly.

Flaxseed Bread

So tasty, you almost forget how good it is for you. Try it. Quite dense, it also makes a great base for appetizers. You'll find spreads galore in The Low-Carb Comfort Food Cookbook.

PREPARATION TIME: 15 minutes. RISING AND BAKING TIME: about 60 minutes. SERVING SIZE: 1 ounce (28 grams). AMOUNT PER SERVING: 3.2 grams of carb, 9.8 grams of protein. TOTAL YIELD: about 22.0 ounces.

		CHO (g)	PRO (g)
1½	cups cold water	0	0
4	tablespoons unsalted butter (½ stick) or coconut oil	0	0
2	packages active dry yeast (or 4 teaspoons)	4.0	8.0
1¾	cups vital wheat gluten	39.2	161.0
¾	cup flaxseed meal	4.8	15.0
¼	cup unprocessed wheat bran	3.0	2.0
½	cup whole almond meal	5.0	10.0
¼	cup dark rye flour	15.0	4.0
¼	cup soy protein powder	0	16.1
	salt to taste (about ½ teaspoon)	0	0
	Total	*71.0*	*216.1*

Please note that this dough requires 1½ cups of water. Heat 1 cup and 2 tablespoons with the butter. Add 6 tablespoons of cold water.

For bread-making steps, follow the directions for Basic White Bread on page 24.

Variation: Flaxseed Bread with Walnuts

Follow the directions for Flaxseed Bread above. Make these changes: increase the water by 2 tablespoons. Add 4 ounces of coarsely chopped walnuts to the dry mix. The walnuts increase the total weight of the loaves to about 26 ounces. The carb count for a single serving (28 grams) drops to 2.9 grams. There is no protein change.

Variation: Flaxseed Bread (Nut-Free)

Follow the directions for Flaxseed Bread above. Make these changes: omit the whole almond meal. Increase the water by 2 tablespoons. Increase the unprocessed wheat bran to ⅔ cup. Increase the soy protein powder to ⅓ cup. Add 4 tablespoons of whey protein powder (natural, zero-carb). Changes in carb grams are negligible; protein counts increase by 1.0 gram per serving.

Sourdough Bread

This nice bread has a mild sourdough flavor.

PREPARATION TIME: 20 minutes. RISING AND BAKING TIME: about 75 minutes. Starter requires 48 hours to ripen.

SERVING SIZE: 1 ounce (28 grams). AMOUNT PER SERVING: 4.2 grams of carb, 8.3 grams of protein. TOTAL YIELD: about 26.0 ounces.

		CHO (g)	PRO (g)
SOURDOUGH STARTER			
⅓	cup enriched unbleached wheat (white) flour	30.7	4.0
¼	teaspoon dry yeast	0.3	0
⅛	teaspoon sugar (cane)	0.5	0
¾	cup warm water	0	0
2	ounces plain yogurt (full-fat)	3.0	3.0
BREAD DOUGH			
¾	cup cold water	0	0
4	tablespoons unsalted butter (½ stick)	0	0
2	packages active dry yeast (or 4 teaspoons)	4.0	8.0
1¾	cups vital wheat gluten	39.2	161.0
⅓	cup dark rye flour	20.0	4.0
½	cup whole almond meal	5.0	10.0
½	cup blanched almond meal	6.0	10.0
¼	cup soy protein powder	0	16.1
	salt to taste (about 1¼ teaspoon)	0	0
	Total	*108.7*	*216.1*

For the starter, combine all the ingredients in a small microwavable container. Whisk briefly until well mixed. Cover and put in a warm place for 48 hours. A cupboard or the top of the fridge are good spots. During this time, whisk the mixture once a day.

When you are ready to make the bread, preheat the oven briefly, as you would for any raised bread (see Basic White Bread on page 24). Stir the starter and put it in the microwave for about 15 seconds, to warm it slightly. Reserve 1 tablespoon of the butter. Heat the water with 3 tablespoons of the butter until the butter melts. Combine the melted butter with the starter in a medium mixing bowl and stir well.

Combine the remaining ingredients in a separate bowl. Stir the dry mix well and work it into the liquid, using a fork. Continue the process as directed for Basic White Bread on page 24.

Pumpkin Bread

An unusual, delicious, moist, lightly sweetened bread with a barely perceptible pumpkin flavor. Really low in carbohydrates too.

PREPARATION TIME: 20 minutes. RISING AND BAKING TIME: about 60 minutes. SERVING SIZE: 1 ounce (28 grams). AMOUNT PER SERVING: 2.3 grams of carb, 8.8 grams of protein. TOTAL YIELD: about 24.0 ounces.

		CHO (g)	PRO (g)
1¼	cups cold water	0	0
4	tablespoons unsalted butter (½ stick) or coconut oil	0	0
½	cup canned pumpkin	3.0	2.0
1	teaspoon Stevia Plus (or equivalent)	0	0
2	packages active dry yeast (or 4 teaspoons)	4.0	8.0
1¾	cups vital wheat gluten	39.2	161.0
¾	cup whole almond meal	7.5	15.0
½	cup flaxseed meal	3.2	10.0
¼	cup soy protein powder	0	16.1
	salt to taste (about ½ teaspoon)	0	0
	Total	*56.9*	*212.1*

Add the pumpkin and Stevia Plus to the yeast mix before adding the dry mix.

For bread-making steps, follow the directions for Basic White Bread on page 24.

Rolls to Go

Rolls swallow up tons of flour; it makes them especially high in carbohydrates. A 2-ounce bagel, as you may know, has a shattering 31 grams of carb; some other rolls of equal weight are worse. This is just to prepare you for the fact that the low-carb rolls in this book—for the same reason—have a carb count that is seemingly high. Even so, it will be much lower than the count for high-carb rolls.

You can make rolls from just about any recipe here, but the yield, when it comes to the number of rolls, is low. One recipe that gives you four small loaves produces only ten or eleven rolls. It is best, therefore, to make rolls from breads with the lowest carb counts. Light Almond Bread (page 26) would give you ten rolls at 7.4 grams of carb each. But they are also delicious.

For best results, use 3½-inch buttered muffin pans for baking rolls. (You will need two.) The rolls need the support from the muffin cup walls as they rise. To make any rolls, simply follow the directions for the bread recipe of your choice. When the time comes to shape the rolls, shape two ropes about 1¾ inches across; cut them in the number of rolls you want to make. Shape the rolls and set them in the cups. Allow rolls to rise for about the same length of time as you would bread. Bake the rolls for 20 to 22 minutes at 350°F or until golden.

(Please note that the best carbohydrate bargain ever for a 3½-inch roll is the Magic Roll. You find Magic Rolls in *The Low-Carb Comfort Food Cookbook*. The rolls are not yeast based but are related to the process that makes cream puffs rise. They are quite delicious.)

Bread Sticks

It is best to use a plain bread recipe for making bread sticks. Light Almond Bread (page 26) is a good choice.

Follow the instructions for the bread you want to use. You can mix and match, if you want, and bake some bread as well as bread sticks.

You can make any number of sticks from one recipe. Bread sticks can be frozen and will keep a long time.

For shaping bread sticks, the dough needs to be fairly firm. Work an extra 2 to 4 tablespoons of soy protein powder into the dough at the end, add more if needed. As a guide, divide the dough into four equal portions and divide each portion into six or eight chunks, as you wish. Twist and elongate the chunks into ropes about ½ to ¾ inch thick and whatever length you like. Place them fairly close together on a cookie sheet with a silicone-coated liner. Allow them to rise for about 30 minutes. Bake the sticks for 18 minutes or until they turn light golden brown. To find out the grams of carb in each stick, divide the number of sticks you end up with by the total number of carbohydrate grams in the recipe.

Restore the bread sticks to crispness by placing them for 15 minutes on a cookie sheet in the oven set at 300°F. A toaster oven will do the same. If desired, roll the dough in a few sesame seeds as you shape the sticks.

Variation: Cheese Bread Sticks

Use the Light Almond Bread recipe on page 26 but make these changes: add ¾ cup of Parmesan cheese to the dry mix. Follow the directions for making Light Almond Bread and also the directions for making Bread Sticks above. This dough will require only a small amount of extra soy protein, if any, for shaping the bread sticks. The cheese adds a total of 27.0 grams of protein to the recipe. The carb change is insignificant.

Pecan Rolls

Completely delicious. Try them. You won't believe they're low-carb.

PREPARATION TIME: 20 minutes. RISING AND BAKING TIME: about 60 minutes.
SERVING SIZE: 1 pecan roll (weight about 1 ounce). AMOUNT PER SERVING:
4.9 grams of carb, 9.1 grams of protein. TOTAL YIELD: 18 to 24 pecan
rolls.

		CHO (g)	PRO (g)
1	cup cold water	0	0
4	tablespoons unsalted butter (½ stick), very soft	0	0
2	teaspoons Stevia Plus (or equivalent)	0	0
2	teaspoons vanilla extract	1.0	0
2	packages active dry yeast (or 4 teaspoons)	4.0	8.0
1	cup vital wheat gluten	22.4	92.0
¼	cup unbleached wheat (white) flour	23.0	3.0
1	cup blanched almond meal	12.0	20.0
¼	cup oat flour	13.0	4.0
½	cup soy protein powder	0	32.2
½	teaspoon ground nutmeg (optional)	0.5	0
	salt, trace	0	0
FILLING			
1	tablespoon unsalted butter, melted	0	0
2	tablespoons xylitol	4.5	0
4	packets Splenda	4.0	0
½	teaspoon ground cinnamon	0.4	0
2	ounces toasted pecans, coarsely chopped	3.2	5.2
	Total	*88.0*	*164.4*

Preheat the oven to 350°F for about 5 minutes and *turn it off*. Butter two 2-inch muffin pans with a capacity of 12 cups each.

Combine ¾ cup of the water and the butter in a medium microwavable mixing bowl and heat in the microwave until the butter melts (this takes about 1 minute). Add the remaining cold water, Stevia Plus, and vanilla extract. Stir in the yeast. Set aside.

Combine all the dry ingredients, except the filling, in a medium microwavable mixing bowl. Stir well. If any ingredients came from the fridge or the freezer, warm the mix in the microwave for about 20 seconds or so to remove the chill.

Pour the dry mix into the yeast mix. Stir with a fork until large lumps form. Take over by hand; the dough will be quite squishy (this is a good time for disposable gloves). Shape the dough into a smooth ball.

Transfer the dough to a large cutting board (14 by 18 inches) or use the countertop. Put a wet kitchen towel beneath the board to keep it from sliding. Roll the dough into a rectangle, approximately 13 by 17 inches. The dough should not be sticky.

For the filling: brush the dough with the melted butter. Mix the sugar with the cinnamon and sprinkle evenly over the sheet of dough. Sprinkle the chopped pecans on top. Lightly press the nuts with your hands into the dough. Roll up the dough into a tight roll about 16 to 17 inches long. If needed, stretch it a bit.

Cut the roll into 18 to 24 equal chunks and put them in the muffin pans. Fill 18 or 24 cups. Set them in the prewarmed oven and let them rise for about 30 to 45 minutes. Turn the oven to 325°F and bake the rolls for about 18 to 20 minutes or until light golden. Do not over-bake. Set them on a cooling rack to cool.

Variation: Glazed Pecan Rolls

Follow the directions for Pecan Rolls above. Since these buns have a relatively high carb count, you may want to use a glaze made from xylitol powdered sugar. It closely resembles regular powdered sugar. Mix 3 tablespoons of xylitol powdered sugar with 2 teaspoons of cream to make a thin paste. Brush the glaze over the rolls while still hot; allow the glaze to dry completely. This adds 0.2 gram of carb to each pecan roll. You can substitute real powdered sugar for the glaze. This adds 1.4 grams of carb to each roll.

Variation: Cinnamon Walnut Rolls

Follow the directions for Pecan Rolls above. Make these changes to the filling: increase the cinnamon to 1 teaspoon. Omit the pecans and use 2 ounces of finely chopped walnuts instead. Changes in gram counts are insignificant.

Raised Doughnuts

You need a deep fryer to make these. This is the only recipe in this book that calls for a fryer. If you do not have one, you may want to test-fry a doughnut in a small pan before investing in a deep fryer for this one recipe.

PREPARATION TIME: 25 minutes. RISING AND BAKING TIME: about 60 minutes. SERVING SIZE: one 1-ounce doughnut. AMOUNT PER SERVING: 6.0 grams of carb, 7.0 grams of protein. TOTAL YIELD: about 16 to 18 doughnuts.

		CHO (g)	PRO (g)
¾	cup cold water	0	0
4	tablespoons unsalted butter (½ stick), very soft	0	0
2	teaspoons vanilla extract	1.0	0
2	packages active dry yeast (or 4 teaspoons)	4.0	8.0
2	teaspoons Stevia Plus (or equivalent)	0	0
¾	cup vital wheat gluten	16.8	69.0
½	cup stone-ground whole wheat flour	36.2	8.0
¼	unbleached wheat (white) flour	23.0	8.0
¼	cup blanched almond meal	2.2	5.0
2	tablespoons soy protein powder	0	8.0
¼	teaspoon ground nutmeg (optional)	0.3	0
1	tablespoon xylitol	1.8	0
2	tablespoons Splenda	3.0	0
	salt, trace	0	0
	coconut oil for deep frying; amount depends on fryer	0	0
SUGAR TOPPING			
3	tablespoons xylitol powdered sugar	5.4	0.0
	Total	*93.7*	*106.0*

Combine 9 tablespoons of the water and the butter in a medium microwavable mixing bowl and heat in the microwave until the butter melts. Add the remaining cold water and the vanilla extract. Stir in the yeast. Set aside.

Combine all the dry ingredients, except for the sugar topping, in a medium mixing bowl and stir well.

Add this mix to the yeast mix. Stir with a fork until large lumps form. Take over by hand and shape the dough into a smooth ball; it will be squishy (this is a good time for disposable gloves). The dough should be soft but firm enough to cut out.

Transfer the dough to a large cutting board or use the countertop.

Pat the dough into a sheet about ¾ inch thick. This is not a sticky dough. If needed, sprinkle a tablespoon of soy protein powder on the board. Cut out small doughnuts, about 2 inches across. Put the doughnuts on a tray or a cutting board. Allow them to rise at room temperature for about 15 minutes and then chill them for about 10 minutes.

Prepare the deep fryer with oil according to the manufacturer's instructions or use coconut oil. Set the temperature to 375°F. Fry the doughnuts until golden brown on one side and turn. Fry on the other side, and remove each doughnut carefully to a layer of paper towels. Roll each doughnut in the sugar topping. Set out on a rack to dry and cool. These doughnuts are best when fresh.

Bread Crumbs from Raised Breads

Making bread crumbs from the plain breads in this book is easy and quick to do. Cut the bread you want to use in fairly thin slices, one-half inch or less. Leave the slices out, until dry, which happens almost overnight, and then run them through the food processor. Five ounces of fresh bread make 4 ounces of dry crumbs or 1¼ cups of crumbs. The carb count depends on the type of bread you use. Light Almond Bread (page 26), used to illustrate the process, has 3.5 grams of carb per ounce and 10.0 grams of protein. You can also mix these crumbs with the bread crumbs you can make from Magic Rolls, a great recipe featured in the *Low-Carb Comfort Food Cookbook*. Store these crumbs in the fridge or the freezer. They keep well.

3

Quick Breads, Muffins, Scones, and Coffee Cakes

Coffee Cake Toppings

Quick breads are wonderful. You can have a lot of fun with these because they are easy to make thanks to the quick action of baking powder and baking soda. Savory breads, coffee cakes, muffins, or tea bread are ready in less than 40 minutes—and usually only 10 minutes of that is preparation time.

Unlike raised breads, quick breads are always at their best the day they are made and perhaps the next. Freezing will preserve them nicely, though.

Most of the recipes in this chapter make relatively small batches, partly for this reason. The batter for the muffin recipes makes 6 large muffins, weighing about 2.6 ounces each (there is some variation due to ingredients). The same batter will also make 9 medium-size muffins, about 1.5 ounces each, or 12 small muffins, about 1.3 ounces each. The yield in the recipes is based on a set of 9 medium muffins. Of course you can change the size of your muffins to suit your tastes.

The amount of batter in the recipes also yields either two 3-by-6-inch loaves or one 12-by-12-inch coffee cake (over 1 inch thick). Coffee cakes with their tempting toppings are about the quickest way to come up with a scrumptious treat. And you can even have scones!

Although most of the items in this chapter are sweet, some are savory. The breads are totally delicious and vary considerably in character. You cannot make a virtually foolproof bread more quickly. Nearly all of the breads can become quick tea breads if desired. Try the slices toasted. Add sweeteners as you like; count the additional carbohydrates.

Quick Light Bread

From breakfast toast to sandwich.

PREPARATION TIME: 10 minutes. BAKING TIME: about 35 to 40 minutes.
SERVING SIZE: 1 slice. AMOUNT PER SERVING: 1.2 grams of carb, 4.5 grams of
   protein. TOTAL YIELD: 2 loaves (20 to 24 slices).

		CHO (g)	PRO (g)
2	ounces cream cheese, very soft	1.6	4.2
4	tablespoons sour cream	2.0	1.2
3	tablespoons unsalted butter		
	(⅜ stick), soft, or coconut oil	0	0
3	eggs, room temperature	1.8	18.0
¼	cup whey protein (natural, zero-carb)	0	20.0
1¼	cup blanched almond meal	15.0	25.0
1	teaspoon baking powder	1.2	0
	salt (about ¼ teaspoon)	0	0
¼	cup whole almond meal	2.5	5.0
¼	cup soy protein powder	0	16.1
	Total:	*24.1*	*89.5*

Preheat the oven to 350°F. Butter two heavy metal 3-by-6-inch
baking pans.

Combine the cream cheese, sour cream, butter, and 1 egg in a
medium mixing bowl. Beat briefly until smooth. Add the remaining
eggs and beat briefly again.

Add to the cream cheese mixture the whey protein, blanched
almond meal, baking powder, and salt. Stir until well mixed. Add the
remaining ingredients and stir again. Spoon the batter into the baking
pans. Bake for about 35 to 40 minutes or until a knife inserted in the
center comes out clean. Remove the bread from the pans and cool it
on a cooling rack. Freeze any bread that isn't going to be used the
same day. Preslice the bread if you like.

Sour Cream Biscuits

Biscuits are very difficult to make with low-carb ingredients. However, if you miss them, these wonderful biscuits come mighty close to the original. They are quick to whisk together.

PREPARATION TIME: 10 minutes. (The dough requires brief chilling.) BAKING TIME: about 15 to 18 minutes.

SERVING SIZE: 1 biscuit. AMOUNT PER SERVING: 4.2 grams of carb, 10.2 grams of protein. TOTAL YIELD: 10 biscuits.

		CHO (g)	PRO (g)
2	ounces cream cheese, very soft	1.6	4.2
5	tablespoons sour cream	2.5	1.5
3	tablespoons unsalted butter (⅜ stick), soft, or coconut oil	0	0
3	eggs, room temperature	1.8	18.0
1¼	cups blanched almond meal	15.0	25.0
1	teaspoon baking powder	1.2	0
¼	teaspoon baking soda	0	0
	salt (about ¼ teaspoon)	0	0
⅓	cup dark rye flour	20.0	5.0
¾	cup soy protein powder	0.0	48.3
	Total	*42.1*	*102.0*

Preheat the oven to 400°F. Use a 12-muffin pan. Butter 10 of the cups, or use liners.

Combine the cream cheese, sour cream, butter, and 1 egg in a medium mixing bowl. Beat briefly until smooth. Add the remaining eggs and beat briefly again.

Add to the cream cheese mixture the almond meal, baking powder, soda, salt, dark rye flour, and soy protein powder. Stir lightly. You want to handle the dough as little as possible.

Refrigerate the dough for about 30 minutes. Put it on a cutting board dusted with soy protein powder. Flatten the dough lightly with your hands and cut ten 2-inch rounds with a cookie cutter, about ¾ inch high. You can also carefully shape the biscuits with your hands. Set them in the muffin pans. You can make 12 smaller biscuits if you wish. Bake the biscuits for about 15 to 18 minutes. Freeze any leftover biscuits. Reheat them in a toaster oven, if you have one; they will taste great.

Quick Brown Bread

Dense, heavy, with a hint of molasses.

PREPARATION TIME: 10 minutes. BAKING TIME: about 35 to 40 minutes.
SERVING SIZE: 1 slice. AMOUNT PER SERVING: 1.6 grams of carb, 3.3 grams of
protein. TOTAL YIELD: 2 loaves (20 to 24 slices).

		CHO (g)	PRO (g)
3	tablespoons hot water	0	0
1	tablespoon blackstrap molasses	17.0	0
1	packet Splenda	1.0	0
1	tablespoon instant coffee powder	0	0
1	tablespoon unsweetened cocoa powder	1.0	1.0
6	tablespoons unsalted butter		
	(¾ stick), soft, or coconut oil	0	0
2	eggs, room temperature	1.2	12.0
½	cup whole almond meal	5.0	10.0
½	cup unprocessed wheat bran	6.0	2.0
1	teaspoon baking powder	1.2	0
	salt (about ¼ teaspoon)	0	0
¼	cup whey protein powder		
	(natural, zero-carb)	0	20.0
⅓	cup soy protein powder	0	21.5
	Total	*32.4*	*66.5*

Preheat the oven to 350°F. Butter 2 heavy metal 3-by-6-inch baking pans.

Combine the water, molasses, Splenda, and instant coffee and cocoa powders in a medium mixing bowl, and stir until the coffee and cocoa powders are dissolved. Beat in the soft butter. Beat in the eggs, one at a time.

Add the almond meal, wheat bran, baking powder, and salt. Stir until well mixed. Add the whey protein powder and the soy protein powder; stir again.

Fill the baking pans. Bake for about 35 to 40 minutes or until a knife inserted in the center comes out clean. Remove the bread from the pans and cool it on a cooling rack. Freeze any bread that isn't going to be used the same day. Preslice the bread if you wish.

Quick Flaxseed Bread (Nut-Free)

A fabulous, heavy bread—delicious and healthy. This is a good candidate for serving with appetizers.

PREPARATION TIME: 10 minutes. BAKING TIME: about 35 to 40 minutes.
SERVING SIZE: 1 slice. AMOUNT PER SERVING: 1.7 grams of carb, 4.1 grams of protein. TOTAL YIELD: 2 loaves (20 to 24 slices).

	CHO (g)	PRO (g)
2 ounces cream cheese, very soft	1.6	4.2
2 tablespoons sour cream	1.0	0.6
4 tablespoons unsalted butter (½ stick), soft, or coconut oil	0	0
3 eggs, room temperature	1.8	18.0
¼ cup whey protein powder (natural, zero-carb)	0	20.0
⅓ cup dark rye flour	20.0	4.0
¾ cup flaxseed meal	4.8	15.0
1 teaspoon baking powder	1.2	0
salt (about ¼ teaspoon)	0	0
¼ cup unprocessed wheat bran	3.0	4.0
¼ cup soy protein powder	0	16.0
Total	*33.4*	*81.8*

Preheat the oven to 350°F. Butter two heavy metal 3-by-6-inch baking pans.

Combine the cream cheese, sour cream, butter, and 1 egg in a medium mixing bowl. Beat until smooth. Beat in the remaining eggs.

Add the whey protein powder, dark rye flour, flaxseed meal, baking powder, and salt. Stir well. Add the wheat bran and the soy protein powder next, and stir until the batter is smooth.

Fill the baking pans. Bake for about 35 to 40 minutes or until a knife inserted in the center comes out clean. Remove the bread from the pans and cool it on a cooling rack. Freeze any bread that isn't going to be used the same day. Preslice the bread if you wish.

Quick Flaxseed Biscuits (Nut-Free)

These delicious biscuits have the added benefit of flaxseed meal. Always keep flaxseed products refrigerated or frozen.

PREPARATION TIME: 10 minutes. (The dough requires brief chilling.) BAKING TIME: about 15 to 18 minutes.

SERVING SIZE: 1 biscuit. AMOUNT PER SERVING: 3.9 grams of carb, 9.3 grams of protein. TOTAL YIELD: 10 biscuits.

		CHO (g)	PRO (g)
2	ounces cream cheese, very soft	1.6	4.0
2	tablespoons sour cream	1.0	0
4	tablespoons unsalted butter (½ stick), soft, or coconut oil	0	0
3	eggs, room temperature	1.8	18.0
¼	cup whey protein powder (instant, zero-carb)	0	20.0
⅓	cup dark rye flour	20.0	5.0
1	teaspoon baking powder	1.2	0
¼	teaspoon baking soda	0	0
½	cup soy protein powder	0	32.2
	salt (about ¼ teaspoon)	0	0
½	cup flaxseed meal	3.2	10.0
½	cup unprocessed wheat bran	6.0	4.0
	Total	*34.8*	*93.2*

Preheat the oven to 400°F. Use a 12-muffin pan. Butter 10 of the cups, or use liners.

Combine the cream cheese, sour cream, butter, and 1 egg in a medium mixing bowl. Beat briefly until smooth. Add the remaining eggs and beat briefly again.

Add the whey protein powder, dark rye flour, baking powder, soda, salt, flaxseed meal, wheat bran, and soy protein powder. Stir lightly. You want to handle the dough as little as possible.

Refrigerate this dough for about 30 minutes. Put it on a cutting board dusted with soy protein powder. Flatten the dough lightly with your hands and cut ten 2-inch rounds with a cookie cutter, about ¾ inch high. You can also carefully shape the biscuits with your hands. If needed, add a bit of soy protein powder. Set them in the muffin pans. You can make 12 smaller biscuits if you wish. Bake the biscuits for about 15 to 18 minutes. Freeze any leftover biscuits. Reheat them in a toaster oven, if you have one; they will taste great.

Quick Cheddar Cheese Bread

Enjoy it with butter and a glass of wine. This bread is great as a base for appetizers.

PREPARATION TIME: 10 minutes. BAKING TIME: about 35 to 40 minutes.
SERVING SIZE: 1 slice. AMOUNT PER SERVING: 1.1 grams of carb, 5.0 grams of protein. TOTAL YIELD: 2 loaves (20 to 24 slices).

		CHO (g)	PRO (g)
2	ounces cream cheese, very soft	1.6	4.2
3	tablespoons unsalted butter (⅜ stick), soft, or coconut oil	0	0
3	eggs, room temperature	1.8	18.0
1	cup sharp cheddar cheese, grated	4.0	24.0
¼	cup whey protein powder (natural, zero-carb)	0	20.0
¾	cup whole almond meal	7.5	15.0
1½	teaspoons baking powder	1.8	0
	salt (about ¼ to ½ teaspoon)	0	0
½	cup unprocessed wheat bran	6.0	4.0
¼	cup soy protein powder	0	16.1
	Total	*22.7*	*101.3*

Preheat the oven to 350°F. Butter two heavy metal 3-by-6-inch baking pans.

Combine the cream cheese, butter, and 1 egg in a medium mixing bowl. Beat well. Add the remaining eggs and mix. Stir in the grated cheddar cheese.

Add the whey protein powder, almond meal, baking powder, and salt. Stir well. Add the wheat bran and soy protein powder.

Fill the baking pans. Bake for 35 to 40 minutes or until a knife inserted in the center comes out clean. Remove the bread from the pans and cool on a cooling rack. If not used promptly, freeze.

Variation: Quick Cheddar Cheese Flatbread

Follow the directions for Quick Cheddar Cheese Bread above. Make these changes: butter a 12-by-12-inch heavy metal baking pan. Preheat the oven to 350°F. Add 1 extra egg to the batter. Spread the batter in the baking pan and level it. Brush the top with 2 teaspoons of olive oil or butter. Sprinkle with ¼ cup of grated Parmesan cheese. (Optional: mix ½ teaspoon of garlic powder into the cheese before sprinkling it on the bread.) Bake the flatbread for about 18 to 20 minutes. Do not overbake. If you cut the bread into 24 pieces, each has 1.0 gram of carb and 4.0 grams of protein.

Quick Sunflower Seed Bread

Dense and deliciously nutty, this is one of my favorites.

PREPARATION TIME: 15 minutes. BAKING TIME: about 35 to 40 minutes.
SERVING SIZE: 1 slice. AMOUNT PER SERVING: 1.2 grams of carb, 5.0 grams of
protein. TOTAL YIELD: 2 loaves (20 to 24 slices).

		CHO (g)	PRO (g)
2	ounces cream cheese, very soft	1.6	4.2
2	tablespoons sour cream	1.0	0.6
4	tablespoons unsalted butter (½ stick), soft, or coconut oil	0	0
3	eggs, room temperature	1.8	18.0
¼	cup whey protein powder (natural, zero-carb)	0	20.0
¾	cup toasted sunflower seeds, coarsely chopped	6.9	18.9
¾	cup whole almond meal	7.5	15.0
1	teaspoon baking powder	1.2	0
	salt (about ¼ to ½ teaspoon)	0	0
½	cup flaxseed meal	3.2	5.0
¼	cup soy protein powder	0	16.0
	Total	23.2	97.7

Preheat the oven to 350°F. Butter two heavy metal 3-by-6-inch baking pans.

Combine the cream cheese, sour cream, butter, and 1 egg in a medium mixing bowl. Beat until smooth. Beat in the remaining eggs.

Add the whey protein powder, sunflower seeds, almond meal, baking powder, and salt. Stir well. Then add the flaxseed meal and the soy protein powder. Stir again.

Fill the baking pans. Bake for about 35 to 40 minutes or until a knife inserted in the center comes out clean. Remove the bread from the pans and cool on a cooling rack. If not used promptly, freeze.

Variation: Quick Sunflower Seed Bread with Dates

Follow the directions for Quick Sunflower Seed Bread above. Make these changes: chop 5 soft dates into very small pieces and add to the bread mix along with the whey powder and sunflower seeds. Bake as directed. This adds 1.3 grams of carb to each slice (of 20).

Quick Fiber Walnut Bread

High in protein. High in fiber. Low in carb. Good for you. Terrific taste.

PREPARATION TIME: 15 minutes. BAKING TIME: about 35 to 40 minutes.
SERVING SIZE: 1 slice. AMOUNT PER SERVING: 1.0 grams of carb, 5.5 grams of protein. TOTAL YIELD: 2 loaves (20 to 24 slices). The loaves have 58.8 grams of fiber. Each slice has approximately 3.0 grams of fiber.

		CHO (g)	PRO (g)
3	ounces cream cheese, very soft	2.4	6.3
4	tablespoons unsalted butter (½ stick), soft, or coconut oil	0	0
4	eggs, room temperature	2.4	24.0
1	tablespoon sour cream	1.0	0.3
½	cup whey protein powder (natural, zero-carb)	0	40.0
1	cup walnut meal	4.0	27.2
1	teaspoon baking powder	1.2	0
	salt (about ¼ to ½ teaspoon)	0	0
¼	cup unprocessed bran	3.0	2.0
½	cup flaxseed meal	3.2	10.0
4	tablespoons psyllium husks	3.2	0
4	tablespoons inulin	0	0
	Total	*20.4*	*109.8*

Preheat the oven to 350°F. Butter two heavy metal 3-by-6-inch baking pans.

Combine the cream cheese, butter, and 1 egg in a medium mixing bowl. Beat the mixture until smooth. Add the remaining eggs and sour cream.

Add the whey protein powder, walnut meal, baking powder, and salt. Stir well. Add the remaining ingredients and stir again until well mixed.

Fill the baking pans. Bake for about 35 to 40 minutes or until a knife inserted in the center comes out clean. Remove the bread from the pans and cool on a cooling rack. If not used promptly, freeze. Preslice the loaves if you wish.

Almond Flaxseed Crackers

Low-carb munching at its best!

PREPARATION TIME: 40 minutes. BAKING TIME: about 26 minutes (requires two cookie sheets).

SERVING SIZE: one 1-inch cracker. AMOUNT PER SERVING: 0.6 gram of carb, 0.8 gram of protein. TOTAL YIELD: about 60 crackers.

	CHO (g)	PRO (g)
4 tablespoons unsalted butter (½ stick), soft	0	0
1 egg, room temperature	0.6	6.0
½ cup oat flour	26.0	8.0
1 teaspoon baking powder	1.8	0
salt (about ⅛ teaspoon or to taste)	0	0
¼ cup flaxseed meal	1.6	5.0
1 cup blanched almond meal	6.0	10.0
¼ cup soy protein powder	0	16.1
Total	*36.0*	*45.1*

Preheat the oven to 350°F. Use two heavy metal large cookie sheets with silicone-coated liners.

Combine the butter and the egg in a medium mixing bowl. Beat until smooth; use a fork or a small whisk.

Add all the remaining ingredients (without combining them first) and stir the dough with a fork until fairly well mixed. Continue with your fingers (you might want to use plastic gloves) and work the dough into a smooth ball.

Shape the dough into balls the size of small grapes and put them on the first cookie sheet, allowing room for flattening the crackers. You need to be able to flatten the crackers with a jar or lid without hitting an adjacent one. First, flatten the balls with your fingertips and nudge them into circles. These crackers need to be extremely thin. The best way to do this is to flatten them with a small, empty, inverted jar with a smooth lid (some vitamin bottles have useful covers), and apply pressure to the cookies. If the dough sticks, rub a hint of soy protein powder on the lid. Prepare the second cookie/cracker sheet while the first is in the oven. Bake for 11 to 13 minutes per batch or until the crackers show a light golden color around the edges. Allow the crackers to dry completely. They are best kept frozen because they contain flaxseed meal.

Everyday Cracker

Try to find a better one! I bet you can't. So enjoy.

PREPARATION TIME: 30 minutes. BAKING TIME: about 26 minutes (requires two cookie sheets).

SERVING SIZE: one 2-inch cracker. AMOUNT PER SERVING: 0.9 gram of carb, negligible protein. TOTAL YIELD: about 60 crackers.

		CHO (g)	PRO (g)
¼	cup hot water	0	0
5	tablespoons unsalted butter (⅝ stick), soft	0	0
⅓	cup oat flour	17.3	5.0
¼	cup stone-ground whole wheat flour	23.0	0
	salt (about ⅛ teaspoon or to taste)	0	0
1¼	cups whole almond meal	12.5	20.0
¼	cup soy protein powder	0	16.1
	Total	*52.8*	*41.1*

Preheat the oven to 350°F. Use two large cookie sheets with silicone-coated liners.

Combine the hot water and the butter in a medium mixing bowl and stir until the butter is melted.

Work in the remaining ingredients (without combining them first) and stir the dough with a fork until fairly well mixed. Continue with your fingers (use disposable gloves if you want) and work the dough into a smooth ball.

Shape the dough into balls the size of very small grapes and put them on a cookie sheet, allowing room for flattening the crackers. If the dough is a little crumbly, add 1 tablespoon or more of raw egg white. You need to be able to flatten each cracker with a jar or a lid without hitting an adjacent one. First, flatten the balls with your fingertips and nudge them into circles. These crackers need to be extremely thin. A good way to flatten them is with a small, empty, inverted jar with a smooth lid (some vitamin bottles have useful covers), and apply pressure to the crackers. If the dough sticks, rub a hint of soy protein powder on the lid. Prepare the second cookie/cracker sheet while the first is in the oven. Bake for 11 to 13 minutes per batch or until the crackers show a light golden color around the edges. Allow the crackers to dry completely. These crackers keep fresh for weeks. They can always be refreshed with a quick trip to the oven, preheated to 350°F, for about 5 to 6 minutes. Just pile the crackers on a cookie sheet before putting them in the oven.

Spice Muffins

Team a muffin with some eggs for a great breakfast or simply grab a muffin or two on the run.

PREPARATION TIME: 10 minutes. BAKING TIME: about 24 to 28 minutes.
SERVING SIZE: 1 medium muffin. AMOUNT PER SERVING: 3.8 grams of carb, 10.0 grams of protein. TOTAL YIELD: Makes 6 large, 9 medium, or 12 small muffins.

		CHO (g)	PRO (g)
2	ounces cream cheese, very soft	1.6	4.2
4	tablespoons unsalted butter (½ stick), soft, or coconut oil	0	0
1	tablespoon sour cream	0.5	0.3
3	eggs, room temperature	1.8	18.0
¼	cup Splenda	6.0	0
3	tablespoons xylitol	5.4	0
1	teaspoon Stevia Plus (or equivalent)	0	0
1	teaspoon vanilla extract	0.5	0
¼	cup whey protein powder (natural, zero-carb)	0	20.0
¾	cup blanched almond meal	9.0	15.0
1	teaspoon baking powder	1.8	0
	salt, trace	0	0
1½	teaspoons ground cinnamon	1.3	0
½	teaspoon ground cloves	0.5	0
½	teaspoon nutmeg	0.5	0
½	cup whole almond meal	5.0	10.0
⅓	cup soy protein powder	0	21.5
	Total	*33.9*	*89.0*

Preheat the oven to 350°F. Butter a heavy metal nonstick 2-inch muffin pan. There will be some sticking, but not much; cleanup is easy. You can also use paper cup liners.

Combine the cream cheese, butter, sour cream, 1 egg, sweeteners, and vanilla extract in a medium mixing bowl. Beat briefly until well mixed and smooth. Beat in the remaining eggs.

Add all the remaining ingredients. Stir until well mixed.

Distribute the batter in muffin cups; a teaspoon works well for this. Fill the cups about ⅔ full.

Bake the muffins for about 24 to 28 minutes or until done and golden brown. Remove muffins from the pan and cool on a cooling rack. If not used the day they are baked, it is best to freeze the muffins. For icings and glazes see page 181.

Cranberry Muffins

Both tart and sweet, these taste terrific.

PREPARATION TIME: 10 minutes. BAKING TIME: about 24 to 28 minutes.
SERVING SIZE: 1 medium muffin. AMOUNT PER SERVING: 5.0 grams of carb,
10.0 grams of protein. TOTAL YIELD: 9 medium muffins.

		CHO (g)	PRO (g)
1	cup cranberries	8.0	1.0
2	ounces cream cheese, very soft	1.6	4.2
4	tablespoons unsalted butter (½ stick), soft, or coconut oil	0	0
3	eggs, room temperature	1.8	18.0
7	tablespoons Splenda	10.5	0
4	tablespoons xylitol	7.2	0
1	teaspoon Stevia Plus (or equivalent)	0	0
1	teaspoon vanilla extract	0.5	0
¼	cup whey protein powder (natural, zero-carb)	0	20.0
¾	cup blanched almond meal	9.0	15.0
1	teaspoon baking powder	1.2	0
	salt, trace	0	0
½	teaspoon cinnamon	0.4	0
½	cup whole almond meal	5.0	10.0
⅓	cup soy protein powder	0	21.5
	Total	*45.2*	*89.7*

Preheat the oven to 350°F. Butter a heavy metal nonstick 2-inch muffin pan. There will be some sticking, but not much; cleanup is easy. You can also use paper cup liners.

You can leave the cranberries whole or, for greater distribution, crush them lightly with a single pulse or so in a processor. Set aside.

Combine the cream cheese, butter, 1 egg, sweeteners, and vanilla extract in a medium mixing bowl. Beat briefly until well mixed and smooth. Beat in the remaining eggs.

Add the whey protein powder, blanched almond meal, baking powder, salt, and cinnamon, and stir well. Add the remaining ingredients and combine until well mixed.

Distribute the batter in muffin cups; a teaspoon works well for this. Fill the cups about ⅔ full.

Bake the muffins for about 24 to 28 minutes or until done and golden brown. Remove them from the pan and cool on a cooling rack. If not used the day they are baked, it is best to freeze the muffins. For icings and glazes see page 181.

Carrot Muffins

Moist and delicious.

PREPARATION TIME: 15 minutes. BAKING TIME: about 24 to 28 minutes.
SERVING SIZE: 1 medium muffin. AMOUNT PER SERVING: 3.9 grams of carb, 11.1 grams of protein. TOTAL YIELD: 6 large, 9 medium, or 12 small muffins.

		CHO (g)	PRO (g)
2	ounces cream cheese, very soft	1.6	4.2
6	tablespoons unsalted butter (¾ stick), soft, or coconut oil	0	0
3	eggs, room temperature	1.8	18.0
¼	cup Splenda	6.0	0
3	tablespoons xylitol	5.4	0
1	teaspoon Stevia Plus (or equivalent)	0	0
1	tablespoon lemon juice	1.3	0
1	cup fresh carrots (about 3 ounces), finely grated	9.0	1.0
¼	cup whey protein powder (natural, zero-carb)	0	20.0
¾	cup whole almond meal	7.5	15.0
1	teaspoon baking powder	1.2	0
3	teaspoons lemon peel	0.8	0
	salt, trace	0	0
⅔	cup soy protein powder	0	42.3
	Total	*34.6*	*100.5*

Preheat the oven to 350°F. Butter a heavy metal nonstick 2-inch muffin pan. There will be a little sticking, but not much; cleanup is easy. You can also use paper cup liners.

Combine the cream cheese, butter, 1 egg, sweeteners, and lemon juice in a medium mixing bowl. Beat briefly until well mixed. The cream cheese should be smooth. Add the grated carrots and mix well.

Add the whey protein powder, whole almond meal, baking powder, lemon peel, and salt. Stir. Add the soy protein powder and stir again until well mixed.

Distribute the batter evenly in muffin cups; a teaspoon works well for this. Fill the cups about ⅔ full. Bake the muffins for about 24 to 28 minutes or until done and golden brown. Remove them from the pan and cool on a cooling rack. If not used the day they are baked, it is best to freeze the muffins.

Zucchini Chocolate Muffins

Moist and chocolatey.

PREPARATION TIME: 15 minutes. BAKING TIME: about 24 to 28 minutes.

SERVING SIZE: 1 medium muffin. AMOUNT PER SERVING: 4.5 grams of carb, 8.1 grams of protein. TOTAL YIELD: 6 large, 9 medium, or 12 small muffins.

	CHO (g)	PRO (g)
1 cup cooked, mashed zucchini (2.5 medium)	5.5	3.0
1 ounce unsweetened baking chocolate	4.0	4.0
2 ounces sugar-free semisweet chocolate	5.4	2.0
3 tablespoons heavy cream	1.2	0.9
2 ounces cream cheese, very soft	1.6	4.2
4 tablespoons unsalted butter (½ stick), soft, or coconut oil	0	0
2 eggs, room temperature	1.2	12.0
¼ cup Splenda	6.0	0
3 tablespoons xylitol	5.4	0
1 teaspoon Stevia Plus (or equivalent)	0	0
¾ cup whole almond meal	7.5	15.0
1 teaspoon baking powder	1.2	0
salt, trace	0	0
1 teaspoon ground cinnamon	0.7	0
½ cup soy protein powder	0	32.2
Total	*39.7*	*73.3*

Preheat the oven to 350°F. Butter a heavy metal nonstick 2-inch muffin pan. There will be a little sticking, but not much; cleanup is easy. You can also use paper cup liners.

Wash, slice, and cook the unpeeled zucchini in a small amount of water until just tender, less than 10 minutes. Mash in a blender or a food processor. Drain well. Measure 1 cup, piled lightly. Set aside.

Put the chocolates and cream in the top of a double boiler and heat over hot water kept at or below a simmer. Stir frequently. When the chocolates are melted, stir until smooth and remove from the heat. Set aside.

Combine the cream cheese, butter, eggs, and sweeteners in a medium mixing bowl. Beat briefly until well mixed. The cream cheese should be smooth. Add the grated zucchini and mix well. Add the remaining ingredients and stir until well mixed.

Distribute the batter evenly in muffin cups; a teaspoon works well for this. Fill the cups about ⅔ full. Bake the muffins for about 24 to 28 minutes or until done and golden brown. Remove them from the pan and cool on a cooling rack. If not used the day they are baked, it is best to freeze the muffins. For icings and glazes see page 181.

All-Seed Muffins

Mingling seeds creates an unusual, lively flavor. Slice and toast these muffins for a marvelous treat.

PREPARATION TIME: 10 minutes. BAKING TIME: about 24 to 28 minutes.
SERVING SIZE: 1 medium muffin. AMOUNT PER SERVING: 3.2 grams of carb,
   10.2 grams of protein. TOTAL YIELD: 6 large, 9 medium, or 12 small
   muffins.

		CHO (g)	PRO (g)
2	ounces cream cheese, very soft	1.6	4.2
6	tablespoons unsalted butter (¾ stick), soft, or coconut oil	0	0
1	tablespoon sour cream	0.5	0.3
3	eggs, room temperature	1.8	18.0
¼	cup Splenda	6.0	0
3	tablespoons xylitol	5.4	0
1	teaspoon Stevia Plus (or equivalent)	0	0
2	teaspoons vanilla extract	1.0	0
¼	cup whey protein powder (natural, zero-carb)	0	20.0
¼	cup toasted, chopped sunflower seeds	2.3	6.3
¼	cup toasted pumpkin seeds, coarsely ground	2.5	10.0
¼	cup sesame seeds	3.0	7.0
1	teaspoon baking powder	1.2	0
	salt, trace	0	0
2	teaspoons lemon peel	0.5	0
½	cup flaxseed meal	3.2	10.0
¼	cup soy protein powder	0	16.1
	Total	*27.4*	*91.9*

Preheat the oven to 350°F. Butter a heavy metal nonstick 2-inch muffin pan. There will be some sticking, but not much; cleanup is easy. You can also use paper cup liners.

Combine the cream cheese, butter, sour cream, 1 egg, sweeteners, and vanilla extract in a medium mixing bowl. Beat until smooth. Beat in the remaining eggs. Stir well. Add the remaining ingredients and stir until well mixed.

Distribute the batter evenly in muffin cups; a teaspoon works well for this. Fill the cups about ⅔ full.

Bake the muffins for about 24 to 28 minutes or until done and golden brown. Remove the muffins from the pan and cool on a cooling rack. If not used the day they are baked, it is best to freeze the muffins.

Banana Sesame Muffins

Two will make a breakfast to last all morning (24 grams of protein).

PREPARATION TIME: 10 minutes. BAKING TIME: about 24 to 28 minutes.
SERVING SIZE: 1 medium muffin. AMOUNT PER SERVING: 5.4 grams of carb, 12.0 grams of protein. TOTAL YIELD: 6 large, 9 medium, or 12 small muffins.

		CHO (g)	PRO (g)
4	tablespoons unsalted butter (½ stick), soft, or coconut oil	0	0
2	tablespoons sour cream	1.0	0.6
3	eggs, room temperature	1.8	18.0
¼	cup Splenda	6.0	0
3	tablespoons xylitol	5.4	0
1	teaspoon Stevia Plus (or equivalent)	0	0
2	teaspoons vanilla extract	1.0	0
⅓	cup mashed bananas (3 ounces)	19.0	1.0
¼	cup whey protein powder (natural, zero-carb)	0	20.0
⅓	cup flaxseed meal	2.1	6.7
1	teaspoon baking powder	1.2	0
	salt, trace	0	0
2	teaspoons lemon peel	0.5	0.0
⅓	cup sesame seeds	4.0	9.0
½	cup whole almond meal	5.0	10.0
⅔	cup soy protein powder	0	42.3
	Total	*47.0*	*107.6*

Preheat the oven to 350°F. Butter a heavy metal nonstick 2-inch muffin pan. There will be some sticking, but not much; cleanup is easy. You can also use paper cup liners.

Combine the butter, sour cream, eggs, sweeteners, and vanilla extract in a medium mixing bowl. Beat briefly until well mixed and smooth. Add the bananas; stir.

Add the whey protein powder, flaxseed meal, baking powder, salt, and lemon peel. Stir well. Add the remaining ingredients and stir again until well mixed.

Distribute the batter evenly in muffin cups; a teaspoon works well for this. Fill the cups about ⅔ full.

Bake the muffins for about 24 to 28 minutes or until golden brown. Remove the muffins from the pan and cool on a cooling rack. If not used the day they are baked, it is best to freeze the muffins.

Hazelnut Almond Muffins

Light and airy. And doubly nutty. Mmmm.

PREPARATION TIME: 15 minutes. BAKING TIME: about 24 to 28 minutes.
SERVING SIZE: 1 medium muffin. AMOUNT PER SERVING: 3.2 grams of carb, 7.5 grams of protein. TOTAL YIELD: 6 large, 9 medium, or 12 small muffins.

		CHO (g)	PRO (g)
2	egg whites	0.6	7.0
5	egg yolks	1.5	14.0
4	tablespoons xylitol	7.2	0
2	tablespoons Splenda	3.0	0
1	teaspoon Stevia Plus (or equivalent)	0	0
2	teaspoons vanilla extract	1.0	0
2	ounces cream cheese, very soft	1.6	4.2
2	tablespoons unsalted butter		
	(½ stick), soft, or coconut oil	0	0
1	cup hazelnut meal	7.6	16.0
1	teaspoon baking powder	1.2	0
2	teaspoons lemon peel	0.5	0
	salt, trace	0	0
½	cup whole almond meal	5.0	10.0
¼	cup soy protein powder	0	16.1
	Total	*29.2*	*67.3*

Preheat the oven to 350°F. Butter a heavy metal nonstick 2-inch muffin pan. There will be a little sticking, but not much; cleanup is easy. You can also use paper cup liners.

In a medium mixing bowl, beat the egg whites until firm but not stiff. Set aside.

Put the egg yolks in a larger mixing bowl and beat until thick and creamy. Add the sweeteners gradually, by the tablespoon, beating well after each addition. Beat in the vanilla extract, cream cheese, and butter.

Stir in the remaining ingredients, alternating them with the beaten egg whites.

Distribute the batter evenly in muffin cups; a teaspoon works well for this. Fill the cups about ⅔ full. Bake the muffins for about 24 to 28 minutes or until light golden brown. Remove them from the pan and cool on a cooling rack. If not used the day they are baked or the next, it is best to freeze the muffins. For icings and glazes see page 181.

Coconut Muffins

For coconut lovers. And who isn't one?

PREPARATION TIME: 15 minutes. BAKING TIME: about 24 to 28 minutes.
SERVING SIZE: 1 medium muffin. AMOUNT PER SERVING: 3.8 grams of carb,
11.8 grams of protein. TOTAL YIELD: 6 large, 9 medium, or 12 small
muffins.

		CHO (g)	PRO (g)
2	ounces cream cheese, very soft	1.6	4.2
6	tablespoons unsalted butter		
	(¾ stick), soft, or coconut oil	0	0
3	eggs, room temperature	1.8	18.0
1	tablespoon sour cream	0.4	0.3
¼	cup Splenda	6.0	0
3	tablespoons xylitol	5.4	0
1	teaspoon Stevia Plus (or equivalent)	0	0
2	teaspoons vanilla extract	1.0	0
¼	cup whey protein powder		
	(natural, zero-carb)	0	20.0
1	cup unsweetened coconut, finely grated	6.0	6.0
1	teaspoon baking powder	1.2	0
2	teaspoons lemon peel	0.5	0
	salt, trace	0	0
¾	cup blanched almond meal	9.0	15.0
⅔	cup soy protein powder	0	42.9
	Total	*32.9*	*106.4*

Preheat the oven to 350°F. Butter a heavy metal nonstick 2-inch muffin pan. There will be a little sticking, but not much; cleanup is easy. You can also use paper cup liners.

Combine the cream cheese, butter, 1 egg, sour cream, sweeteners, and vanilla extract in a medium mixing bowl. Beat briefly until well mixed and the cream cheese is smooth. Beat in the remaining eggs.

Add the whey protein powder, coconut, baking powder, lemon peel, and salt. Stir well. Add the remaining ingredients and stir again until well mixed.

Distribute the batter evenly in muffin cups; a teaspoon works well for this. Fill the cups about ⅔ full. Bake the muffins for about 24 to 28 minutes or until golden brown. Remove the muffins from the pan and cool on a cooling rack. If not used the day they are baked or the next, it is best to freeze the muffins.

Banana Coconut Muffins

Try this tasty combination. These have a deliciously tropical flavor.

PREPARATION TIME: 15 minutes. BAKING TIME: about 24 to 28 minutes.
SERVING SIZE: 1 medium muffin. AMOUNT PER SERVING: 5.2 grams of carb,
11.2 grams of protein. TOTAL YIELD: 6 large, 9 medium, or 12 small
muffins.

		CHO (g)	PRO (g)
2	ounces cream cheese, very soft	1.6	4.2
6	tablespoons unsalted butter		
	(¾ stick), soft, or coconut oil	0	0
3	eggs, room temperature	1.8	18.0
1	tablespoon sour cream	0.4	0.3
¼	cup Splenda	6.0	0
3	tablespoons xylitol	5.4	0
1	teaspoon Stevia Plus (or equivalent)	0	0
2	teaspoons vanilla extract	1.0	0
⅓	cup mashed bananas (3 ounces)	19.0	1.0
¼	cup whey protein powder		
	(natural, zero-carb)	0	20.0
¾	cup unsweetened coconut, grated	4.5	4.5
1	teaspoon baking powder	1.2	0
2	teaspoons lemon peel	0.5	0
	salt, trace	0	0
½	cup whole almond meal	5.0	10.0
⅔	cup soy protein powder	0	42.9
	Total	*48.4*	*100.9*

Preheat the oven to 350°F. Butter a heavy metal nonstick 2-inch
muffin pan. There will be a little sticking, but not much; cleanup is
easy. You can also use paper cup liners.

Combine the cream cheese, butter, 1 egg, sour cream, sweeteners,
and vanilla extract in a medium mixing bowl. Beat briefly until well
mixed and smooth. Beat in the remaining eggs. Stir in the bananas.

Add the whey protein powder, coconut, baking powder, lemon
peel, and salt. Stir well. Add the remaining ingredients and stir again
until well mixed.

Distribute the batter evenly in muffin cups; a teaspoon works well
for this. Fill the cups ⅔ full. Bake the muffins for about 24 to 28 minutes or until golden brown. Remove the muffins from the pan and
cool on a cooling rack. If not used the day they are baked or the next,
it is best to freeze the muffins.

Peanut Butter Chocolate Muffins

A delightful combination. High in protein too.

PREPARATION TIME: 10 minutes. BAKING TIME: about 24 to 28 minutes.
SERVING SIZE: 1 medium muffin. AMOUNT PER SERVING: 5.0 grams of carb, 13.3 grams of protein. TOTAL YIELD: 6 large, 9 medium, or 12 small muffins.

		CHO (g)	PRO (g)
2	ounces sugar-free semisweet chocolate	5.4	4.0
2	tablespoons heavy cream	0.8	0.6
2	ounces cream cheese, very soft	1.6	4.2
4	tablespoons unsalted butter (½ stick), soft, or coconut oil	0	0
⅓	cup natural peanut butter	13.3	19.0
3	eggs, room temperature	1.8	18.0
¼	cup Splenda	6.0	0
3	tablespoons xylitol	5.4	0
1	teaspoon Stevia Plus (or equivalent)	0	0
2	teaspoons vanilla extract	1.0	0
¼	cup whey protein powder (natural, zero-carb)	0	20.0
½	cup blanched almond meal	6.0	10.0
1	teaspoon baking powder	1.2	0
	salt, trace	0	0
2	teaspoons lemon peel	0.5	0
½	cup walnut meal	2.0	12.0
½	cup soy protein powder	0	32.2
	Total	*45.0*	*120.0*

Preheat the oven to 350°F. Butter a heavy metal nonstick 2-inch muffin pan. There will be some sticking, but not much; cleanup is easy. You can also use paper cup liners.

In a small microwavable bowl combine the chocolate and heavy cream and microwave for a few seconds until the chocolate is melted. Stir until smooth and set aside. You can also do this in a double boiler over hot water; always keep the water at or below a simmer. Set aside.

In a large bowl, combine the cream cheese, butter, peanut butter, 2 eggs, sweeteners, and vanilla extract. Beat briefly until well mixed and smooth. Beat in the remaining egg.

Add the whey protein powder, almond meal, baking powder, salt, and lemon peel. Stir well. Add the remaining dry ingredients and stir again until well mixed.

Carefully add the chocolate mix to the batter, stirring only lightly so that dark ribbons of chocolate will still be visible. Distribute the batter evenly in muffin cups; a teaspoon works well for this. Fill the cups about ⅔ full.

Bake the muffins for about 24 to 28 minutes or until golden brown. Remove them from the pan and cool on a cooling rack. If not used the day they are baked, it is best to freeze the muffins.

Variation: Peanut Butter Muffins with Chocolate Chips

Follow the directions for Peanut Butter Chocolate Muffins above. Make these changes: omit the chocolate. Instead, add 2 ounces of sugar-free semisweet or milk chocolate chips to the batter before baking. The carb count remains unchanged.

Peanut Butter Flaxseed Muffins (Nut-Free)

A filling proposition: loaded with healthy nutrition and delightful flavor.

PREPARATION TIME: 10 minutes. BAKING TIME: about 24 to 28 minutes.
SERVING SIZE: 1 medium muffin. AMOUNT PER SERVING: 4.7 grams of carb, 11.8 grams of protein. TOTAL YIELD: 6 large, 9 medium, or 12 small muffins.

		CHO (g)	PRO (g)
2	ounces cream cheese, very soft	1.6	4.2
2	tablespoons unsalted butter (¼ stick), soft, or coconut oil	0	0
⅓	cup natural peanut butter	13.3	19.0
3	eggs, room temperature	1.8	18.0
2	teaspoons vanilla extract	1.0	0
¼	cup Splenda	6.0	0
3	tablespoons xylitol	5.4	0
1	teaspoon Stevia Plus (or equivalent)	0	0
¼	cup whey protein powder (natural, zero-carb)	0	20.0
¾	cup flaxseed meal	4.8	15.0
1	teaspoon baking powder	1.2	0
	salt, trace	0	0
2	teaspoons lemon peel	0.5	0
½	cup sesame seeds	6.0	14.0
¼	cup soy protein powder	0	16.1
	Total	*41.6*	*106.3*

Preheat the oven to 350°F. Butter a heavy metal nonstick 2-inch muffin pan. There will be some sticking, but not much; cleanup is easy. You can also use paper cup liners.

Combine the cream cheese, butter, peanut butter, 2 eggs, vanilla extract, and sweeteners in a medium mixing bowl. Beat briefly until well mixed and smooth. Beat in the remaining egg.

Add the whey protein powder, flaxseed meal, baking powder, salt, and lemon peel. Stir well. Add the remaining ingredients and stir again until well mixed.

Distribute the batter evenly in muffin cups; a teaspoon works well for this. Fill the cups about ⅔ full.

Bake the muffins for about 24 to 28 minutes or until golden brown. Remove them from the pan and cool on a cooling rack. If not used the day they are baked, it is best to freeze the muffins.

Hazelnut Muffins

A special treat if you are fond of hazelnuts. Nutritious, too.

PREPARATION TIME: 10 minutes. BAKING TIME: about 24 to 28 minutes.

SERVING SIZE: 1 medium muffin. AMOUNT PER SERVING: 2.9 grams of carb, 9.8 grams of protein. TOTAL YIELD: 6 large, 9 medium, or 12 small muffins.

		CHO (g)	PRO (g)
2	ounces cream cheese, very soft	1.6	4.2
4	tablespoons unsalted butter (½ stick), soft, or coconut oil	0	0
3	eggs, room temperature	1.8	18.0
2	teaspoons vanilla extract	1.0	0
¼	cup Splenda	6.0	0
3	tablespoons xylitol	5.4	0
1	teaspoon Stevia Plus (or equivalent)	0	0
¼	cup whey protein powder (natural, zero-carb)	0	20.0
¾	cup hazelnut meal	5.7	12.0
1	teaspoon ground cinnamon	0.7	0
½	teaspoon ground cloves	0.5	0
1	teaspoon baking powder	1.2	0
	salt, trace	0	0
½	cup flaxseed meal	3.2	10.0
¼	cup soy protein powder	0	16.1
	Total	*26.1*	*80.3*

Preheat the oven to 350°F. Butter a heavy metal nonstick 2-inch muffin pan. There will be some sticking, but not much; cleanup will be easy. You can also use paper cup liners.

Combine the cream cheese, butter, 1 egg, vanilla extract, and sweeteners in a medium mixing bowl. Beat briefly until well mixed and smooth. Beat in the remaining eggs.

Add the whey protein powder, hazelnut meal, cinnamon, cloves, baking powder, and salt. Stir well. Add the remaining ingredients and stir again until well mixed.

Distribute the batter evenly in muffin cups; a teaspoon works well for this. Fill the cups about ⅔ full.

Bake the muffins for about 24 to 28 minutes or until golden brown. Remove them from the pan and cool on a cooling rack. If not used the day they are baked, it is best to freeze the muffins.

Poppy Seed Muffins

Filled with those luscious little seeds, this recipe is a winner.

PREPARATION TIME: 10 minutes. BAKING TIME: about 24 to 28 minutes.
SERVING SIZE: 1 medium muffin. AMOUNT PER SERVING: 3.5 grams of carb, 11.1 grams of protein. TOTAL YIELD: 6 large, 9 medium, or 12 small muffins.

		CHO (g)	PRO (g)
3	tablespoons poppy seeds	3.6	5.0
3	tablespoons heavy cream	1.2	0.9
1	ounce cream cheese, very soft	0.8	2.1
4	tablespoons unsalted butter (½ stick), soft, or coconut oil	0	0
3	eggs, room temperature	1.8	18.0
1	tablespoon lemon juice	1.3	0
2	teaspoons vanilla extract	1.0	0
¼	cup Splenda	6.0	0
3	tablespoons xylitol	5.4	0.0
1	teaspoon Stevia Plus (or equivalent)	0	0
¼	cup whey protein powder (natural, zero-carb)	0	20.0
½	cup blanched almond meal	6.0	10.0
1	teaspoon baking powder	1.2	0
	salt, trace	0	0
3	teaspoons lemon peel	0.8	0
½	cup walnut meal	2.0	12.0
½	cup soy protein powder	0	32.2
	Total	*31.1*	*100.2*

Preheat the oven to 350°F. Butter a heavy metal nonstick 2-inch muffin pan. There will be some sticking, but not much; cleanup is easy. You can also use paper cup liners.

Put the poppy seeds through a coffee grinder, then soak them in the heavy cream. Set aside.

Combine the cream cheese, butter, 1 egg, lemon juice, vanilla extract, and sweeteners in a medium mixing bowl. Beat briefly until well mixed and smooth. Beat in the remaining eggs and the poppy seeds. Add the remaining ingredients and stir well.

Distribute the batter evenly in muffin cups; a teaspoon works well for this. Fill the cups about ⅔ full.

Bake the muffins for about 24 to 28 minutes or until golden brown. Remove them from the pan and cool on a cooling rack. If not used the day they are baked, it is best to freeze the muffins.

Chocolate Orange Macadamia Nut Muffins

These muffins are sublime! Who would have thought they were good for you?

PREPARATION TIME: 10 minutes. BAKING TIME: about 24 to 28 minutes.
SERVING SIZE: 1 medium muffin. AMOUNT PER SERVING: 5.2 grams of carb, 11.3 grams of protein. TOTAL YIELD: 6 large, 9 medium, or 12 small muffins.

	CHO (g)	PRO (g)
1 ounce unsweetened baking chocolate	4.0	4.0
2 ounces sugar-free semisweet chocolate	5.4	2.0
3 tablespoons heavy cream	1.2	0.9
2 ounces cream cheese, very soft	1.6	4.0
6 tablespoons unsalted butter (¾ stick), soft, or coconut oil	0	0
3 eggs, room temperature	1.8	18.0
1 teaspoon orange extract (or as desired)	1.0	0
1 teaspoon lemon extract (or as desired)	1.0	0
2 teaspoons vanilla extract	1.0	0
¼ cup Splenda	6.0	0
3 tablespoons xylitol	5.4	0
1 teaspoon Stevia Plus (or equivalent)	0	0
¼ cup whey protein powder (natural, zero-carb)	0	20.0
5 ounces roasted macadamia nuts, finely chopped	7.5	11.0
½ cup blanched almond meal	6.0	10.0
1 teaspoon baking powder	1.2	0
4 teaspoons orange peel	0.8	0
salt, trace	0	0
½ cup macadamia nut meal	2.6	4.0
½ cup soy protein powder	0	32.2
Total	*46.5*	*106.1*

Preheat the oven to 350°F. Butter a heavy metal nonstick 2-inch muffin pan. There will be some sticking, but not much; cleanup will be easy. You can also use paper cup liners.

Melt the chocolates and the cream in the top of a double boiler; keep the water at or below a simmer. Stir until smooth and remove from the heat. Allow to cool.

Combine the cream cheese, butter, 2 eggs, lemon and orange extracts, vanilla extract, and sweeteners in a medium mixing bowl.

Beat briefly until well mixed and smooth. Beat in the remaining egg. Stir in the chocolate mixture.

Add the whey protein powder, macadamia nuts, almond meal, baking powder, orange peel, and salt. Stir well. Add the remaining ingredients and stir again until well mixed.

Distribute the batter evenly in muffin cups; a teaspoon works well for this. For 9 muffins, fill each cup about ⅔ full.

Bake the muffins for about 24 to 28 minutes or until golden brown. Remove them from the pan and cool on a cooling rack. If not used the day they are baked, it is best to freeze the muffins.

Oatmeal Almond Muffins

This muffin has the most carbs. Still, a regular muffin of the same weight has about 20.0 or more grams of carb.

PREPARATION TIME: 10 minutes. BAKING TIME: about 24 to 28 minutes.
SERVING SIZE: 1 medium muffin. AMOUNT PER SERVING: 6.7 grams of carb,
  11.9 grams of protein. TOTAL YIELD: 6 large, 9 medium, or 12 small
  muffins.

	CHO (g)	PRO (g)
¾ cup rolled oats, toasted	34.5	7.0
8 tablespoons unsalted butter (1 stick), soft, or coconut oil	0	0
3 eggs, room temperature	1.8	18.0
¼ cup Splenda	6.0	0
3 tablespoons xylitol	5.4	0
1 teaspoon Stevia Plus (or equivalent)	0	0
2 teaspoons vanilla extract	1.0	0
¼ cup whey protein powder (natural, zero-carb)	0	20.0
¾ cup sliced almonds, toasted	7.8	18.0
1 teaspoon baking powder	1.2	0
salt, trace	0	0
2 teaspoons lemon peel	0.5	0
½ cup walnut meal	2.0	12.0
½ cup soy protein powder	0	32.2
Total	*60.2*	*107.2*

To toast the oats, heat a heavy skillet over medium heat. Add the oats and stir constantly until oats become golden. Remove instantly from the skillet (to avoid scorching oats while they sit in the hot pan) and set aside.

Preheat the oven to 350°F. Butter a heavy metal nonstick 2-inch muffin pan. There will be some sticking, but not much; cleanup is easy. You can also use paper cup liners.

Combine the butter, 2 eggs, sweeteners, and vanilla extract in a medium mixing bowl. Beat briefly until well mixed and smooth. Beat in the remaining egg. Add the remaining ingredients and stir until well mixed.

Distribute the batter evenly in muffin cups; a teaspoon works well for this. For 9 muffins, fill each cup about ⅔ full.

Bake the muffins for about 24 to 28 minutes or until golden brown. Remove them from the pan and cool on a cooling rack. If not used the day they are baked, it is best to freeze the muffins.

High-Fiber Walnut Muffins

High in protein. High in fiber. Good for you. And wait until you taste them!

PREPARATION TIME: 10 minutes. BAKING TIME: about 24 to 28 minutes.

SERVING SIZE: 1 medium muffin. AMOUNT PER SERVING: 3.4 grams of carb, 10.0 grams of protein. TOTAL YIELD: 6 large, 9 medium, or 12 small muffins. Each medium muffin has 6.0 grams of fiber.

		CHO (g)	PRO (g)
3	ounces cream cheese, very soft	2.4	6.3
4	tablespoons unsalted butter (½ stick), soft, or coconut oil	0	0
4	eggs, room temperature	2.4	24.0
2	teaspoons vanilla extract	1.0	0
¼	cup Splenda	6.0	0
3	tablespoons xylitol	5.4	0
1	teaspoon Stevia Plus (or equivalent)	0	0
¼	cup whey protein powder (natural, zero-carb)	0	20.0
1¼	cup walnut meal	5.0	30.0
1	teaspoon baking powder	1.2	0
	salt, trace	0	0
2	teaspoons lemon peel	0.5	0
½	cup flaxseed meal	3.2	10.0
4	tablespoons psyllium husks	3.2	0
4	tablespoons inulin	0	0
	Total	*30.3*	*90.3*

Preheat the oven to 350°F. Butter a heavy metal nonstick 2-inch muffin pan. There will be some sticking, but not much; cleanup will be easy. You can also use paper cup liners.

Combine the cream cheese, butter, 2 eggs, vanilla extract, and sweeteners in a medium mixing bowl. Beat briefly until well mixed and smooth. Beat in the remaining eggs.

Add the whey protein powder, walnut meal, baking powder, salt, and lemon peel. Stir well. Add the remaining ingredients and stir again until well mixed.

Distribute the batter evenly in muffin cups; a teaspoon works well for this. For 9 muffins, fill each cup about ⅔ full.

Bake the muffins for about 24 to 28 minutes or until golden brown. Remove them from the pan and cool on a cooling rack. If not used the day they are baked, it is best to freeze the muffins.

High-Fiber Bran Muffins (Nut-Free)

Bran? It's not exactly everybody's favorite stuff—but this combination might really appeal to your taste buds.

PREPARATION TIME: 10 minutes. BAKING TIME: about 24 to 28 minutes.
SERVING SIZE: 1 medium muffin. AMOUNT PER SERVING: 4.3 grams of carb, 7.4 grams of protein. TOTAL YIELD: 6 large, 9 medium, or 12 small muffins. Each medium muffin has 7.0 grams of fiber.

		CHO (g)	PRO (g)
2	ounces cream cheese, very soft	1.6	4.2
4	tablespoons unsalted butter (½ stick), soft, or coconut oil	0	0
4	eggs, room temperature	2.4	24.0
1	tablespoon sour cream	0.5	0.3
2	teaspoons vanilla extract	1.0	0
¼	cup Splenda	6.0	0
3	tablespoons xylitol	5.4	0
1	teaspoon Stevia Plus (or equivalent)	0	0
¼	cup soy protein powder	0	16.1
1	cup unprocessed wheat bran	12.0	8.0
1	teaspoon baking powder	1.2	0
	salt, trace	0	0
2	teaspoons lemon peel	0.5	0
½	cup toasted sesame seeds	6.0	14.0
4	tablespoons psyllium husks	3.2	0
4	tablespoons inulin	0	0
	Total	*39.8*	*66.6*

Preheat the oven to 350°F. Butter a heavy metal nonstick 2-inch muffin pan. There will be some sticking, but not much; cleanup will be easy. You can also use paper cup liners.

Combine the cream cheese, butter, 2 eggs, sour cream, vanilla extract, and sweeteners in a medium mixing bowl. Beat briefly until well mixed and smooth. Beat in the remaining eggs.

Add the soy protein powder, wheat bran, baking powder, salt, and lemon peel. Stir well. Add the remaining ingredients and stir again until well mixed.

Distribute the batter evenly in muffin cups; a teaspoon works well for this. For 9 muffins, fill each cup about ⅔ full.

Bake the muffins for about 24 to 28 minutes or until golden brown. Remove them from the pan and cool on a cooling rack. If not used the day they are baked, it is best to freeze the muffins.

Pecan Blueberry Muffins

Sound pretty good? They taste even better!

PREPARATION TIME: 10 minutes. BAKING TIME: about 24 to 28 minutes.
SERVING SIZE: 1 medium muffin. AMOUNT PER SERVING: 5.4 grams of carb, 9.0 grams of protein. TOTAL YIELD: 6 large, 9 medium, or 12 small muffins.

		CHO (g)	PRO (g)
4	ounces coarsely ground pecans, toasted	7.2	10.4
2	ounces cream cheese, very soft	1.6	4.0
2	tablespoons unsalted butter (¼ stick), soft, or coconut oil	0	0
3	eggs, room temperature	1.8	18.0
¼	cup Splenda	6.0	0
3	tablespoons xylitol	5.4	0
1	teaspoon Stevia Plus (or equivalent)	0	0
1	teaspoon vanilla extract	0.5	0
¾	cup whole almond meal	7.5	15.0
1	teaspoon baking powder	1.2	0
	salt, trace	0	0
2	teaspoons lemon peel	0.5	0
1	teaspoon ground cinnamon	0.7	0
¼	cup soy protein powder	0	16.1
1	cup fresh blueberries	16.0	2.0
	Total	*48.4*	*65.5*

Preheat the oven to 350°F. Butter a heavy metal nonstick 2-inch muffin pan. There will be some sticking, but not much; cleanup is easy. You can also use paper cup liners.

Toast the pecans. Rather than chop the pecans as is usually done, run them through a food processor, but pulse only once. Keep the nuts coarse. Set aside.

Combine the cream cheese, butter, 1 egg, sweeteners, and vanilla extract in a medium mixing bowl. Beat briefly until well mixed and smooth. Beat in the remaining eggs.

Add the remaining ingredients, including the pecans but not the blueberries, and stir until well mixed. Fold the blueberries in last. Distribute the batter in muffin cups; a teaspoon works well for this. Fill the cups about ⅔ full.

Bake the muffins for about 24 to 28 minutes or until golden brown. Remove them from the pan and cool on a cooling rack. If not used the day they are baked, it is best to freeze the muffins. For icings and glazes see page 181.

Scones with Currants

If you miss scones, here they are to enjoy again. The currants add 1.2 grams of carb to each scone. You may choose to omit them for a treat even lower in carb grams.

PREPARATION TIME: 15 minutes. BAKING TIME: about 16 to 20 minutes. The dough requires brief chilling.

SERVING SIZE: 1 scone. AMOUNT PER SERVING: 5.0 grams of carb, 8.2 grams of protein. TOTAL YIELD: 12 scones.

		CHO (g)	PRO (g)
2	eggs, room temperature	1.8	18.0
8	tablespoons unsalted butter (1 stick), soft	0	0
2	teaspoons vanilla extract	1.0	0
¼	cup Splenda	6.0	0
3	tablespoons xylitol	5.4	0
1	teaspoon Stevia Plus (or equivalent)	0	0
1	cup blanched almond meal	12.0	20.0
¼	cup dark rye flour	15.0	4.0
½	cup walnut meal	2.0	13.6
1	teaspoon baking powder	1.2	0
	salt, trace	0	0
3	teaspoons lemon peel	0.7	0
¾	cup soy protein powder	0	48.3
2	tablespoons currants (optional)	14.0	0
	Total	*58.5*	*97.9*

Preheat the oven to 350°F. Line a large cookie sheet with a silicone-coated mat.

Separate the eggs. Set the yolks aside. In a medium mixing bowl beat the egg whites with a portable electric beater until they hold firm but still somewhat soft peaks. Set aside.

Combine the egg yolks, butter, vanilla extract, and sweeteners in a medium mixing bowl. Beat the batter until it is thick and creamy.

Combine all the other ingredients in a separate bowl, but reserve ½ cup of the soy protein powder for later use. Add about half of this dry mix to the butter-egg mixture and stir until smooth. Work in the egg whites. A fork is handy for this job. Finish with the remaining dry mix.

This dough needs to be just firm enough to handle. Chill it for about 10 minutes. Sprinkle a tablespoon or so of the soy protein powder on a cutting board that can readily hold two 6-inch circles. Put the dough on the board. Work in a little soy protein powder at a time and stop when the dough can be shaped.

Divide the dough in two portions. Pat each into a 6-inch circle, about ½ to ¾ inch thick. Cut each circle into six wedges (change the number and size if you like). With a cake server or a spatula, lift the wedges and transfer them separately to the cookie sheet. Bake the scones for about 16 to 20 minutes or until light golden. Cool on a cooling rack. These scones freeze well.

Variation: Glazed Scones

Follow the directions for Scones with Currants above. You have two choices. You can apply a glaze made with powdered cane sugar or one made with xylitol powdered sugar. Mix 2 tablespoons of regular powdered sugar with 2 teaspoons of heavy cream to make a thin paste. If you use xylitol powdered sugar, you can increase the sugar in the glaze to 3 tablespoons. Make a similar thin paste. Apply either glaze while the scones are still hot and allow the glaze to dry completely. The cane sugar glaze adds 1.4 gram of carb to each scone, the xylitol glaze adds 0.5 gram to each scone.

Variation: Scones with Blueberries

Follow the directions for making Scones with Currants above. Make these changes: replace the currants with ⅔ cup of fresh or frozen blueberries. The added carb count per scone is 0.9 gram.

Variation: Scones with Cranberries

Follow the directions for making Scones with Currants above. Make these changes: replace the currants with ⅔ cup of finely chopped cranberries. The added carb count per scone is 0.7 gram.

Quick Sour Cream Coffee Cake

This is as good as it gets. You do not really need a topping, but if you want one they begin on page 92.

PREPARATION TIME: 15 minutes. BAKING TIME: about 16 to 18 minutes.
SERVING SIZE: ½ of yield. AMOUNT PER SERVING: 4.4 grams of carb, 6.0 grams of protein. TOTAL YIELD: one 9-by-13-inch coffee cake.

		CHO (g)	PRO (g)
5	tablespoons unsalted butter (⅝ stick), very soft	0	0
3	tablespoons xylitol	5.4	0
5	tablespoons Splenda	7.5	0
1	teaspoon Stevia Plus (or equivalent)	0	0
2	eggs, room temperature	1.2	12.0
2	teaspoons vanilla extract	1.0	0
⅓	cup sour cream	2.7	1.6
½	cup oat flour	26.0	8.0
	salt, trace	0	0
2	teaspoons grated lemon peel	0.5	0
1	teaspoon baking powder	1.2	0
¼	teaspoon baking soda	0	0
¼	cup whole almond meal	2.5	5.0
½	cup blanched almond meal	6.0	10.0
½	cup soy protein powder	0	32.2
	Total	*54.0*	*68.8*

Preheat the oven to 350°F. Butter a 9-by-13-inch (or similar) glass baking dish. Glass is best for cutting the cake inside the pan.

Reserve 1 tablespoon of the butter and combine the rest with the sweeteners, eggs, and vanilla extract in a medium mixing bowl. Beat until thick and creamy. Beat in the sour cream.

Stir in the oat flour, salt, lemon peel, baking powder, and baking soda along with the blanched almond meal, mixing well. Finish by adding the almond meal and soy protein powder.

Spread the batter evenly in the baking dish and level it out. Melt the reserved butter and brush it lightly over the batter. Choose a topping and spread it evenly over the batter. If feasible, press down lightly on the topping before baking. Topping recipes begin on page 92. Bake the cake for 16 to 18 minutes. Do not overbake. Cool the coffee cake in the baking dish.

Serve within a day or two. Promptly freeze leftover pieces. Remove them from the baking dish and wrap them in aluminum foil.

Quick Basic Coffee Cake

Put a tasty topping on this cake; it's hard to beat for a quick-to-make snack.

PREPARATION TIME: 15 minutes. BAKING TIME: about 16 to 18 minutes.
SERVING SIZE: ¹⁄₁₂ of yield. AMOUNT PER SERVING: 4.2 grams of carb, 6.0 grams of protein. TOTAL YIELD: one 9-by-13-inch coffee cake.

		CHO (g)	PRO (g)
5	tablespoons unsalted butter (⅝ stick), very soft	0	0
3	tablespoons xylitol	5.4	0
5	tablespoons Splenda	7.5	0
1½	teaspoons Stevia Plus (or equivalent)	0	0
2	eggs, room temperature	1.2	12.0
2	teaspoons vanilla extract	1.0	0
½	cup oat flour	26.0	8.0
	salt, trace	0	0
2	teaspoons grated lemon peel	0.5	0
1	teaspoon baking powder	1.2	0
½	cup blanched almond meal	6.0	10.0
¼	cup whole almond meal	2.5	10.0
½	cup soy protein powder	0	32.2
	Total	*50.3*	*72.2*

Preheat the oven to 350°F. Butter a 9-by-13-inch (or similar) glass baking dish. Glass is best for cutting the cake inside the pan.

Reserve 1 tablespoon of the butter and combine the rest with the sweeteners, 1 egg, and vanilla extract in a medium mixing bowl. Beat until thick and smooth. Add the remaining egg and beat in.

Stir in all the other ingredients in two portions. Mix until well combined.

Distribute the batter evenly in the baking dish and level it out. Melt the reserved butter and brush the batter lightly with it. Choose streusel or another topping. Topping recipes begin on page 92. Spread the topping evenly over the cake and, where feasible, press it down lightly. Bake for 16 to 18 minutes. Do not overbake. Cool the coffee cake in the baking dish.

Serve within a day or two. Promptly freeze leftover pieces. Remove them from the baking dish and wrap them in aluminum foil.

Nut-Free Coffee Cake

Combine with the Toffee Coconut Topping (page 95) and no one will miss the nuts. A delicious treat.

PREPARATION TIME: 15 minutes. BAKING TIME: about 16 to 18 minutes.
SERVING SIZE: ½ of yield. AMOUNT PER SERVING: 4.9 grams of carb, 6.2 grams of protein. TOTAL YIELD: one 9-by-13-inch coffee cake.

		CHO (g)	PRO (g)
5	tablespoons unsalted butter (⅝ stick), very soft	0	0
3	tablespoons xylitol	5.4	0
5	tablespoons Splenda	7.5	0
1½	teaspoons Stevia Plus (or equivalent)	0	0
2	eggs, room temperature	1.2	12.0
2	teaspoons vanilla extract	1.0	0
½	cup oat flour	26.0	8.0
	salt, trace	0	0
2	teaspoons grated lemon peel	0.5	0
1	teaspoon baking powder	1.2	0
½	cup soy milk powder	10.0	18.0
½	cup unprocessed wheat bran	6.0	4.0
½	cup soy protein powder	0	32.2
	Total	*58.8*	*74.2*

Preheat the oven to 350°F. Butter a 9-by-13-inch (or similar) glass baking dish. Glass is best for cutting the cake inside the pan.

Reserve 1 tablespoon of the butter and combine the rest with the sweeteners, 1 egg, and the vanilla extract in a medium mixing bowl. Beat until thick and smooth. Add the remaining egg and beat in.

Stir in all the other ingredients in two portions. Mix until well combined.

Spread the batter evenly in the baking dish and level it out. Melt the reserved butter and brush it lightly over the batter. Use Toffee Coconut Topping on page 95. Spread the topping evenly over the batter and press it down lightly. Bake for 16 to 18 minutes. Do not overbake. Cool the coffee cake in the baking dish.

Serve within a day or two. Promptly freeze any leftover pieces. Remove them from the baking dish and wrap them in aluminum foil.

Coconut Coffee Cake

This one is simply scrumptious.

PREPARATION TIME: 15 minutes. BAKING TIME: about 16 to 18 minutes.
SERVING SIZE: 1/12 of yield. AMOUNT PER SERVING: 3.2 grams of carb, 4.1 grams of protein. TOTAL YIELD: one 9-by-13-inch coffee cake.

		CHO (g)	PRO (g)
5	tablespoons unsalted butter (5/8 stick), very soft	0	0
3	tablespoons xylitol	5.4	0
5	tablespoons Splenda	7.5	0
1½	teaspoons Stevia Plus (or equivalent)	0	0
2	eggs, room temperature	1.2	12.0
2	teaspoons vanilla extract	1.0	0
¼	cup oat flour	13.0	4.0
	salt, trace	0	0
2	teaspoons grated lemon peel	0.5	0
1	teaspoon baking powder	1.2	0
1¼	cups unsweetened coconut, finely grated	7.5	7.5
¼	cup whole almond meal	2.5	10.0
¼	cup soy protein powder	0	16.1
	Total	*39.6*	*49.6*

Preheat the oven to 350°F. Butter a 9-by-13-inch (or similar) glass baking dish. Glass is best for cutting the cake inside the pan.

Reserve 1 tablespoon of the butter and combine the rest with the sweeteners, 1 egg, and the vanilla extract in a medium mixing bowl. Beat until thick and smooth. Add the remaining egg and beat in.

Stir in all the other ingredients in two portions. Mix until well combined.

Spread the batter evenly in the baking dish and level it out. Melt the reserved butter and brush it lightly over the batter. Choose streusel or another topping. Topping recipes begin on page 92. Spread the topping evenly over the batter and, where feasible, press it down lightly. Bake for 16 to 18 minutes. Do not overbake. Cool the coffee cake in the baking dish.

Serve within a day or two. Promptly freeze any leftover pieces. Remove them from the baking dish and wrap them in aluminum foil.

Streusel Topping

Everyone likes this, and nothing could be easier to put together.

PREPARATION TIME: 5 minutes.

SERVING SIZE: 1/12 of yield. AMOUNT PER SERVING: 1.5 grams of carb, 1.0 gram of protein. TOTAL YIELD: topping for one 9-by-13-inch coffee cake.

		CHO (g)	PRO (g)
2	tablespoons unsalted butter (¼ stick)	0	0
4	tablespoons DiabetiSweet Brown Sugar Substitute	7.2	0
1	tablespoon unbleached wheat (white) flour	5.8	0
½	teaspoon ground cinnamon	0.4	0
1	cup finely chopped walnuts	4.0	24.0
	Total	*17.4*	*24.0*

Put all the ingredients in one small mixing bowl and work together with your fingers until they become coarse and crumbly. Spread the topping over the coffee cake and press down lightly.

Toasted Pecan Topping

Great pecan taste, quick to make.

PREPARATION TIME: 5 minutes.

SERVING SIZE: ¹⁄₁₂ of yield. AMOUNT PER SERVING: 1.2 grams of carb, 0.9 gram
of protein. TOTAL YIELD: topping for one 9-by-13-inch coffee cake.

	CHO (g)	PRO (g)
1 tablespoon unsalted butter (⅛ stick), melted	0	0
1 teaspoon vanilla extract	0.5	0
4 tablespoons DiabetiSweet Brown Sugar Substitute	7.2	0
4 ounces coarsely ground pecans, toasted	7.2	10.4
Total	*14.9*	*10.4*

Heat a skillet over medium heat. Melt the butter, but do not allow it
to brown. Stir in the vanilla extract and brown sugar. Add the pecans.
Stir briefly and remove the topping from the pan. Sprinkle the topping
on coffee cakes, pies, ice cream, custards, and puddings, and press it
down lightly where feasible. If you don't use the topping immediately, cover and store it in the fridge.

Upside-Down Macadamia Topping

The surprise is baked right into the coffee cake.

PREPARATION TIME: 10 minutes.
SERVING SIZE: ½ of yield. AMOUNT PER SERVING: 1.3 grams of carb; less than 1.0 gram of protein. TOTAL YIELD: topping for one 9-by-13-inch coffee cake.

		CHO (g)	PRO (g)
4	tablespoons unsalted butter (½ stick)	0	0
5	tablespoons DiabetiSweet Brown Sugar Substitute	9.0	0
2	teaspoons vanilla extract	0.5	0
½	teaspoon ground cinnamon	0.4	0
4	ounces toasted macadamia nuts, finely chopped	6.8	8.8
	Total	*16.7*	*8.8*

Melt the butter in a 1-quart skillet over medium heat. Stir in the brown sugar, vanilla extract, and cinnamon. Cook for about 2 minutes. Add the macadamia nuts and stir for another minute. Pour this mixture in the bottom of a buttered 9-by-13-inch glass baking dish. Put the coffee cake batter gently on top and bake as directed. Turn the cake upside-down when baked.

Toffee Coconut Topping

On a low-carb diet? Tasting this, you'd never know it.

PREPARATION TIME: 5 minutes.
SERVING SIZE: ½ of yield. AMOUNT PER SERVING: 1.2 grams of carb, no protein. TOTAL YIELD: topping for one 9-by-13-inch coffee cake.

	CHO (g)	PRO (g)
4 tablespoons unsalted butter (½ stick)	0	0
2 teaspoons vanilla extract	0.5	0
½ teaspoon ground cinnamon	0.4	0
3 tablespoons water	0	0
5 tablespoons DiabetiSweet Brown Sugar Substitute	9.0	0
¾ cup finely grated unsweetened coconut	4.5	4.5
Total	*14.4*	*4.5*

Combine the butter, vanilla extract, cinnamon, water, and brown sugar over low heat in a heavy-bottomed 1-quart saucepan. Cook for 2 minutes, stirring constantly. Remove from the heat and stir in the coconut. Allow the topping to cool slightly and then spread it over the coffee cake batter. Press down lightly on the topping.

Baked Hazelnut Topping

Nutty, comforting, good. Mmm.

PREPARATION TIME: 5 minutes.

SERVING SIZE: ½ of yield. AMOUNT PER SERVING: 1.9 grams of carb, negligible protein. TOTAL YIELD: topping for one 9-by-13-inch coffee cake.

		CHO (g)	PRO (g)
3	egg yolks	0.9	8.4
2	teaspoons vanilla extract	0.5	0
1	teaspoon ground cinnamon	0.7	0
	salt, trace	0	0
5	tablespoons DiabetiSweet Brown Sugar Substitute	9.0	0
½	teaspoon baking powder	0.6	0
1½	teaspoons unbleached wheat (white) flour	2.9	0
4	ounces toasted hazelnuts, coarsely chopped	7.6	3.0
	Total	*22.2*	*11.4*

Combine the egg yolks, vanilla extract, cinnamon, and salt in a medium mixing bowl. Beat vigorously until the egg yolks are thick and creamy. Add the brown sugar by the tablespoon and beat well after each addition. Beat in the baking powder and flour. Stir in the nuts. Spread the topping evenly over the coffee cake.

4

COOKIES AND BARS

Cookies delight us with their textures, whether chewy, soft, or crunchy. Cookies' textures often result from creaming butter, sugar, and eggs. Of the sweeteners here, only xylitol imitates real sugar. With few exceptions, the sweeteners you use in this chapter *will* make a difference. The recipes include xylitol, Splenda, and Stevia Plus—and the cookies will be very good—but for best results I prefer to use xylitol and Stevia Plus alone in most cookie recipes. If you want to do that, too, simply increase the xylitol to ⅓ cup and leave out the Splenda. There is virtually no change in the carb count, and you might get an extra cookie or two.

These cookies are mostly quickies from beginning to end. Most recipes yield the number of cookies that will fit on one cookie sheet, if sometimes a bit snugly. Some require two sheets.

Most cookies need to be shaped by hand. Often, the finished dough will be just right to process at once. Sometimes it may need to be chilled; cookie dough can be slightly unpredictable. This has to do with the large number of eggs used in the recipes. Eggs tend to vary in weight, even if you consistently use "large" eggs, as recommended. There's enough difference to cause some batches of cookie dough to come out a little softer than others. Brief chilling will take care of that. If you cannot wait, gently work a small amount of soy protein powder into the dough—a tablespoon or two. If you leave cookie dough in the fridge for a longer period than the recipe specifies, let the dough regain room temperature until it gets to a point where it is soft enough to shape into balls.

Vanilla Cookies

If your kids love eating vanilla cookies from the box, here is a treat they may like even better.

PREPARATION TIME: 20 minutes. (The dough may need brief chilling.)
BAKING TIME: about 24 to 28 minutes (requires two cookie sheets).
SERVING SIZE: one 1-inch cookie. AMOUNT PER SERVING: 0.7 gram of carb, 1.1 grams of protein. TOTAL YIELD: about 72 cookies.

		CHO (g)	PRO (g)
6	tablespoons unsalted butter (¾ stick), very soft	0	0
2	eggs, room temperature	1.2	12.0
5	tablespoons Splenda	7.5	0
3	tablespoons xylitol	5.4	0
1	teaspoon Stevia Plus (or equivalent)	0	0
2	teaspoons vanilla	1.0	0
1½	cups fine, blanched almond meal	18.0	30.0
⅓	cup oat flour	17.3	5.0
½	cup soy protein powder	0	32.2
1	teaspoon baking powder	1.2	0
2	teaspoons lemon peel	0.5	0
	salt, trace	0	0
	Total	*52.1*	*79.2*

Preheat the oven to 350°F. Use two large cookie sheets with silicone-coated liners.

In a medium mixing bowl, combine the butter, eggs, sweeteners, and vanilla extract; beat the mixture until thick, smooth, and creamy.

Combine the dry ingredients in a separate bowl and mix well. Work this mix in two portions into the butter-egg batter; stir well after each addition. If the dough is too soft to shape, chill it for 10 to 15 minutes or work in an extra 1 or 2 tablespoons of soy protein powder.

Shape the dough into balls the size of small to medium grapes, and put them on the cookie sheets. The cookies will expand. Flatten each cookie with your fingertips. Bake them for 12 to 14 minutes per batch or until light golden, then transfer to a cooling rack. These cookies freeze well.

Variation: Anise Cookies

Follow the directions for Vanilla Cookies above. Make these changes: add 1 or 1½ teaspoons of anise extract—the amount depends on how strong an anise flavor you like—along with the vanilla extract. The change in carb count is insignificant.

Chocolate Cookies

Here is a sumptuous chocolate cookie, designed for chocolate lovers.

PREPARATION TIME: 20 minutes. (The dough needs brief chilling.) BAKING
  TIME: about 24 to 28 minutes (requires two cookie sheets).
SERVING SIZE: one 2-inch cookie. AMOUNT PER SERVING: 1.52 grams of carb,
  2.0 grams of protein. TOTAL YIELD: about 32 cookies.

		CHO (g)	PRO (g)
1	ounce unsweetened baking chocolate	4.0	4.0
2	ounces sugar-free semisweet chocolate	5.4	2.0
4	tablespoons heavy cream	1.6	1.2
4	tablespoons unsalted butter (½ stick), very soft	0	0
1	egg, room temperature	0.6	6.0
1	egg yolk, room temperature	0.3	2.0
5	tablespoons Splenda	7.5	0
4	tablespoons xylitol	7.2	0
1	teaspoon Stevia Plus (or equivalent)	0	0
2	teaspoons vanilla extract	1.0	0
1½	cups whole almond meal	15.0	25.0
½	cup soy protein powder	0	32.0
1	teaspoon baking powder	1.2	0
	salt, trace	0	0
	Total	*42.5*	*72.0*

Preheat the oven to 350°F. Use two large cookie sheets with silicone-coated liners. These cookies need to be flattened out and will expand quite a bit.

Put the chocolates and the cream in a double boiler over water kept at or below a simmer. Stir frequently until the chocolate is melted. Remove from the heat and set aside.

In a medium mixing bowl, combine the butter, egg, egg yolk, sweeteners, and vanilla extract; beat the mixture until it is thick, smooth, and creamy. Add the melted chocolate.

Combine the dry ingredients in a separate bowl and mix well. Stir into the butter-egg batter. Chill the dough for 30 minutes.

Shape the dough into balls the size of medium grapes and space them well apart on the cookie sheets. Flatten them with your fingertips. For a smooth surface, press down on the dough with a smooth lid. Use a smidgen of soy protein on the lid if the dough sticks. Bake the cookies until done, 12 to 14 minutes per batch, and then transfer them to a cooling rack. These cookies freeze well.

Hazelnut Cookies

A soft, chewy cookie bursting with the wonderful flavor of hazelnuts.

PREPARATION TIME: 25 minutes. (The dough needs brief chilling.) BAKING TIME: about 13 minutes.

SERVING SIZE: one 2-inch cookie. AMOUNT PER SERVING: 1.1 grams of carb; 2.2 grams of protein. TOTAL YIELD: about 32 cookies.

		CHO (g)	PRO (g)
5	egg yolks, room temperature	1.5	14.0
5	tablespoons Splenda	7.5	0
3	tablespoons xylitol	5.4	0
1	teaspoon Stevia Plus (or equivalent)	0	0
2	teaspoons vanilla extract	1.0	0
2	cups hazelnut meal	15.2	32.0
2	tablespoons whey protein powder (natural, zero-carb)	0	10.0
2	tablespoons soy protein powder	0	8.0
1	teaspoon baking powder	1.2	0
2	teaspoons lemon peel	0.5	0
30	whole hazelnuts (optional)	4.0	6.0
	salt, trace	0	0
	Total	*36.3*	*70.0*

Preheat the oven to 350°F. Use one large cookie sheet with a silicone liner.

Separate the eggs and save the whites. In a medium mixing bowl, combine the egg yolks, sweeteners, and vanilla extract. Beat the mixture until thick, smooth, and creamy; it may take 30 seconds with a portable electric mixer.

Combine all the dry ingredients except for the whole hazelnuts in a small bowl; stir. Fold the dry mix gently into the egg-butter batter. This is a slightly sticky dough that requires chilling for about 15 minutes or more.

Shape the dough into walnut-size balls and set them on the cookie sheet, allowing for some expansion. Flatten the cookies slightly with your fingertips and top each with a hazelnut, if desired. Bake until the cookies begin to show some coloring around the edges, about 13 minutes. Do not overbake. Transfer the cookies to a cooling rack. These chewy cookies tend to become dry within a day or two. It is best to freeze them promptly.

Pfeffernüsse

Yum. These cookies, popular holiday treats, are enjoyable at any time. Made with a touch of pepper and other spices, they are soft and chewy. They are especially good with a hint of xylitol powdered sugar glaze.

PREPARATION TIME: 20 minutes. (The dough requires brief chilling.) BAKING TIME: about 15 minutes.

SERVING SIZE: 1 cookie. AMOUNT PER SERVING: 1.4 grams of carb, 1.0 gram of protein. TOTAL YIELD: about 30 cookies.

		CHO (g)	PRO (g)
1	egg, room temperature	0.6	6.0
4	egg yolks, room temperature	1.2	11.2
5	tablespoons Splenda	7.5	0
3	tablespoons xylitol	5.4	0
1	teaspoon Stevia Plus (or equivalent)	0	0
2	teaspoons vanilla extract	1.0	0
¼	teaspoon anise extract	0.3	0
½	cup blanched almond meal	6.0	10.0
1½	cups whole almond meal	12.5	25.0
½	cup soy protein powder	0	16.1
½	teaspoon white pepper (more if you like)	0.3	0
½	teaspoon ground nutmeg	0.3	0
½	teaspoon ground cloves	0.3	0
1½	teaspoons ground cinnamon	1.2	0
1	teaspoon baking powder	1.2	0
1	teaspoon lemon peel	0.3	0
	trace of salt	0	0

GLAZE (OPTIONAL)

		CHO (g)	PRO (g)
3	tablespoons xylitol powdered sugar*	3.6	0
3	teaspoons heavy cream	0.4	0
	Total	*42.1*	*68.3*

Preheat the oven to 350°F. Use one large cookie sheet with a silicone-coated liner.

Separate 4 of the eggs and reserve the yolks. In a medium mixing bowl, combine the whole egg, 4 egg yolks, sweeteners, and vanilla extract. Beat the mixture until thick and creamy, about 30 seconds.

Combine the dry ingredients in a small bowl and stir thoroughly. It

*If you choose to use regular powdered sugar, follow the same directions and use the same amounts. The carb count for 1 cookie (of 30) rises by 0.8 gram of carb.

is important to distribute the spices well. Fold the dry mix gently into the egg batter. This is a slightly sticky dough that requires chilling for about 15 minutes or a little longer. If needed, add a little soy protein powder.

Shape the dough into walnut-size balls and set them on the cookie sheet. Allow some room for expansion. Flatten each cookie with your fingertips. Bake the cookies until they become golden, about 15 minutes. Do not overbake. Transfer the cookies to a cooling rack.

Apply the sugar glaze while the cookies are still warm. Mix the powdered sugar with the heavy cream. Brush thinly over the top of each cookie. Allow the glaze to harden completely. Do not freeze cookies until the glaze is completely dry. The cookies are soft and chewy but will dry out quickly. They are best kept frozen.

Macadamia Nut Biscotti

Biscotti are truly easy to make, even though they are baked twice. Great munchies.

PREPARATION TIME: 20 minutes. (The dough needs chilling.) BAKING TIME: 30 minutes for the first baking; the second baking takes several hours, largely unattended.

SERVING SIZE: one 2-inch biscotti. AMOUNT PER SERVING: 1.0 gram of carb, 2.2 grams of protein. TOTAL YIELD: about 36 biscotti.

		CHO (g)	PRO (g)
6	tablespoons unsalted butter (¾ stick), very soft	0	0
3	ounces cream cheese, very soft	2.4	6.3
2	eggs, room temperature	1.2	12.0
5	tablespoons Splenda	7.5	0
3	tablespoons xylitol	5.4	0
1	teaspoon Stevia Plus (or equivalent)	0	0
2	teaspoons vanilla extract	1.0	0
1	cup macadamia nut meal*	5.2	4.0
¾	cup toasted macadamia nuts, coarsely ground	5.1	6.6
¾	cup blanched almond meal	9.0	15.0
½	cup soy protein powder	0.0	32.2
1	teaspoon baking powder	1.2	0
2	teaspoons lemon peel	0.5	0
	salt, trace	0	0
	Total	*38.5*	*76.1*

Preheat the oven to 325°F. Line a large cookie sheet with a silicone-coated liner.

In a medium mixing bowl, combine the butter, cream cheese, eggs, sweeteners, and vanilla extract. Beat until thick and creamy.

Combine the remaining ingredients in a separate bowl and mix well. Add to the butter-egg batter and stir until well blended. Refrigerate the dough for about 30 minutes.

Shape the dough into 3 or 4 rolls, each about 2 inches in diameter. Put these on the cookie sheet and bake them for about 30 minutes or until they begin to show some faint coloring. It is normal for these rolls to split open a bit on top. Allow the rolls to cool; they will be easier to handle.

For the next step—you can do it hours later or the next day—set

*If you do not have macadamia nut meal, you may use blanched almond meal instead.

the oven to the lowest temperature setting. Put the rolls on a cutting board and slice them into thirty-six ¾-inch wide, or slightly less, slices. Set these upright on the cookie sheet and return them to the oven. What happens next depends on your oven temperature. If it is around 150°F, you can keep the biscotti in the oven until they completely dry, which may take several hours. Check the biscotti a few times during the first two hours. If they show no signs of turning color, you can leave them alone until done. If there is browning, remove the biscotti and let them dry at room temperature, unless the humidity is very high. Cover them with a paper towel or a lightweight kitchen towel. Once the biscotti are dry, they will keep for several weeks. There is no need to freeze them.

Variation: Spice Biscotti

Though the directions are nearly the same as for Macadamia Nut Biscotti above, note the following changes in ingredients.

SERVING SIZE: one 2-inch biscotti. AMOUNT PER SERVING: 1.2 grams of carb, 3.0 grams of protein. TOTAL YIELD: about 36 biscotti.

		CHO (g)	PRO (g)
6	tablespoons unsalted butter (¾ stick), very soft	0	0
3	ounces cream cheese, very soft	2.4	6.3
2	eggs, room temperature	1.2	12.0
5	tablespoons Splenda	7.5	0
3	tablespoons xylitol	5.4	0
1	teaspoon Stevia Plus (or equivalent)	0	0
2	teaspoons vanilla extract	1.0	0
1	teaspoon ground cinnamon	0.7	0
½	teaspoon ground cloves	0.5	0
1½	cups blanched almond meal	18.0	30.0
½	cup whole almond meal	5.0	10.0
¾	cup soy protein powder	0	48.9
1	teaspoon baking powder	1.2	0
2	teaspoons lemon peel	0.5	0
	salt, trace	0	0
	Total	*43.4*	*107.2*

Macadamia Nut Cookies

Everyone will love these elegant cookies. Great for teatime—or anytime.

PREPARATION TIME: 25 minutes. (The dough may need brief chilling.) BAKING TIME: about 24 to 28 minutes (requires two cookie sheets).
SERVING SIZE: 1 cookie. AMOUNT PER SERVING: 1.0 gram of carb, 1.8 grams of protein. TOTAL YIELD: about 34 cookies.

		CHO (g)	PRO (g)
6	tablespoons unsalted butter (¾ stick), very soft	0	0
1	egg, room temperature	0.6	6.0
5	tablespoons Splenda	7.5	0
3	tablespoons xylitol	5.4	0
1	teaspoon Stevia Plus (or equivalent)	0	0
2	teaspoons vanilla extract	1.0	0
1½	cups toasted macadamia nuts, finely chopped	10.2	13.2
½	cup macadamia nut meal*	2.6	4.0
⅓	cup blanched almond meal	4.0	7.0
½	cup soy protein powder	0	32.2
½	teaspoon ground nutmeg (optional)	0.3	0
1	teaspoon baking powder	1.2	0
2	teaspoons lemon peel	0.5	0
	salt, trace		
	Total	*33.3*	*62.4*

Preheat the oven to 350°F. Use two cookie sheets with silicone-coated liners.

Combine the butter, egg, sweeteners, and vanilla extract in a medium mixing bowl and beat until thick, smooth, and creamy.

Combine all the other ingredients, including the toasted macadamia nuts, in another mixing bowl and mix well. Work the dry mix in two stages into the egg batter. If the dough is too soft to shape by hand, chill it for about 10 to 15 minutes or add 1 to 2 tablespoons of soy protein powder to the dough.

Form balls about the size of small walnuts and put them on the cookie sheet, allowing room for expansion. Flatten each cookie with your fingertips. If you want them to be smooth on top—they will look more attractive—use a small, smooth, 2-inch lid (some vitamin

---

*If you do not have macadamia nut meal, replace it with blanched almond meal. This adds 0.1 gram of carb to each cookie (of 34).

bottles have useful lids) and apply pressure to the cookies. If the dough sticks a little, rub a hint of soy protein powder on the lid. Bake the cookies until they are light golden, about 12 to 14 minutes per batch.

Cool the cookies on a cooling rack. The cookies will keep well at room temperature for several days. They can also be frozen.

Variation: Macadamia Nut Cookies with Chocolate Chips

Follow the directions for Macadamia Nut Cookies above. Make these changes: add 1½ ounces of sugar-free semisweet or milk chocolate chips to the dough at the end. There is some increase in the number of cookies. The change in carb count is negligible.

Chocolate Almond Cookies

Great anytime and a special treat during the holiday season.

PREPARATION TIME: 30 minutes. (The dough requires brief chilling.) BAKING TIME: about 22 to 28 minutes (requires two cookie sheets).

SERVING SIZE: one 2-inch cookie. AMOUNT PER SERVING: 1.4 grams of carbs, 2.3 grams of protein. TOTAL YIELD: about 34 cookies.

		CHO (g)	PRO (g)
2	ounces semisweet, sugar-free chocolate	5.4	4.0
2	tablespoons heavy cream	0.8	0
1	egg, room temperature	0.6	6.0
2	egg yolks, room temperature	0.6	5.6
5	tablespoons Splenda	7.5	0
3	tablespoons xylitol	5.4	0
1	teaspoon Stevia Plus (or equivalent)	0	0
2	teaspoons vanilla extract	1.0	0
½	cup blanched almond meal	6.0	10.0
1½	cups whole almond meal	12.5	25.0
⅓	cup soy protein powder	0	21.5
½	teaspoon ground nutmeg	0.3	0
½	teaspoon ground cloves	0.5	0
2	teaspoons ground cinnamon	1.4	0
1	teaspoon baking powder	1.2	0
	salt, trace	0	0
	Total	*43.2*	*72.6*

Preheat the oven to 350°F. Use two cookie sheets with silicone-coated liners.

Put the chocolate and the heavy cream in a small, microwavable bowl and microwave until the chocolate is melted, about 20 seconds. You can also do this in a small bowl set atop a double boiler over hot water kept at or below a simmer. Remove from the heat. Stir until smooth and set aside.

Combine the egg, egg yolks, sweeteners, and vanilla extract in a medium mixing bowl and beat until thick, smooth, and creamy. Save the extra egg whites in the fridge to use in other dishes. Stir the melted chocolate into the egg mixture and combine thoroughly.

Combine the remaining ingredients in a mixing bowl and stir until well mixed; the spices must be well distributed. Fold or stir the dry ingredients in two portions gently into the egg-chocolate mixture. Chill the dough for about 10 to 15 minutes.

Shape the dough into balls the size of small walnuts and set on the cookie sheet, allowing for expansion. Using your fingertips, flatten the cookies to about half their thickness. Bake the cookies for about 11 to 14 minutes per batch or until done. Do not overbake. Cool them on a cooling rack. These cookies will dry out fairly quickly. They can be frozen.

Almond Crispies

Oh so very good, these cookies may well be worth the little extra fuss required in making them. Use only Splenda with this recipe.

PREPARATION TIME: 25 to 30 minutes (excludes roasting time for almonds).
BAKING TIME: about 40 minutes (requires two cookie sheets).
SERVING SIZE: one 2.5-inch cookie. AMOUNT PER SERVING: 1.6 grams of carb, 2.5 grams of protein. TOTAL YIELD: about 34 cookies.

		CHO (g)	PRO (g)
3	tablespoons unsalted butter (⅜ stick), very soft	0	0
1	egg, room temperature	0.6	6.0
2	egg yolks, room temperature	0.6	5.6
10	tablespoons Splenda	15.0	0
2	teaspoons vanilla extract	1.0	0
2	tablespoons oat flour	6.5	2.0
½	teaspoon baking powder	0.6	0
2	teaspoons lemon peel	0.5	0
	salt, trace	0	0
3	cups sliced almonds, toasted	31.2	72.0
	Total	*56.5*	*84.4*

Preheat the oven to 300°F. Use two large cookie sheets with silicone-coated liners.

Put the soft butter in a medium mixing bowl. Add the egg, egg yolks, Splenda, and vanilla extract. Beat until thick and creamy. Stir in the oat flour, baking powder, lemon peel, and salt. Add the sliced almonds and stir until the almonds are evenly coated with the batter.

If the dough is a bit sticky, chill it for 10 minutes. With a spoon or a fork, place mounds the size of large grapes on the cookie sheet. Flatten the cookies with a fork—these cookies should be thin and crisp. Nudge them with a fork or your fingertips into a circular shape, 2½ inches across. Bake for about 20 minutes per batch or until light golden; do not overbake. Transfer the cookies to a cooling rack.

The finished cookies should be dry and crisp; they will be chewy after baking. Reduce the oven temperature to its lowest setting, about 150°F. Set all of the cookies on a single cookie sheet—some overlapping is fine. Return the cookies to the oven for about 5 hours or longer, until crisp. Check the cookies every hour. There should be no further browning. If there is, remove the tray from the oven and allow the cookies to air-dry. Once dry, store them in an airtight container.

Pumpkin Seed Cookies

A fabulously tasty cookie and healthy treat.

PREPARATION TIME: 20 minutes. (The dough may require brief chilling.)
    BAKING TIME: about 11 to 15 minutes.
SERVING SIZE: one 2-inch cookie. AMOUNT PER SERVING: 1.1 grams of carb,
    2.9 grams of protein. TOTAL YIELD: about 32 cookies.

		CHO (g)	PRO (g)
5	tablespoons unsalted butter (⅝ stick), very soft	0	0
1	egg, room temperature	0.3	6.0
5	tablespoons Splenda	7.5	0
3	tablespoons DiabetiSweet Brown Sugar Substitute*	5.4	0
1	teaspoon Stevia Plus (or equivalent)	0	0
2	teaspoons vanilla extract	1.0	0
½	cup blanched almond meal	6.0	10.0
½	cup whole almond meal	5.0	10.0
¼	cup flaxseed meal	1.6	5.0
½	cup soy protein powder	0	32.2
¾	cup toasted pumpkin seeds, coarsely ground	7.5	30.0
1	teaspoon baking powder	1.2	0
2	teaspoons lemon peel	0.5	0
	salt, trace	0	0
	Total	*36.0*	*93.2*

Preheat the oven to 350°F. Use one large cookie sheet with a silicone-coated liner.

In a medium mixing bowl, combine the butter, egg, sweeteners, and vanilla extract and beat until thick and creamy.

Combine all the remaining ingredients, including pumpkin seeds, in a separate bowl and mix well. Work the dry mix in two portions into the egg batter; finish by hand. If the dough is too soft to handle, chill for about 10 to 15 minutes. You can also add 1 or 2 tablespoons of soy protein powder to firm up the dough for immediate shaping.

Roll the dough into balls about the size of walnuts and place them on the cookie sheet, allowing for some expansion. With your fingertips, flatten the cookies to about half their height. Bake them for about 11 to 15 minutes or until they take on a touch of golden color. Cool them on a rack. It is best to freeze these cookies as they contain flaxseed meal.

*If you do not have this brown sugar, use xylitol instead.

All-Seed Wonder Cookies

Incredibly delicious and nutritious.

PREPARATION TIME: 20 minutes. (The dough may need brief chilling.)
 BAKING TIME: 24 minutes (requires two cookie sheets).
SERVING SIZE: one 2-inch cookie. AMOUNT PER SERVING: 1.3 grams of carb,
 3.0 grams of protein. TOTAL YIELD: about 42 cookies.

		CHO (g)	PRO (g)
4	tablespoons unsalted butter (½ stick), very soft	0	0
1	egg, room temperature	0.6	6.0
1	egg yolk, room temperature	0.3	2.8
5	tablespoons Splenda	7.5	0
3	tablespoons DiabetiSweet Brown Sugar Substitute*	5.4	0
1	teaspoon Stevia Plus (or equivalent)	0	0
2	teaspoons vanilla extract	1.0	0
¼	cup flaxseeds	2.1	7.0
1	cup whole almond meal	10.0	20.0
¼	cup whey protein powder (natural, zero-carb)	0	20.0
1	teaspoon baking powder	1.2	0
½	cup sesame seeds	6.0	14.0
½	cup toasted pumpkin seeds, coarsely crushed	5.0	20.0
¼	cup toasted sunflower seeds	2.3	6.7
2	teaspoons lemon peel	0.5	0
	salt, trace	0	0
	Total	*41.9*	*96.0*

Preheat the oven to 350°F. Use two large cookie sheets lined with silicone-coated liners.

Put the butter, egg, egg yolk, sweeteners, and vanilla extract in a medium mixing bowl. Beat until thick and creamy.

Combine all the remaining ingredients in a separate bowl and stir well. Work the dry mix in two portions into the egg batter. If the dough is a little soft, chill it for 10 to 15 minutes. You can also work 1 or 2 tablespoons of soy protein powder into the dough if you do not want to wait.

Form the dough into balls the size of small walnuts. Put them on the cookie sheet, allowing room for expansion. With your fingertips,

*If you do not have this brown sugar, substitute xylitol instead.

pat the cookies down to about half their height. Bake each batch for about 12 minutes or until the cookies take on a little golden color. Place them on a cooling rack. The cookies tend to dry out within a day or two. Because they contain flaxseed meal, it's best to freeze them.

Flaxseed Cookies

You will love them. And they have only 1 gram of carb per cookie!

PREPARATION TIME: 20 minutes. (The dough may need brief chilling.)
BAKING TIME: about 10 to 14 minutes.
SERVING SIZE: one 2-inch cookie. AMOUNT PER SERVING: 1.0 gram of carb,
1.8 grams of protein. TOTAL YIELD: about 32 cookies.

		CHO (g)	PRO (g)
6	tablespoons unsalted butter (¾ stick), very soft	0	0
1	egg, room temperature	0.6	6.0
5	tablespoons Splenda	7.5	0
3	tablespoons xylitol	5.4	0
1	teaspoon Stevia Plus (or equivalent)	0	0
2	teaspoons vanilla extract	1.0	0
¾	cup flaxseed meal	4.8	15.0
1	cup whole almond meal	10.0	20.0
¼	cup soy protein powder	0	16.1
1	teaspoon baking powder	1.2	0
1	teaspoon lemon peel	0.3	0
	salt, trace	0	0
	Total	*30.8*	*57.1*

Preheat the oven to 350°F. Use a large cookie sheet with a silicone-coated liner.

In a medium mixing bowl, combine the butter, egg, sweeteners, and vanilla extract and beat until thick and creamy.

Combine the remaining ingredients in a separate small bowl and mix well. Work the dry mix in two portions into the egg batter. If the dough is too soft to shape into cookies, chill it for about 10 to 15 minutes. You can also add 1 or 2 tablespoons of soy protein powder to firm up the dough right away.

Roll the dough into balls about the size of walnuts and place them on the cookie sheet, allowing for some expansion. With your fingertips, flatten the cookies to almost half their height. Bake them about 10 to 14 minutes or until they take on a touch of golden color. Cool them on a cooling rack. These cookies are deliciously crunchy. Keep the cookies frozen because they contain flaxseed meal.

Sandy Pecan Balls

Mighty good. Lightly sweetened, they are rolled in xylitol.

PREPARATION TIME: 20 minutes. (The dough requires brief chilling.) BAKING TIME: about 12 to 15 minutes.

SERVING SIZE: one ½-ounce cookie. AMOUNT PER SERVING: 1.5 grams of carbs, negligible protein. TOTAL YIELD: 30 cookies.

		CHO (g)	PRO (g)
6	tablespoons unsalted butter (¾ stick), soft	0	0
1	egg yolk	0.3	2.8
2	tablespoons xylitol	5.6	0
3	tablespoons Splenda	3.0	0
½	teaspoon Stevia Plus (or equivalent)	0	0
2	teaspoons vanilla extract	1.0	0
3	ounces toasted pecans, finely crushed	5.4	7.8
½	cup oat flour	26.0	8.0
	salt, trace	0	0
SUGAR FOR ROLLING			
2	tablespoons xylitol	3.6	0
	Total	*44.9*	*18.6*

Preheat the oven to 350°F. Use a large cookie sheet with a silicone-coated liner.

In a medium mixing bowl, combine the butter, egg yolk, sweeteners, and vanilla extract; beat briefly, just until well mixed and creamy.

Add the pecans, oat flour, and salt. Stir the mixture until it is fairly well combined. Continue with your hands (disposable gloves are good to use for this) until you have a smooth dough. Chill the dough for about 15 minutes.

Shape the dough into balls the size of walnuts and place them on the cookie sheet. Bake the pecan balls for about 12 to 15 minutes or until they show a bit of golden color.

To make the sugar, put 2 tablespoons of xylitol in a small bowl. Roll each cookie lightly in the sugar for a dusting and then put the cookies on a cooling rack. Somewhat crumbly, these cookies will dry out fairly quickly and need careful handling. They can be frozen.

Coconut Cookies

Always popular. Real comfort food!

PREPARATION TIME: 15 minutes. (The dough may require brief chilling.)
BAKING TIME: about 10 to 13 minutes.
SERVING SIZE: one 2-inch cookie. AMOUNT PER SERVING: 1.1 grams of carb,
2.0 grams of protein. TOTAL YIELD: about 32 cookies.

		CHO (g)	PRO (g)
8	tablespoons unsalted butter (1 stick), very soft	0	0
1	large egg, room temperature	0.6	6.0
5	tablespoons Splenda	7.5	0
3	tablespoons xylitol	5.4	0
1	teaspoon Stevia Plus (or equivalent)	0	0
2	teaspoons vanilla extract	1.0	0
1¼	cups unsweetened coconut, finely grated	7.5	7.5
1	teaspoon baking powder	1.2	0
1	cup blanched almond meal	12.0	20.0
½	cup soy protein powder	0	32.2
2	teaspoons lemon peel	0.5	0
	salt, trace	0	0
	Total	*35.7*	*65.7*

Preheat the oven to 350°F. Use a large cookie sheet with a silicone-coated liner.

Put the butter, egg, sweeteners, and vanilla extract in a medium mixing bowl and beat until thick and creamy.

Combine the remaining ingredients in a separate bowl. Add the dry mix in two portions to the butter-egg batter. If the dough is too soft to handle, chill it for 10 to 15 minutes or work 1 or 2 tablespoons of soy protein powder into the dough.

Roll the dough into walnut-size balls and place them on the cookie sheet, allowing for expansion. Pat each cookie down slightly with your finger tips. Bake for 10 to 13 minutes or until done. The cookies should remain quite light in color. Cool them on a cooling rack. These cookies are slightly chewy to begin with, but they will become crunchy within a day or two if not stored in a tightly covered container or frozen.

Coconut Pecan Crispies

You could also call them the big surprise cookies; self-discipline may go out the window. But they are low in carb count.

PREPARATION TIME: 25 minutes. BAKING TIME: 22 to 28 minutes (requires two cookie sheets).

SERVING SIZE: one 2½-inch cookie. AMOUNT PER SERVING: 0.8 gram of carb, negligible protein. TOTAL YIELD: about 30 cookies.

	CHO (g)	PRO (g)
1 cup coconut, finely grated	6.0	6.0
3 ounces toasted pecans, finely chopped	5.4	7.8
½ cup heavy cream	3.2	2.4
5 tablespoons Splenda	7.5	0
3 tablespoons xylitol	5.4	0
1 teaspoon Stevia Plus (or equivalent)	0	0
salt, trace	0	0
2 teaspoons vanilla extract	1.0	0
1 egg white	0.3	3.5
Total	*28.7*	*19.7*

Preheat the oven to 350°F. Line two large cookie sheets with parchment paper.

Combine the coconut and the pecans in a medium mixing bowl and stir.

Put the heavy cream, sweeteners, vanilla extract, and salt in a small bowl and stir until thoroughly mixed. Pour this liquid over the coconut-pecan mixture and stir until the two are well combined.

Beat the egg white until firm but not stiff. Stir the egg white into the batter and mix thoroughly. With a fork or a spoon, remove chunks of batter about the size of cherries and place them on the parchment paper.

Use your fingertips to flatten the cookies to about 2.5 inches in diameter and as thin as you can make them. Bake the cookies for about 11 to 14 minutes per batch or until the edges are lightly brown.

Let the cookies cool and harden slightly before attempting to remove them from the parchment paper; they tend to break easily while warm. Allow them to dry completely exposed to air, or return them to the oven and set it at its lowest setting for another hour or two. Check to make sure the cookies are not turning darker. Once dry, keep them in a tightly closed container. These cookies keep for a long time.

Hermits

Just try them and see for yourself. These are glorious cookies.

PREPARATION TIME: 20 minutes. (The dough may need brief chilling.)
BAKING TIME: about 12 to 14 minutes.
SERVING SIZE: one 1¼-inch cookie. AMOUNT PER SERVING: 1.7 grams of carb,
2.0 grams of protein. TOTAL YIELD: about 32 cookies.

		CHO (g)	PRO (g)
6	tablespoons unsalted butter (¾ stick), very soft	0	0
1	egg, room temperature	0.6	6.0
5	tablespoons Splenda	7.5	0
3	tablespoons xylitol	5.4	0
1	teaspoon Stevia Plus (or equivalent)	0	0
2	teaspoons vanilla extract	1.0	0
¼	cup sour cream	2.0	1.2
½	cup blanched almond meal	6.0	10.0
¾	cup whole almond meal	7.5	15.0
⅔	cup soy protein powder	0	42.3
1	teaspoon baking powder	1.2	0
½	teaspoon ground cinnamon	0	0
¼	teaspoon ground cloves	0.3	0
	salt, trace	0	0
3	tablespoons currants	21.0	1.0
2	ounces finely chopped, toasted pecans	3.6	5.2
	Total	*55.5*	*80.7*

Preheat the oven to 350°F. Line a large cookie sheet with a silicone-coated liner.

In a medium mixing bowl, combine the butter, egg, sweeteners, and vanilla extract. Beat until thick and creamy. Stir in the sour cream.

Combine the remaining ingredients in a separate bowl and stir well. Stir these into the butter-egg batter. If the dough is too soft to handle, chill it for about 10 to 15 minutes or work in an extra tablespoon or two of soy protein powder.

Form cherry-size balls and put them on the cookie sheet. Flatten each slightly with your fingertips. Bake the cookies for 12 to 14 minutes or until they turn light golden. Do not overbake. Cool them on a cooling rack. These cookies are chewy. It is best to freeze them within a day or two or they are likely to dry out.

Honey Spice Cookies

These are perfect holiday cookies—soft, almost cakelike. The honey bites into the carb budget, but these are too good to miss out on. Many will ask for them again and again, holiday or not.

PREPARATION TIME: 20 minutes. (The dough may need chilling.) BAKING TIME: about 24 to 28 minutes (requires two cookie sheets).

SERVING SIZE: one 1¾-inch cookie. AMOUNT PER SERVING: 1.9 grams of carb, 2.2 grams of protein. TOTAL YIELD: about 42 cookies.

	CHO (g)	PRO (g)
2 tablespoons honey	34.0	0
1 tablespoon lemon juice	1.3	0
¼ cup Splenda	6.0	0
2 tablespoons xylitol	3.6	0
1 teaspoon Stevia Plus (or equivalent)	0	0
1 egg, room temperature	0.6	6.0
1 egg yolk, room temperature	0.3	2.8
2 teaspoons vanilla extract	1.0	0
¾ cup whole almond meal	7.5	15.0
¼ oat flour	13.0	4.0
¾ cup blanched almond meal	9.0	15.0
¾ cup soy protein powder	0	48.9
1 teaspoon baking soda	1.0	0
1 teaspoon ground cinnamon	0.7	0
½ teaspoon ground cloves	0.5	0
¼ teaspoon ground nutmeg	0.3	0
salt, trace	0	0
Total	*78.8*	*91.7*

Preheat the oven to 325°F. Line two cookie sheets with silicone-coated liners.

In a microwavable, medium mixing bowl, combine the honey and the lemon juice (if the honey is too hard to get out, warm it slightly before measuring). Microwave for a few seconds until the mixture becomes almost watery. Beat until smooth.

Let the honey cool slightly. Beat in the sweeteners, egg, egg yolk, and vanilla extract.

In a separate bowl, combine all the other ingredients and stir well. Add these to the honey-egg mixture in two portions. Stir well after each addition. Chill the dough if it is too soft to handle. Shape the dough into cherry-size balls and place them on the cookie sheet. Flatten each cookie slightly with your fingertips. Bake the cookies for 12 to 14 minutes per batch or until they turn faintly golden. It is important to watch these cookies; they can easily get overbaked and become dark on the bottom. They are meant to be soft, almost cake-like. Cool them on a cooling rack. It is best to freeze the cookies within a day or two or they will dry out.

Variation: Honey Spice Cookies with Chocolate Glaze

Follow the directions for Honey Spice Cookies above. To make the glaze, follow the directions for Chocolate Glaze on page 185. The glaze adds about 0.2 gram of carb per cookie.

Variation: Honey Spice Cookies with Powdered Sugar Glaze

Follow the directions for Honey Spice Cookies above. To make the glaze, follow the directions for Powdered Low-Carb Sugar Glaze on page 186. The glaze adds about 0.2 gram of carb per cookie.

Oatmeal Cookies

Grandma could have made these. The oats drive these cookies pretty much to the top of the carb list. Still, it's better to eat these than the real thing.

PREPARATION TIME: 20 minutes. (The dough may need brief chilling.) BAKING TIME: about 12 to 14 minutes.

SERVING SIZE: one 2-inch cookie. AMOUNT PER SERVING: 2.4 grams of carb, 2.3 grams of protein. TOTAL YIELD: about 30 cookies.

		CHO (g)	PRO (g)
6	tablespoons unsalted butter (¾ stick), very soft	0	0
1	egg, room temperature	0.6	6.0
5	tablespoons Splenda	7.5	0
3	tablespoons xylitol	5.4	0
1	teaspoon Stevia Plus (or equivalent)	0	0
2	teaspoons vanilla extract	1.0	0
1	cup rolled oats	46.0	10.0
1	cup whole almond meal	10.0	20.0
½	cup soy protein powder	0	32.2
1	teaspoon baking powder	1.2	0
2	teaspoons lemon peel	0.5	0
	salt, trace	0	0
	Total	72.2	68.2

Preheat the oven to 350°F. Line a large cookie sheet with a silicone-coated liner.

In a medium mixing bowl, combine the butter, egg, sweeteners, and vanilla extract. Beat until thick and creamy.

Combine the remaining dry ingredients in a separate bowl and mix well. Add to the egg batter in two portions and stir until well mixed. If the dough is too soft to shape, refrigerate for about 10 to 15 minutes or work in an extra tablespoon or two of soy protein powder.

Shape the dough into small walnut-size balls and put them on the cookie sheet, allowing for some expansion. Flatten each cookie slightly with your fingertips. Bake the cookies for about 12 to 14 minutes or until light golden. Cool them on a cooling rack. To keep the cookies chewy, it is best to freeze them and thaw as needed.

Orange Chocolate Chip Cookies

Low-carb? You bet. But simply divine!

PREPARATION TIME: 25 minutes. (The dough may need brief chilling.) BAKING TIME: about 12 to 15 minutes.
SERVING SIZE: one 2-inch cookie. AMOUNT PER SERVING: 1.5 grams of carb, 2.1 grams of protein. TOTAL YIELD: about 30 cookies.

		CHO (g)	PRO (g)
6	tablespoons unsalted butter (¾ stick), very soft	0	0
5	tablespoons Splenda	7.5	0
3	tablespoons xylitol	5.4	0
1	teaspoon Stevia Plus (or equivalent)	0	0
1	egg, room temperature	0.6	6.0
1	egg yolk, room temperature	0.3	2.8
2	teaspoons vanilla extract	1.0	0
1	teaspoon orange extract (or to taste)	0.5	0
½	cup oat flour	13.0	4.0
½	cup blanched almond meal	6.0	10.0
½	cup whole almond meal	2.5	5.0
1	teaspoon baking powder	1.2	0
½	cup soy protein powder	0	32.2
1	teaspoon lemon peel	0.3	0
1½	ounces sugar-free semisweet chocolate chips	4.1	3.0
	salt, trace	0	0
	Total	*42.4*	*63.0*

Preheat the oven to 350°F. Line a large cookie sheet with a silicone-coated liner.

Combine the butter, sugars, egg, egg yolk, and vanilla extract in a medium mixing bowl. Beat until thick and creamy.

Combine the remaining ingredients, including chocolate chips, in a separate bowl and mix well. Add to the egg batter in two portions. If the dough is too soft to handle, chill it in the fridge for 10 to 15 minutes or work 1 to 2 tablespoons of soy protein powder into the dough.

Shape the dough into balls the size of walnuts and put them on the cookie sheet, allowing for some expansion. Flatten the cookies slightly with your fingertips. Bake them for about 12 to 15 minutes or until they take on a hint of golden color. Transfer the cookies to a cooling rack and cool. These cookies are best kept frozen.

Old-fashioned "Sugar Cookies"

Comforting indeed.

PREPARATION TIME: 20 minutes. (The dough may need brief chilling.)
BAKING TIME: about 24 to 30 minutes (requires two cookie sheets).
SERVING SIZE: one 2½-inch cookie. AMOUNT PER SERVING: 1.4 grams of carb,
2.0 grams of protein. TOTAL YIELD: about 30 cookies.

		CHO (g)	PRO (g)
6	tablespoons unsalted butter (¾ stick), very soft	0	0
1	egg yolk	0.3	2.8
5	tablespoons Splenda	7.5	0
3	tablespoons xylitol	5.4	0
1	teaspoon Stevia Plus (or equivalent)	0	0
2	teaspoons vanilla extract	1.0	0
¼	cup oat flour	13.0	4.0
½	cup blanched almond meal	6.0	10.0
½	cup whole almond meal	5.0	10.0
½	cup soy protein powder	0	32.2
1	teaspoon baking powder	1.2	0
2	teaspoons lemon peel	0.5	0
	salt, trace	0	0
GLAZE			
1	egg white	0.3	3.0
3	teaspoons xylitol	1.8	0
	Total	*42.0*	*62.2*

Preheat the oven to 350°F. Line two cookie sheets with silicone-coated liners.

In a medium mixing bowl, combine the butter, egg yolk, sweeteners, and vanilla extract. Beat until thick and creamy.

Combine the remaining ingredients, except for those in the glaze, in a separate bowl and mix well. Add to the egg batter and stir until well mixed. If the dough is too soft to shape, refrigerate it for about 10 to 15 minutes or work in a tablespoon or two of soy protein powder.

Shape the dough into walnut-size balls and place on the cookie sheets, allowing room for the cookies to expand to about 2.5 inches. Press down on each cookie with your fingertips to flatten it and have it spread out to about 2 inches. These cookies will look more attractive if they are smooth on top. A good way to do this is to use a small, 2-inch lid (some vitamin bottles have useful lids) and apply pressure to the cookies. If the dough sticks, rub a hint of soy protein powder on the lid.

For the glaze, beat the egg white with a few drops of water and brush lightly over each cookie. Sprinkle each with about ⅛ teaspoon of xylitol. Bake the cookies for about 12 to 15 minutes per batch or until they turn a light golden color. Transfer them gently to a cooling rack; these cookies are quite fragile while warm. These cookies keep extremely well; they also can be frozen.

Shortbread

Low-carb shortbread that really tastes like shortbread? See for yourself.

PREPARATION TIME: 20 minutes. (The dough needs brief chilling.) BAKING TIME: about 22 to 26 minutes (requires two cookie sheets).

SERVING SIZE: one 2-inch cookie. AMOUNT PER SERVING: 1.3 grams of carb, 1.4 grams of protein. TOTAL YIELD: about 38 cookies.

		CHO (g)	PRO (g)
8	tablespoons unsalted butter (1 stick), very soft	0	0
1	egg yolk	0.3	2.8
5	tablespoons Splenda	7.5	0
3	tablespoons xylitol	5.4	0
1	teaspoon Stevia Plus (or equivalent)	0	0
2	teaspoons vanilla extract	1.0	0
⅓	cup oat flour	17.3	5.3
¾	cup blanched almond meal	9.0	15.0
½	cup whole almond meal	5.0	10.0
⅓	cup soy protein powder	0	21.5
2	teaspoons lemon peel	0.5	0
	salt, trace	0	0
	Total	*46.0*	*54.6*

Preheat the oven to 350°F. Line two cookie sheets with silicone-coated liners.

In a medium mixing bowl, combine the butter, egg yolk, sweeteners, and vanilla extract. Beat or stir just until mixed.

Combine remaining ingredients and stir them into the butter-egg mix in two portions. Take over by hand and shape the dough into a smooth ball. Chill the dough for about 10 to 15 minutes.

Form balls the size of large grapes and place them on a cookie sheet. Flatten each cookie slightly with your fingertips. These cookies will look much more attractive with a smooth surface. You can do this with a small, smooth 2-inch lid (some vitamin bottles have useful lids). Apply enough pressure to the cookies just to make them smooth; they should not be thin. If the dough sticks, rub a hint of soy protein powder on the lid.

Bake the cookies for about 11 to 13 minutes per batch or until they turn slightly golden around the edges. Transfer them to a cooling rack and cool. These cookies are extremely fragile until they cool and harden. They keep extremely well; they also can be frozen.

Carrot Cookies

What cookie can you make today? How about moist, chewy carrot cookies?

PREPARATION TIME: 25 minutes. (The dough will need brief chilling.)
   BAKING TIME: about 12 to 14 minutes.

SERVING SIZE: one 2-inch cookie. AMOUNT PER SERVING: 1.5 grams of carb,
   1.3 gram of protein. TOTAL YIELD: about 30 cookies.

		CHO (g)	PRO (g)
⅓	cup cooked carrots, mashed	6.0	0
6	tablespoons unsalted butter		
	(¾ stick), very soft	0	0
5	tablespoons Splenda	7.5	0
3	tablespoons xylitol	5.4	0
1	teaspoon Stevia Plus (or equivalent)	0	0
1	egg yolk, room temperature	0.3	2.8
2	teaspoons vanilla extract	1.0	0
¼	cup dark rye flour	15.0	4.0
¾	cup whole almond meal	7.5	15.0
¼	cup soy protein powder	0	16.1
1	teaspoon baking powder	1.2	0
1	teaspoon lemon peel	0.3	0
	salt, trace	0	0
	Total	*44.2*	*37.9*

Cut up 2 or 3 medium carrots and steam them until very tender. Mash the carrots in a blender or a processor. Set aside ⅓ cup of the mashed carrots to cool. (You can do this hours or a day ahead of time.)

Combine the butter, sweeteners, egg yolk, and vanilla extract in a medium mixing bowl. Beat until thick and creamy. Stir the mashed carrots into the batter.

Combine the dry ingredients in a separate bowl and stir well. Add the dry mix to the carrot-egg batter and mix thoroughly. Chill the dough for about 10 to 15 minutes. If needed, add a little soy protein powder.

Form walnut-size balls and place them on a cookie sheet. Flatten slightly with your fingertips. Bake the cookies for about 12 to 14 minutes or until they turn golden. Transfer the cookies to a cooling rack and cool. These cookies freeze well.

Peanut Butter Cookies

Great ones. Just like when we were kids!

PREPARATION TIME: 15 minutes. (The dough needs to be chilled briefly.) BAKING TIME: about 12 to 15 minutes (double if you need two cookie sheets).

SERVING SIZE: one 2-inch cookie. AMOUNT PER SERVING: 1.8 grams of carb, 3.3 grams of protein. TOTAL YIELD: about 30 cookies.

		CHO (g)	PRO (g)
½	cup peanut butter, smooth	20.0	28.0
3	tablespoons unsalted butter (⅜ stick), soft	0	0
1	egg yolk	0.3	2.8
5	tablespoons Splenda	7.5	0
3	tablespoons DiabetiSweet Brown Sugar Substitute	5.4	0
1	teaspoon Stevia Plus (or equivalent)	0	0
2	teaspoons vanilla extract	1.0	0
1½	cup whole almond meal	12.5	25.0
½	cup soy protein powder	0	32.2
1	teaspoon baking powder	1.2	0
2	teaspoons lemon peel	0.5	0
	salt, trace	0	0
1½	ounces lightly chopped, salted peanuts	6.0	10.5
	Total	*54.4*	*98.5*

Preheat the oven to 350°F. Use a large cookie sheet with a silicone-coated liner.

Combine the peanut butter, butter, egg yolk, sweeteners, and vanilla extract in a medium mixing bowl. Beat until thick and creamy.

Combine the remaining ingredients, except for the peanuts, in a mixing bowl and stir until mixed. Work the dry mix into the peanut-butter batter in two portions; stir in the peanuts last. Chill the dough for about 10 to 15 minutes.

Make balls about the size of walnuts and place them on the cookie sheet. Flatten them with the tines of a fork. If you flatten the cookies quite a bit to give them the traditional peanut butter cookie appearance, they won't fit on one cookie sheet and you will need bake them in two batches. Bake for 12 to 15 minutes per batch (if you use two cookie sheets) or until the cookies take on a golden color. Set them on a cooling rack to cool. Handle gently; the cookies are quite fragile while warm. These cookies tend to dry out; it is best to freeze them.

Halloween Cookies

Nice treats—for Halloween or any time of the year.

PREPARATION TIME: 15 minutes. (The dough requires about 45 minutes of chilling.) BAKING TIME: about 12 to 15 minutes.

SERVING SIZE: one 2-inch cookie. AMOUNT PER SERVING: 1.2 grams of carb, 2.3 grams of protein. TOTAL YIELD: about 30 cookies.

		CHO (g)	PRO (g)
4	tablespoons unsalted butter (½ stick), soft	0	0
1	egg yolk, room temperature	0.3	2.8
5	tablespoons Splenda	7.5	0
3	tablespoons xylitol	5.4	0
1	teaspoon Stevia Plus (or equivalent)	0	0
2	teaspoons vanilla extract	1.0	0
½	cup canned pumpkin	4.0	2.0
¾	cup whole almond meal	7.5	15.0
½	cup soy protein powder	0	16.1
¾	cup finely chopped walnuts	4.0	27.0
1	teaspoon baking soda	1.2	0
1	teaspoon ground cinnamon	0.7	0
½	teaspoon ground cloves	0.5	0
½	teaspoon ground nutmeg	0.3	0
1½	ounces sugar-free chocolate chips	4.0	1.5
	salt, trace	0	0
	Total	*36.4*	*64.4*

Preheat the oven to 350°F. Use a large cookie sheet with a silicone-coated liner.

Combine the butter, egg yolk, sweeteners, vanilla extract, and pumpkin in a medium mixing bowl. Beat until thick and creamy.

Combine all the other ingredients, including the chocolate chips, in a mixing bowl and stir until well mixed. Work the dry mix into the pumpkin batter in two portions; finish by hand. Chill dough for about 45 minutes or until firm enough to handle. If the dough still is not firm, add more soy protein powder to it.

Form walnut-size balls and set them on a cookie sheet. Allow for expansion. Flatten the cookies slightly with your fingertips. Bake for 12 to 15 minutes or until the cookies are golden. Set them on a cooling rack to cool. These cookies are soft and chewy. Keep them frozen to prevent drying out.

Soy Grit Cookies

High in protein and delicious.

PREPARATION TIME: 15 minutes. (The dough may need brief chilling.)
BAKING TIME: about 12 to 15 minutes.

SERVING SIZE: one 2-inch cookie. AMOUNT PER SERVING: 1.3 grams of carb, 3.3 grams of protein. TOTAL YIELD: about 32 cookies.

	CHO (g)	PRO (g)
5 tablespoons unsalted butter (⅝ stick), soft	0	0
1 egg, room temperature	0.6	6.0
5 tablespoons Splenda	7.5	0
3 tablespoons xylitol	5.4	0
1 teaspoon Stevia Plus (or equivalent)	0	0
2 teaspoons vanilla extract	1.0	0
¾ cup soy grit (defatted, ground soy nuts)	21.0	57.0
½ cup soy protein powder	0	32.2
½ cup whole almond meal	5.0	10.0
1 teaspoon baking powder	1.2	0
3 teaspoons lemon peel	0.8	0
salt, trace	0	0
Total	*42.5*	*105.2*

Preheat the oven to 350°F. Use a large cookie sheet with a silicone-coated liner.

Combine the butter, egg, sweeteners, and vanilla extract in a medium mixing bowl. Beat until thick and creamy.

Combine the remaining ingredients in a mixing bowl and stir until well mixed. Add the dry mix in two portions to the butter-egg batter; finish by hand. If the dough is too soft to shape, chill it for about 10 minutes. You can add 1 or 2 tablespoons of soy protein powder, as needed, and skip the chilling.

Form balls about the size of walnuts and put them on the cookie sheet, allowing for expansion. Flatten the cookies slightly with your fingertips. Bake them for 12 to 15 minutes or until they have a light golden color. Set them on a cooling rack to cool. Handle gently; the cookies break very easily while warm. These cookies freeze well.

Variation: Soy Grit Cookies with Dates

Follow the directions for Soy Grit Cookies above. Make these changes: chop 5 dates into very tiny pieces. Work these into the butter-egg mix before adding the dry mix. This adds 0.8 gram of carb to each cookie.

Sesame Coconut Cookies

For sesame lovers—and coconut lovers.

PREPARATION TIME: 15 minutes. (The dough may need brief chilling.)
BAKING TIME: about 12 to 15 minutes.
SERVING SIZE: one 2-inch cookie. AMOUNT PER SERVING: 1.3 grams of carb,
2.3 grams of protein. TOTAL YIELD: about 30 cookies.

		CHO (g)	PRO (g)
5	tablespoons unsalted butter (⅝ stick), soft	0	0
1	egg, room temperature	0.6	6.0
5	tablespoons Splenda	7.5	0
3	tablespoons xylitol	5.4	0
1	teaspoon Stevia Plus (or equivalent)	0	0
2	teaspoons vanilla extract	1.0	0
1¼	cups whole almond meal	12.5	25.0
2	tablespoons whey protein powder (natural, zero-carb)	0	10.0
¼	cup soy protein powder	0	16.1
½	cup unsweetened coconut, finely grated	3.0	3.0
½	cup toasted sesame seeds	6.0	14.0
1	teaspoon baking powder	1.2	0
	salt, trace	0	0
	Total	*37.2*	*68.1*

Preheat the oven to 350°F. Use a large cookie sheet with a silicone-coated liner.

Combine the butter, egg, sweeteners, and vanilla extract in a medium mixing bowl and beat until thick and creamy.

Combine all the other ingredients, including sesame seeds and coconut, in a separate bowl and stir well. Stir the dry mix in two portions into the egg batter. If the dough is too soft to handle, chill it for about 10 to 15 minutes or work in a tablespoon or two of soy protein powder as needed.

Form walnut-size balls and set them on the cookie sheet. Allow for expansion. Flatten the cookies slightly with your fingertips. Bake for 12 to 15 minutes or until the cookies are golden. Set them on a cooling rack to cool. These cookies are soft and chewy. It is best to freeze the cookies to prevent drying out.

Meringue Kisses

Did you think you could never have these again? Well, now you can. They are easy to make, although meringue can be a bit cantankerous at times. Avoid making these kisses on humid days. The kisses are wonderful for nibbling and for complementing many desserts. Meringue requires lots of xylitol, so be cautious in how many kisses you eat. An electric stand mixer is helpful as the meringue needs a lot of whipping.

PREPARATION TIME: 30 minutes. BAKING TIME: several hours.
SERVING SIZE: 1 meringue kiss. AMOUNT PER SERVING: 0.5 gram of carb, negligible protein. TOTAL YIELD: about 50 kisses.

		CHO (g)	PRO (g)
3	egg whites, room temperature	0.9	10.5
	salt, trace	0	0
1	teaspoon vanilla extract	0.5	0
¾	cup xylitol (ground fine)	21.6	0
	Total	*23.0*	*10.5*

Preheat the oven to 150°F or the *lowest setting* you have available. Use a large cookie sheet and line it with parchment paper, the best choice, or with wax paper.

Put the egg whites, a smidgen of salt, and vanilla extract in the bowl of an electric stand mixer. Beat until the egg whites are quite firm. Gradually add the xylitol, about a teaspoon at a time. Slow the mixer as you add the xylitol. Resume speed after each addition.

With two teaspoons, drop the meringue kisses fairly close together on the parchment-lined cookie sheet. All 50 should fit. Make them about the size of Hershey kisses or not much bigger. You can also pipe the meringue through a pastry bag. The result will be lovely; the effort is a little messy, though, and you lose a fair amount of the meringue.

Place the kisses in the oven and check after two to three hours. Essentially all the kisses do is dry out and harden. The kisses should remain white. If they have taken on some color, the temperature is too high. Keep the door slightly ajar with a wooden spoon or other prop and check again within another hour. If you are using wax paper, peel the kisses off the paper as soon as they are firm enough. (If you don't, the wax paper eventually will stick to the bottoms of the kisses and is nearly impossible to get off.) Return the kisses to the bare cookie sheet and continue the drying process for as long as may be needed. If the kisses have been in the oven for several hours but still are not dry all the way through, let them sit in the oven overnight. Turn the oven off, close the door, and leave on the oven light. If needed, let the kisses continue to dry at room temperature the next day, but this works only if the humidity is low. Dry meringue kisses can be stored in an airtight container.

Variation: Hazelnut Meringue Kisses

Follow the directions for Meringue Kisses above. Make these changes: when the meringue has been whipped sufficiently, stir in 1¼ cups of hazelnut meal. Set the nut meringue in small heaps on the cookie sheet lined with parchment or wax paper. Despite the addition of the nuts, the increase in volume is not all that great. You might get 55 kisses or so. Allow a bit more space for these kisses; they do not increase much in volume, but they do tend to flatten out on their own. If you get 55 kisses, each has an extra 0.2 gram of carb. Protein count remains under 1.0 gram per kiss.

Walnut Power Bars

High protein and great taste. Two small bars and two eggs give you a nice, high-protein breakfast with over 30 grams of protein. Just pop them in the toaster oven for a few minutes while you cook the eggs. They are good munchies at any time.

PREPARATION TIME: 25 minutes. BAKING TIME: about 20 to 25 minutes.
SERVING SIZE: One 2-by-3-inch bar. AMOUNT PER SERVING: 2.2 grams of carb; 10.9 grams of protein. TOTAL YIELD: 20 bars.

		CHO (g)	PRO (g)
8	tablespoons unsalted butter (1 stick), very soft	0	0
5	tablespoons Splenda	7.5	0
3	tablespoons xylitol	5.4	0
1	teaspoon Stevia Plus (or equivalent)	0	0
3	eggs	1.8	18.0
2	teaspoons vanilla	1.0	0
¾	cup whole almond meal	7.5	15.0
1	cup whey protein powder (natural, zero-carb)	0	80.0
½	cup flaxseed meal	1.6	5.0
½	cup soy protein powder	0	32.2
1	teaspoon baking powder	1.2	0
1	teaspoon ground cinnamon	0.7	0
3	teaspoons grated lemon peel	0.8	0
	salt, trace	0	0
10	ounces coarsely chopped walnuts	10.0	68.0
	Total	*37.5*	*218.2*

Preheat the oven to 350°F. Lightly butter a 9-by-13-inch (or similar) glass baking pan.

Combine the butter, sweeteners, 1 egg, and vanilla extract. Beat until thick and creamy. Add the remaining eggs, 1 at a time. The batter will be thin.

Combine all the other ingredients, except for the walnuts, in a separate bowl and mix well. Stir the dry mix into the butter-egg batter in two portions and mix thoroughly. Add the walnuts last. Spread the batter evenly in the baking pan. Bake for about 20 to 25 minutes or until done. Do not overbake. The bars will have a shiny top. Allow them to cool. Cut into 20 oblong pieces (or whatever size and number you want—but make adjustments if gram counts are affected). If desired, add Powdered Low-Carb Sugar Glaze (page 186).

Because they contain flaxseed meal, keep the bars frozen.

Brownies

These brownies are moist and wonderful beyond belief. Whenever unsweetened chocolate is used in a recipe, as it is here, a little extra sweetener seems to be required.

PREPARATION TIME: 20 minutes. BAKING TIME: about 20 to 24 minutes.
SERVING SIZE: 1 brownie. AMOUNT PER SERVING: 2.1 grams of carb, 2.6 grams of protein. TOTAL YIELD: about 36 brownies.

		CHO (g)	PRO (g)
8	tablespoons unsalted butter (1 stick)	0	0
4	ounces unsweetened baking chocolate	16.0	16.0
4	eggs, room temperature	2.4	24.0
5	tablespoons xylitol	9.0	0
9	tablespoons Splenda	12.0	0
1	teaspoon Stevia Plus (or equivalent)	0	0
2	teaspoons vanilla extract	1.0	0
½	cup whole almond meal	5.0	10.0
1	teaspoon baking powder	1.2	0
½	cup soy protein powder	0	32.0
	salt, trace	0	0

TOPPING

		CHO (g)	PRO (g)
2	ounces walnuts, coarsely chopped	2.0	13.0
	Total	*48.6*	*95.0*

Preheat the oven to 325°F. Butter a 12-inch-square glass baking dish or similar pan.

Combine the butter and the chocolate in a microwavable bowl and microwave briefly until the chocolate is melted. Stir the mixture until smooth and set aside to cool. You can also do this in a double boiler set over hot water that is kept at or below a simmer. Set aside and let cool.

Put the eggs in the bowl of an electric stand mixer (works best) or other large mixing bowl and beat until thick and creamy. Add the sweeteners gradually by the tablespoon and beat well after each addition.

Stir in the vanilla extract and gently stir in the melted, cooled chocolate mixture. Except for the walnuts, add all the remaining ingredients to the bowl, folding them gently into the batter. Pour the batter into the baking dish or pan. Sprinkle the walnuts on top. Press down lightly on them.

Bake for about 20 to 24 minutes or until done. This is not always easy to tell. The brownies are best if they are neither underbaked nor overbaked. A knife should come out clean when inserted in the brownies. Allow the brownies to cool. Cut them in serving pieces and wrap them loosely in aluminum foil and freeze or keep them in the fridge for a few days. These brownies make a yummy dessert if served with a dollop of whipped cream.

Variation: Brownies with Chocolate Icing

Follow the directions for Brownies above. Make these changes: put 3 ounces of sugar-free, semisweet chocolate, 2 tablespoons of butter, and 2 tablespoons of heavy cream in a microwavable bowl and microwave until the chocolate is melted. Stir until smooth, and beat for a few moments until creamy. You can also do this in a double boiler set over hot water kept at or below a simmer. Spread this mix over the brownies and sprinkle pecans on top. This adds 0.2 gram of carb to each brownie (of 36).

Pecan Bars

Glorious, rich cookies with a topping of pecans, hazelnuts, and currants.

PREPARATION TIME: 35 minutes. (The dough requires brief chilling.) BAKING TIME: about 15 to 20 minutes.

SERVING SIZE: ¼₄ of yield. AMOUNT PER SERVING: 3.6 grams of carb, 2.5 grams of protein. TOTAL YIELD: 24 bars.

		CHO (g)	PRO (g)
COOKIE BASE			
6	tablespoons unsalted butter (¾ stick), soft	0	0
1	egg yolk, room temperature	0.3	2.8
2	tablespoons xylitol	3.6	0
4	tablespoons Splenda	3.0	0
½	teaspoon Stevia Plus (or equivalent)	0	0
1	teaspoon vanilla extract	0.5	0
¼	cup dark rye flour	15.0	4.0
¾	cup blanched almond meal	9.0	15.0
¼	cup soy protein powder	0	16.1
	salt, trace	0	0
FILLING			
2	egg yolks	0.6	5.0
¼	cup DiabetiSweet Brown Sugar Substitute	7.2	0
7	tablespoons Splenda	10.0	0
2	tablespoons lemon juice	2.6	0
1	teaspoon vanilla extract	0.5	0
2	teaspoons oat flour	2.2	0
½	teaspoon baking powder	0.6	0
	salt, trace	0	0
3	ounces toasted pecans, coarsely chopped	5.4	7.8
2	ounces hazelnuts, finely chopped	3.8	8.0
2	tablespoons currants	14.0	1.0
	Total	*78.3*	*59.7*

Preheat the oven to 325°F. Lightly butter a 8-by-13-inch or similar size glass baking dish or baking pan.

Combine the butter, egg yolk, sweeteners, and vanilla extract in a medium mixing bowl and stir until well mixed.

Stir in the remaining ingredients, except for the filling, and form the dough into a ball. Chill for about 10 minutes. Pat the dough out in the bottom of the baking dish and level it. Set aside.

Make the filling: in another medium mixing bowl, beat the egg yolks, sweeteners, lemon juice, and vanilla extract until well mixed. Stir in the oat flour, baking powder, and salt. Add the pecans, hazelnuts, and currants. Mix well. Spread this mix evenly over the cookie base. Bake for 15 to 20 minutes or until done. Do not overbake. Cool completely before cutting into 24 bars. If you cut more or fewer pieces, recalculate the carb count. Wrap the bars in aluminum foil and store them in the fridge or the freezer.

Coconut Bars with Chocolate Chips

Who would not love these?

PREPARATION TIME: 35 minutes. (The dough requires brief chilling.) BAKING
TIME: about 15 to 20 minutes.

SERVING SIZE: ¼₄ of yield. AMOUNT PER SERVING: 2.7 grams of carb,
2.6 grams of protein. TOTAL YIELD: 24 bars.

		CHO (g)	PRO (g)
COOKIE BASE			
6	tablespoons unsalted butter (¾ stick), soft	0	0
1	egg yolk, room temperature	0.3	2.0
2	tablespoons xylitol	3.6	0
4	tablespoons Splenda	3.0	0
½	teaspoon Stevia Plus (or equivalent)	0	0
1	teaspoon vanilla extract	0.5	0
¼	cup dark rye flour	15.0	4.0
¾	cup blanched almond meal	9.0	15.0
¼	cup soy protein powder	0	16.1
	salt, trace	0	0
FILLING			
2	egg yolks	0.6	5.6
¼	cup DiabetiSweet Brown Sugar Substitute	7.2	0
7	teaspoons Splenda	10.5	0
2	teaspoons lemon juice	1.0	0
1	teaspoon vanilla extract	0.5	0
	salt, trace	0	0
¾	cup finely grated, unsweetened coconut	4.5	4.5
3	ounces coarsely ground hazelnuts	5.1	12.0
1½	ounces sugar-free chocolate chips	4.0	3.0
	Total:	*64.8*	*62.2*

Preheat the oven to 325°F. Lightly butter a 12-by-12 or similar size
glass baking dish or baking pan.

Combine the butter, egg yolk, sweeteners, and vanilla extract in a
medium mixing bowl and stir until well mixed.

Stir in the remaining ingredients and shape into a ball. Chill the
dough for about 10 minutes. Pat the dough out in the bottom of the
baking dish and level it. Set aside.

Make the filling: in another medium mixing bowl, beat the egg yolks, sweeteners, lemon juice, vanilla extract, and salt until thick and light colored.

Add the coconut, hazelnuts, and chocolate chips. Stir well and cover the cookie base with the filling. Bake for 15 to 20 minutes or until done. Do not overbake. Cool the bars completely before cutting. When cool, cut them into 24 bars. If you cut more or fewer pieces, recalculate the carb count. Wrap the bars in aluminum foil and store them in the fridge or the freezer.

5

CAKES AND PIES

When you glance at the contents for this chapter, with its over-whelming variety and long list of all sorts of cakes, including cheesecakes you bake, cheesecakes you make in the fridge, several cream pies, icings and fillings galore, real pastry pie shells, and other mouthwatering delights, you might wonder for a moment if you are really holding a low-carb cookbook in your hands. But it is not just the names of these cakes and pies that sound inviting and irresistible—just wait until you actually make one of them and taste it, which obviously is the heart of the matter. You may have a hard time convincing your friends that the slice of Best Yellow Cake, or Carrot Cake, or Devil's Food Cake, or Mocha Swirl Cheesecake, or any other cake or pie in this chapter, can truly taste like the beloved "real thing" you miss so much—yet have just a fraction of the high carb grams.

The secret is in selecting and combining the ingredients so that they duplicate or imitate the palate-pleasing texture and flavor of what carbohydrate addicts love so dearly and refuse to give up. You won't have to. It is easy to make everything in this chapter. With very few exceptions, most recipes are quickly assembled too. Cup-cakes are listed as a variation under a few cakes. However, you can turn virtually any recipe into cupcakes. They are convenient for freezing and for grabbing a quick, ready-made snack. So keep that in mind as you work with these recipes. Another nice feature of these low-carb recipes is that the cakes and (baked) cheesecakes freeze well. For easy access, preslice them prior to freezing.

Keep in mind too that with only some exceptions, altering the proportions of sweeteners to suit you—by either increasing or decreasing the total amounts—will not adversely affect a recipe.

Best Yellow Cake

A wonderful, rich loaf cake, almost like a pound cake, that creates a base for a great variety of delicious snacks.

PREPARATION TIME: 20 minutes. BAKING TIME: about 35 to 45 minutes.

SERVING SIZE: 1 slice. AMOUNT PER SERVING: 2.1 grams of carb, 3.0 grams of protein. TOTAL YIELD: about 30 slices.

		CHO (g)	PRO (g)
3	egg whites	0.9	10.5
8	tablespoons unsalted butter (1 stick), very soft		0
¼	cup xylitol	7.2	0
7	tablespoons Splenda	10.5	0
1½	teaspoons Stevia Plus (or equivalent)	0	0
3	eggs, room temperature	1.8	18.0
2	teaspoons vanilla extract	1.0	0
¼	cup dark rye flour	15.0	4.0
¼	cup oat flour	13.0	4.0
	salt, trace (about ⅛ teaspoon)	0	0
2	teaspoons grated lemon peel	0.6	0
1	teaspoon baking powder	1.2	0
1	cup blanched almond meal	12.0	20.0
½	cup soy protein powder	0	32.2
	Total	*63.2*	*88.7*

Preheat the oven to 350°F. Butter three heavy metal 3-by-6-inch baking pans. For extra easy removal of the cake, put a 1½-inch-wide wax paper strip inside each pan with the ends sticking out about 2 inches above the pan on the long ends. The 3 loaves will rise to about 2½ inches. If you want a bigger cake, bake the cake in two 3-by-6-inch baking pans. Carb counts rise to 2.8 grams per slice and 5.0 grams of protein, based on 20 slices.

In a medium mixing bowl, beat the egg whites until they form firm but still soft peaks. Set aside.

Combine the soft butter, sweeteners, 1 egg, and vanilla extract in a medium mixing bowl; beat until thick and creamy. Add the remaining eggs one at a time and beat well.

Add the rye flour, oat flour, salt, lemon peel, baking powder, and about half of the almond meal to the batter and stir until well mixed. Add the remaining almond meal and the soy protein powder alternately with the beaten egg whites. Mix well.

Spoon the batter evenly into the baking pans. Bake for about 35 to 45 minutes or until light golden. A knife inserted in the center should come out clean. Cool the cake on a cooling rack. Carefully loosen the cake loaves around the sides and make sure the bottom does not stick. If you used wax paper, loosen the sides of the loaves and pull them out by the ends of the paper. Transfer them to a cooling rack. Allow the cake to cool completely before cutting. This cake freezes well.

This cake is delicious plain, but it's even better with a glaze. Powdered Low-Carb Sugar Glaze is on page 186 and Chocolate Glaze is on page 185.

Variation: Spice Cake

Follow the directions for Best Yellow Cake above. Make these changes: add the following spices to the dry ingredients when you mix them and blend in well: 1 teaspoon of ground cinnamon, ½ teaspoon of ground ginger, ¼ teaspoon of ground nutmeg, and ¼ teaspoon of cardamom. The changes in carb count are insignificant.

Variation: Yellow Cake with Currants

Follow the directions for Best Yellow Cake above. Make these changes: add 3 tablespoons of currants to the batter at the end before spooning it into the pans. Distribute the currants throughout the batter. This adds 0.7 gram of carb per slice of cake (of 30).

Variation: Yellow Cake with Chocolate Chips

Follow the directions for Best Yellow Cake above. Make these changes: add 2 ounces of sugar-free, semisweet, or milk chocolate chips to the batter at the end. Distribute them well throughout the batter. This adds 0.2 gram of carb per slice of cake (of 30).

Lemon Poppy Seed Cake

Full of poppy seeds and with a lively lemon flavor. Great with the Powdered Low-Carb Sugar Glaze on page 186.

PREPARATION TIME: 20 minutes. BAKING TIME: about 35 to 45 minutes.
SERVING SIZE: 1 slice. AMOUNT PER SERVING: 2.1 grams of carb, 3.0 grams of protein. TOTAL YIELD: about 30 slices.

		CHO (g)	PRO (g)
3	tablespoons poppy seeds	3.6	5.0
¼	cup heavy cream	1.6	1.2
3	egg whites	0.9	10.0
8	tablespoons unsalted butter, (1 stick) very soft	0	0
5	tablespoons xylitol	9.0	0
9	tablespoons Splenda	13.5	0
1½	teaspoons Stevia Plus (or equivalent)	0	0
3	eggs, room temperature	1.8	18.0
2	teaspoons vanilla extract	1.0	0
⅓	cup oat flour	17.3	5.0
	salt, trace	0	0
1	tablespoon grated lemon peel	0.8	0
1	tablespoon grated orange peel	0.9	0
1	teaspoon baking powder	1.2	0
¾	cup blanched almond meal	9.0	15.0
¼	cup whole almond meal	2.5	5.0
½	cup soy protein powder	0	32.2
	Total	*63.1*	*91.4*

Preheat the oven to 350°F. Butter three heavy metal 3-by-6-inch baking pans. For extra easy removal of the cake, put a 1½-inch-wide wax paper strip inside each pan with the ends sticking out about 2 inches at the long ends of the pan. The 3 loaves will rise to about 2½ inches. For a larger cake, bake the cake in two bake pans. The cake will rise quite high.

If possible, grind the poppy seeds in a coffee grinder or a blender a day early and soak them in the heavy cream. Otherwise do this about an hour before baking.

In a medium mixing bowl, beat the egg whites until they form firm but still soft peaks. Set aside.

Combine the butter, sweeteners, 1 egg, and vanilla extract in a medium mixing bowl; beat until thick and creamy. Add the remaining eggs one at a time and beat well. Stir in the soaked poppy seeds.

Add the oat flour, salt, lemon peel, orange peel, baking powder, and about half of the blanched almond meal to the batter and stir until well mixed. Add the remaining blanched almond meal, whole almond meal, and soy protein powder alternately with the beaten egg whites. Mix well.

Spoon the batter evenly into the baking pans. Bake for about 35 to 45 minutes or until light golden. A knife inserted in the center should come out clean. Cool the cake on a cooling rack. Carefully loosen the cake loaves around the sides and make sure the bottoms do not stick. If you used wax paper, loosen the sides of the loaves and pull them out by the ends of the paper. Allow the cake to cool completely before cutting. This cake freezes well.

Marzipan Cake

This cake is made with a few ounces of almond paste, the wonderful almond concoction that gives us marzipan. Enjoy but eat sparingly, since it's relatively high in carb grams. Great with the Chocolate Glaze on page 185.

PREPARATION TIME: 20 minutes. BAKING TIME: about 35 to 45 minutes.
SERVING SIZE: 1 slice. AMOUNT PER SERVING: 3.8 grams of carb, 3.4 grams of protein. TOTAL YIELD: about 30 slices.

		CHO (g)	PRO (g)
4	egg whites	1.2	14.0
6	tablespoons unsalted butter (¾ stick), soft	0	0
4	tablespoons xylitol	7.2	0
7	tablespoons Splenda	10.5	0
1½	teaspoons Stevia Plus (or equivalent)	0	0
3½	ounces pure almond paste	60.0	10.0
3	eggs, room temperature	1.8	18.0
2	teaspoons vanilla extract	1.0	0
1	teaspoon almond extract (or to taste)	1.0	0
¼	cup oat flour	13.0	4.0
	salt, trace (about ⅛ teaspoon)	0	0
1	teaspoon baking powder	1.2	0
1	cup blanched almond meal	12.0	20.0
¼	cup whole almond meal	2.5	5.0
½	cup soy protein powder	0	32.2
	Total	*111.4*	*103.2*

Preheat the oven to 350°F. Butter three heavy metal 3-by-6-inch baking pans. For easy removal of the cakes, put a 1½-inch-wide wax paper strip inside each pan with the ends sticking out about 2 inches at the long ends of the pan. The 3 loaves will rise to about 2¾ inches.

The amount of almond paste used in this cake is equal to ½ of a 7-ounce package of pure almond paste, sold in many stores. Shave small pieces, less than pea size, off the paste to get it well distributed in the cake.

In a medium mixing bowl, beat the egg whites until they form firm but still soft peaks. Set aside.

Combine the butter, sweeteners, and almond paste in a medium mixing bowl; beat until the almond paste is smooth. Add 1 egg and the extracts. Beat until thick and creamy. Add the remaining eggs one at a time and beat well.

Add the oat flour, salt, baking powder, and blanched almond meal to the batter and stir until well mixed. Add the whole almond meal and the soy protein powder alternately with the beaten egg whites. Mix well.

Spoon the batter evenly into the baking pans. Bake for about 35 to 45 minutes or until light golden. A knife inserted in the center should come out clean. Cool the cake on a cooling rack. Carefully loosen the loaves around the sides and make sure the bottoms do not stick. If you used wax paper, loosen the sides of the loaves and pull them out by the ends of the paper. Allow the cake to cool completely before cutting. This cake freezes well.

Chocolate Marble Cake

Ah, how rich, how chocolatey . . . how low in carb!

PREPARATION TIME: 20 minutes. BAKING TIME: about 35 to 45 minutes.
SERVING SIZE: 1 slice. AMOUNT PER SERVING: 2.2 grams of carb, 3.4 grams of
  protein. TOTAL YIELD: about 30 slices.

		CHO (g)	PRO (g)
1	ounce unsweetened baking chocolate	4.0	4.0
2	ounces sugar-free semisweet chocolate	5.4	2.0
¼	cup heavy cream	1.6	1.2
4	egg whites	1.2	14.0
8	tablespoons unsalted butter (1 stick), very soft	0	0
4	tablespoons xylitol	7.2	0
7	tablespoons Splenda	10.5	0
1½	teaspoons Stevia Plus (or equivalent)	0	0
3	eggs, room temperature	1.8	18.0
2	teaspoons vanilla extract	1.0	0
⅓	cup oat flour	17.3	5.0
	salt, trace (about ⅛ teaspoon)	0	0
1	teaspoon baking powder	1.2	0
1	cup blanched almond meal	12.0	20.0
¼	cup whole almond meal	2.5	5.0
½	cup soy protein powder	0	32.2
	Total	*65.7*	*100.4*

Preheat the oven to 350°F. Butter three heavy metal 3-by-6-inch baking pans. For extra easy removal of the cakes, put a 1½-inch-wide wax paper strip inside each pan with the ends sticking out about 2 inches at the long ends of the pan. The 3 loaves will rise to about 2¾ inches. For larger loaves, use two small pans. (The cakes will rise high.)

Put the chocolates and the heavy cream in a double boiler over hot water kept at or below a simmer. Stir occasionally. When all the chocolate is melted, stir until smooth. Remove from the heat and set aside.

In a medium mixing bowl, beat the egg whites until they form firm but still soft peaks. Set aside.

Combine the butter, sweeteners, 1 egg, and the vanilla extract in a medium mixing bowl; beat until thick and creamy. Add the remaining eggs one at a time and beat well.

Add the oat flour, salt, baking powder, and blanched almond meal to the batter; stir until well mixed. Add the whole almond meal and the soy protein powder alternately with the beaten egg whites. Mix well.

Remove about half of the batter from the mixing bowl and put it in another bowl. Stir in the melted chocolate.

As you spoon the batter in the pans, alternate dark and light batters. Bake for about 35 to 45 minutes or until light golden. A knife inserted in the center should come out clean. Cool the cake on a cooling rack. Carefully loosen the cake loaves around the sides and make sure the bottoms do not stick. If you used wax paper, loosen the sides of the loaves and pull them out by the ends of the paper. Allow the cake to cool completely before cutting. This cake freezes well. It tastes especially good with Chocolate Glaze (page 185).

Zucchini Chocolate Cake

How to entertain them today? Why not try a zucchini chocolate cake? It is an incredibly delicious combination.

PREPARATION TIME: 20 minutes. BAKING TIME: about 35 to 40 minutes. SERVING SIZE: ⅒ of yield. AMOUNT PER SERVING: 6.1 grams of carb, 9.9 grams of protein. TOTAL YIELD: one single- or two-layer cake.

		CHO (g)	PRO (g)
1	cup cooked zucchini, pureed (about 2.5 medium)	5.5	3.0
1	ounce unsweetened baking chocolate	4.0	4.0
1	ounce sugar-free semisweet or milk chocolate	2.8	1.0
¼	cup heavy cream	1.6	1.2
2	egg whites	0.6	7.0
2	tablespoons unsalted butter (¼ stick), very soft	0	0
5	tablespoons xylitol	7.2	0
9	tablespoons Splenda	13.5	0
1½	teaspoons Stevia Plus (or equivalent)	0	0
2	eggs, room temperature	1.2	12.0
2	teaspoons vanilla extract	1.0	0
¼	cup oat flour	13.0	4.0
	salt, trace	0	0
1	teaspoon ground cinnamon	0.7	0
½	teaspoon ground cloves	0.5	0
1	teaspoon baking powder	1.2	0
1	cup whole almond meal	10.0	20.0
¾	cup soy protein powder	0	48.9
	Total	*62.8*	*101.1*

Preheat the oven to 350°F. For a single-layer cake, use a 9-inch springform pan. For two layers, use an 8-inch pan. You can also use a 9-by-13-inch glass baking dish. Butter the pan of your choice.

Wash, slice, and cook the unpeeled zucchini in a small amount of water until just tender, for less than 10 minutes. Puree it in a blender or food processor. Drain until ready to use. Measure 1 cup, piled lightly. Set aside.

Put the chocolates and the heavy cream in the top of a double boiler and cook over hot water kept at or below a simmer. Stir frequently. When the chocolate is melted, stir until smooth and remove from the heat. Set aside.

In a medium mixing bowl, beat the egg whites until they form firm but still soft peaks. Set aside.

Combine the butter, sweeteners, 1 egg, and vanilla extract in a medium mixing bowl; beat until thick and creamy. Add the remaining eggs one at a time and beat well. Stir in the cooked zucchini.

Add the oat flour, salt, spices, baking powder, and about half of the almond meal to the batter and stir until well mixed. Add the remaining almond meal and the soy protein powder alternately with the beaten egg whites. Mix well.

Take about half of the batter out of the mixing bowl and put it into another. Add the chocolate to this bowl and stir. Return the mix to the main batter and stir lightly, leaving ribbons.

Spoon the batter evenly into your chosen baking pan and bake for about 35 to 40 minutes. A knife inserted in the center should come out clean. Carefully loosen the cake around the sides. If you used a springform pan, wait to remove the cake from the springform bottom or simply leave it in place. Cool the cake, then refrigerate. This cake freezes well. See page 181 for a choice of icings.

Orange Breakfast Cake

This has all the protein you need for breakfast or a healthy snack. This cake uses both cooked whole eggs and fresh eggs. It is loaded with orange flavor and is rich and moist.

PREPARATION TIME: 20 minutes. BAKING TIME: about 35 to 40 minutes.
SERVING SIZE: ¹⁄₁₅ of yield. AMOUNT PER SERVING: 4.5 grams of carb, 8.9 grams of protein. TOTAL YIELD: about 15 pieces.

		CHO (g)	PRO (g)
5	hard-boiled eggs, peeled	3.0	30.0
2	egg whites	0.6	7.0
6	tablespoons unsalted butter (¾ stick), very soft	0	0
5	tablespoons xylitol	7.2	0
9	tablespoons Splenda	13.5	0
1½	teaspoons Stevia Plus (or equivalent)	0	0
3	eggs, room temperature	1.8	18.0
2	teaspoons vanilla extract	1.0	0
1	teaspoon orange extract (or to taste)	0.5	0
½	cup oat flour	26.0	8.0
	salt, trace	0	0
1	tablespoon finely grated orange peel	1.0	0
1	tablespoon finely grated lemon peel	1.0	0
1	teaspoon baking powder	1.2	0
1	cup whole almond meal	10.0	20.0
¾	cup soy protein powder	0	48.9
	Total	*66.8*	*131.9*

Preheat the oven to 350°F. Butter a 9-by-13-inch glass baking dish. Mash the hard-boiled eggs in a processor.

In a medium mixing bowl, beat the egg whites until they form firm but still soft peaks. Set aside.

Combine the butter, sweeteners, 1 egg, and vanilla extract in a medium mixing bowl; beat until thick and creamy. Add the remaining eggs one at a time and beat well. Add the mashed hard-boiled eggs. Stir well. Add the oat flour, salt, orange and lemon peels, baking powder, and about half of the almond meal to the batter and stir until mixed. Add the remaining almond meal and the soy protein powder alternately with the beaten egg whites. Mix well.

Spoon the batter evenly into the baking dish and bake for about 35 to 40 minutes. A knife inserted in the center should come out clean. Frost with Orange Crème Icing (page 182). Refrigerate the cake when cool. This cake can be frozen.

What-to-Do-with-Egg-Yolks Cake

It's not a leftover kind of cake, it's fabulous—rich, moist, and mellow. So save up your egg yolks.

PREPARATION TIME: 20 minutes. BAKING TIME: about 35 to 40 minutes.
SERVING SIZE: ⅟₁₅ of yield. AMOUNT PER SERVING: 4.5 grams of carb, 7.2 grams of protein. TOTAL YIELD: about 15 pieces.

		CHO (g)	PRO (g)
3	egg whites	0.6	10.5
8	egg yolks	2.4	22.4
5	tablespoons xylitol	7.2	0
8	tablespoons unsalted butter (1 stick), very soft	0	0
9	tablespoons Splenda	13.5	0
1½	teaspoons Stevia Plus (or equivalent)	0	0
2	teaspoons vanilla extract	1.0	0
¼	cup sour cream	2.0	1.2
⅓	cup oat flour	17.3	5.0
	salt, trace	0	0
2	teaspoons lemon peel, finely grated	0.5	0
1	teaspoon baking powder	1.2	0
1	cup whole almond meal	10.0	20.0
¾	cup soy protein powder	0	48.9
	Total	*55.7*	*108.0*

Preheat the oven to 350°F. Butter a 9-by-13-inch glass baking dish or an 8- or 9-inch springform pan.

In a medium mixing bowl, beat the egg whites until firm but not stiff. Set aside.

Put the egg yolks in a medium mixing bowl and beat until thick and creamy. Add the xylitol by the tablespoon, beating well after each addition. Set aside.

In another bowl, combine the butter, remaining sweeteners, and vanilla extract; beat until thick and creamy. Combine this with the egg mixture and stir well. Add the sour cream.

Add the oat flour, salt, lemon peel, baking powder, and about half of the almond meal to the batter and stir until well mixed. Add the remaining almond meal and soy protein powder alternately with the beaten egg whites.

Spoon the batter evenly into the baking dish or a springform pan and bake for about 35 to 40 minutes. A knife inserted in the center should come out clean. A chocolate icing or glaze goes well with this cake (see page 181 for icings). Refrigerate the cake when cool. It can also be frozen.

Featherlight Hazelnut Almond Torte

This is indescribably good. It is so good, in fact, that even though it tends to sag in the middle, you will forgive it. Baking the cake as 2 separate layers prevents much sagging. Try this one for sure. It uses only xylitol. An electric stand mixer is useful here.

PREPARATION TIME: 20 minutes. BAKING TIME: about 35 to 40 minutes.
SERVING SIZE: ⅒ of yield. AMOUNT PER SERVING: 3.6 grams of carb, 5.3 grams of protein. TOTAL YIELD: 1 double-layer 8-inch cake.

		CHO (g)	PRO (g)
5	eggs, separated, room temperature	3.0	30.0
1	teaspoon vanilla extract	1.0	0
	salt, trace	0	0
1	teaspoon lemon peel	0.3	0
½	cup xylitol	14.4	0
3	tablespoons oat flour	9.8	2.0
½	cup hazelnut meal	3.8	8.0
⅓	cup whole almond meal	3.3	13.3
	Total	*35.8*	*53.3*

Preheat the oven to 325°F. If possible, use two 8-inch springform pans for this cake. Otherwise use two 8- or 9-inch cake pans. Put wax paper in the bottoms of the pans. Butter the pans you use. You can also bake this cake in a buttered 9-by-13-inch glass dish.

Put the egg whites in a large mixing bowl and put the egg yolks in a medium mixing bowl.

Beat the egg whites until they are firm but not stiff. Set aside. Add the vanilla extract, salt, and lemon peel to the egg yolks and beat them until thick and creamy. Gradually add the xylitol by the tablespoon, and continue beating after each addition. This should become a thick mass.

Stir the oat flour, hazelnut meal, and almond meal gently into the egg yolk mixture. With a spatula, transfer the egg yolk mixture to the egg whites and combine carefully.

Pour the batter into the springform pans. Bake for about 35 to 40 minutes. Cool the cake on a rack. The cake tends to sag slightly while baking; it can get worse when it is cooling. The best frosting for this cake is sweetened whipped cream. (See Whipped Cream Sauce, page 253.) You could cover the cake with it and fill the crater in the middle, if you have one. This cake is so good, no one will mind.

Fruitcake

Regular fruitcake ranks high on the no-no list. If you miss it, here is one that might help you stay away from the other. It is not really low-carb, but it is at least acceptable as an occasional holiday treat.

PREPARATION TIME: 20 minutes. BAKING TIME: about 45 to 55 minutes.
SERVING SIZE: 1 slice. AMOUNT PER SERVING: 5.4 grams of carb, 3.2 grams of
  protein. TOTAL YIELD: about 30 slices.

		CHO (g)	PRO (g)
3	egg whites	1.2	10.5
8	tablespoons unsalted butter (1 stick), very soft	0	0
½	cup DiabetiSweet Brown Sugar Substitute	14.4	0
1⅓	teaspoons Stevia Plus (or equivalent)	0	0
3	eggs, room temperature	1.8	18.0
2	teaspoons vanilla extract	1.0	0
2	tablespoons rum	0	0
1	tablespoon lemon peel	0.8	0
1	tablespoon orange peel	0.9	0
¼	cup oat flour	13.0	4.0
	salt, trace (about ⅛ teaspoon)	0	0
1	teaspoon baking powder	1.2	0
½	cup blanched almond meal	6.0	10.0
¼	cup whole almond meal	2.5	5.0
¼	cup soy protein powder	0	16.1
½	cup currants	48.0	2.0
10	dates, chopped fine	50.0	3.0
½	cup toasted sunflower seeds (optional)	6.0	12.6
4	ounces toasted pecan halves	7.2	10.4
3	ounces sugar-free chocolate chips	8.1	3.0
	Total	*162.1*	*94.6*

Preheat the oven to 325°F. Butter three heavy metal 3-by-6-inch baking pans. For easy removal of the cake, put a 1½-inch-wide wax paper strip inside each pan with the ends sticking out about 2 inches at the long ends of the pan. The 3 loaves will rise quite high because of all the extra ingredients. You may also consider baking the fruitcake in minimuffin pans with liners.

In a medium mixing bowl, beat the egg whites until they form firm but still soft peaks. Set aside.

Combine the butter, sweeteners, 1 egg, vanilla extract, rum, lemon peel, and orange peel in a medium mixing bowl; beat until thick and creamy. Add the remaining eggs one at a time and beat well.

Add the oat flour, salt, baking powder, and blanched almond meal to the batter and stir until well mixed. Add the whole almond meal and the soy protein powder alternately with the beaten egg whites. Mix well.

Fold in the currants, finely chopped dates, sunflower seeds (if using), pecans, and chocolate chips. Spoon the batter into the cake pans or minimuffin pans and bake for about 45 to 55 minutes or until lightly browned.

Cool the cake on a cooling rack. This cake can be frozen.

Chiffon Cake

This is a light, airy cake, the perfect companion to lush frostings and icings. It is high in protein too. The quickest way to make this cake is to turn it into a sheet cake and pile a nice frosting on top. It also makes a small 8-inch layer cake.

PREPARATION TIME: 20 minutes. BAKING TIME: about 35 to 40 minutes.
SERVING SIZE: ⅟₁₅ of yield. AMOUNT PER SERVING: 4.5 grams of carb, 13.0 grams of protein. TOTAL YIELD: about 15 pieces.

		CHO (g)	PRO (g)
6	egg whites	1.8	21.0
4	tablespoons unsalted butter (½ stick), very soft, or coconut oil	0	0
7	tablespoons Splenda	10.5	0
4	tablespoons xylitol	7.2	0
1⅓	teaspoons Stevia Plus (or equivalent)	0	0
3	eggs, room temperature	1.8	18.0
2	teaspoons vanilla extract	1.0	0
¼	cup dark rye flour	15.0	5.0
⅓	cup oat flour	20.0	5.0
2	teaspoons lemon peel, grated	0.5	0
	salt, trace	0	0
1	teaspoon baking powder	1.2	0
¾	cup blanched almond meal	9.0	15.0
⅔	cup soy protein powder	0	42.3
	Total	*68.0*	*106.3*

Preheat the oven to 350°F. Lightly butter a 9-by-13-inch glass baking dish or similar dish for a sheet cake. For a small layer cake use two 8-inch cake pans or two springform pans.

In a large mixing bowl, beat the egg whites until they form firm but still soft peaks. Set aside.

Combine the soft butter, sweeteners, 1 egg, and vanilla extract in a medium mixing bowl; beat until thick and creamy. Add the remaining eggs one at a time and beat well.

Add the dark rye flour, oat flour, lemon peel, salt, baking powder, and about half of the almond meal to the batter and stir until well mixed. Add the remaining almond meal and the soy protein powder alternately with the beaten egg whites. Mix well.

Distribute the batter evenly in the glass baking dish. Bake for about 35 to 40 minutes or until light golden. A knife inserted in the center should come out clean. Put the cake on a rack to cool. Icing recipes begin on page 181.

Boston Cream Pie

This is a good old-fashioned treat, updated to be as healthy as possible.

PREPARATION TIME: 20 minutes. BAKING TIME: about 35 to 45 minutes.
SERVING SIZE: ¹⁄₁₀ of yield. AMOUNT PER SERVING: 8.2 grams of carb, 10.3 grams of protein. TOTAL YIELD: one 8-inch double-layer cake.

		CHO (g)	PRO (g)
3	egg whites	0.9	10.5
6	tablespoons unsalted butter (¾ stick), very soft	0	0
5	tablespoons xylitol	9.0	0
9	tablespoons Splenda	13.5	0
1⅓	teaspoons Stevia Plus (or equivalent)	0.0	0
3	eggs, room temperature	1.8	18.0
2	teaspoons vanilla extract	1.0	0
⅓	cup oat flour	17.3	5.0
	salt, trace (about ⅛ teaspoon)	0	0
2	teaspoons lemon peel	0.5	0
1	teaspoon baking powder	1.2	0
¾	cup blanched almond meal	9.0	15.0
½	cup whole almond meal	5.0	10.0
½	cup soy protein powder	0	32.2
FILLING			
4	ounces cream cheese, very soft	3.2	8.4
¾	cup heavy cream	4.8	3.6
1	teaspoon vanilla extract	1.0	0
	salt, trace	0	0
2	tablespoons sour cream	1.0	0.6
3	tablespoons xylitol	5.4	0
5	tablespoons Splenda	7.5	0
	Total	*82.1*	*103.2*

Preheat the oven to 350°F. Butter an 8-inch springform pan.

In a medium mixing bowl, beat the egg whites until they form firm but still soft peaks. Set aside.

Combine the butter, sweeteners, 1 egg, and vanilla extract in a medium mixing bowl; beat until thick and creamy. Add the remaining eggs one at a time and beat well.

Add the oat flour, salt, lemon peel, baking powder, and blanched almond meal to the batter. Stir until well mixed. Add the whole almond meal and the soy protein powder alternately with the beaten egg whites. Mix well.

Pour the batter into the pan and bake for about 35 to 45 minutes or until light golden. A knife inserted in the center should come out clean. Put the cake on a cooling rack. Before removing the spring-form collar, slide a knife around the outside edge. Slide the cake carefully off the bottom onto a cake platter. You can also freeze this cake, if you wish, and have it ready for the day when you want to make the filling. If you freeze the cake, loosen it from the pan bottom, but leave it in place. Put the cake briefly in the freezer to harden. Then put the cake in a disposable pie pan, wrap it in aluminum foil, and freeze. To thaw, position the cake on a cake tray and put it in the fridge.

To prepare the filling, put the cream cheese, 2 tablespoons of the heavy cream, vanilla extract, salt, sour cream, and the sweeteners in a medium mixing bowl. Beat with a portable electric mixer (or use an electric stand mixer) until the cream cheese is smooth and extremely thick and fluffy. It should increase greatly in volume. Beat the remaining heavy cream until quite firm and combine it with the cream cheese mix.

Carefully slice the cake in two layers. Thickly pile the filling between the two layers, about an inch or so high. For a frosting, you can select Chocolate Icing (page 182) or Chocolate Glaze (page 185). Apply the frosting carefully. Cover the pie and refrigerate. Remove it from the fridge about 45 minutes before serving. The pie will keep for several days. Add the gram counts for the frosting.

Variation: Lemon Pie

Follow the directions for Boston Cream Pie above. Make these changes: add 2 tablespoons of lemon juice to the batter along with the vanilla extract. Increase the lemon peel to 1 tablespoon and add 1 tablespoon of grated orange peel. Frost and fill the cake with Lemon Crème Icing (page 182). A serving size that is ⅒ of the cake has about 11.0 grams of carb and 11.3 grams of protein. The frosting is included in these counts.

Macadamia Nut Cake

Macadamias add a buttery crunch to this scrumptious cake.

PREPARATION TIME: 20 minutes. BAKING TIME: about 35 to 45 minutes.
SERVING SIZE: ⅛ of yield. AMOUNT PER SERVING: 5.5 grams of carb, 10.7
grams of protein. TOTAL YIELD: one 8-inch double-layer cake.

		CHO (g)	PRO (g)
3	egg whites	0.9	10.5
6	tablespoons unsalted butter (¾ stick), very soft	0	0
5	tablespoons xylitol	9.0	0
9	tablespoons Splenda	13.5	0
1⅓	teaspoons Stevia Plus (or equivalent)	0	0
3	eggs, room temperature	1.8	18.0
2	teaspoons vanilla extract	1.0	0.0
¾	cup macadamia nut meal	3.9	6.0
	salt, trace	0	0
2	teaspoons lemon peel	0.5	0
1	teaspoon baking powder	1.2	0
½	cup whole almond meal	5.0	10.0
1	cup toasted macadamia nuts, finely chopped	6.8	8.8
½	cup soy protein powder	0	32.2
	Total	*43.6*	*85.5*

Preheat the oven to 350°F. Butter an 8-inch springform pan.

In a medium mixing bowl, beat the egg whites until they form firm but still soft peaks. Set aside.

Combine the butter, sweeteners, 1 egg, and vanilla extract in a medium mixing bowl; beat until thick and creamy. Add the remaining eggs one at a time and beat well.

Add the macadamia nut meal, salt, lemon peel, and baking powder to the batter and stir until well mixed. Add the almond meal, toasted macadamia nuts, and soy protein powder alternately with the beaten egg whites. Mix well.

Spoon the batter into the springform pan and bake for about 35 to 45 minutes or until light golden. A knife inserted in the center should come out clean. Put the cake on a cooling rack. Before removing the collar, slide a knife around the outside edge. Slide the cake carefully off the bottom onto a cake platter. You can also freeze this cake, if you wish, and have it ready for the day when you want to fill and frost it. If you choose to freeze the cake, loosen it from the pan bottom, but leave it in place. Put it briefly in the freezer to harden. Then put the cake in a disposable pie pan, wrap it in aluminum foil, and freeze. To thaw, position the cake on a cake tray and put it in the fridge. Icings begin on page 181. Add the gram counts for any frosting you choose.

Orange Coconut Cake

Ah, yummy orange and coconut together. A great way to finish any meal.

PREPARATION TIME: 20 minutes. BAKING TIME: about 35 to 45 minutes.
SERVING SIZE: ¹⁄₁₀ of yield. AMOUNT PER SERVING: 5.9 grams of carb, 8.3 grams of protein. TOTAL YIELD: one 8-inch double-layer cake.

		CHO (g)	PRO (g)
3	egg whites	0.9	10.5
6	tablespoons unsalted butter		
	(¾ stick), very soft	0	0
5	tablespoons xylitol	9.0	0
9	tablespoons Splenda	13.5	0
1½	teaspoons Stevia Plus (or equivalent)	0	0
3	eggs, room temperature	1.8	18.0
2	teaspoons vanilla extract	1.0	0
1	teaspoon orange extract (or as desired)	0.5	0
⅓	cup oat flour	17.3	5.0
	salt, trace (about ⅛ teaspoon)	0	0
1	tablespoon lemon peel	1.0	0
	tablespoon orange peel	1.0	0
1	teaspoon baking powder	1.2	0
1¼	cup unsweetened coconut, finely		
	grated	7.5	7.5
½	cup whole almond meal	5.0	10.0
½	cup soy protein powder	0	32.2
	Total	*59.7*	*83.2*

Preheat the oven to 350°F. Butter an 8-inch springform pan.

In a medium mixing bowl, beat the egg whites until they form firm but still soft peaks. Set aside.

Combine the butter, sweeteners, one egg, vanilla extract, and orange extract in a medium mixing bowl; beat until thick and creamy. Add the remaining eggs one at a time and beat well.

Add the oat flour, salt, lemon peel, orange peel, baking powder, and about half of the grated coconut to the batter and stir until well mixed. Add the remaining coconut flakes, almond meal, and soy protein powder alternately with the beaten egg whites. Mix well.

Spoon the batter into the springform pan and bake for about 35 to 45 minutes or until light golden. A knife inserted in the center should come out clean. Place the cake on a cooling rack. Before removing the collar, slide a knife around the outside edge. Slide the cake carefully off the bottom onto a cake platter. You can also freeze this cake, if you wish. To freeze, loosen the cake from the pan bottom, but keep it in place. Put it briefly in the freezer to harden. Then put the cake in a disposable pie pan, wrap it in aluminum foil, and freeze. To thaw, position the cake on a cake tray and put in the fridge. Frost with Orange Crème Icing (page 182). Add the gram counts for it.

Devil's Food Cake

When was the last time you had this? Here it is to enjoy again.

PREPARATION TIME: 20 minutes. BAKING TIME: about 35 minutes.
SERVING SIZE: 1/10 of yield. AMOUNT PER SERVING: 6.3 grams of carb, 11.0 grams of protein. TOTAL YIELD: one 8-inch layer cake.

		CHO (g)	PRO (g)
8	tablespoons unsalted butter (1 stick)	0	0
4	ounces unsweetened baking chocolate	16.0	16.0
5	eggs, room temperature	3.0	30.0
5	tablespoons xylitol	9.0	0
9	tablespoons Splenda	13.0	0
2	teaspoons Stevia Plus (or equivalent)	0	0
2	teaspoons vanilla extract	1.0	0
2/3	cup almond meal	6.7	8.0
1/4	cup oat flour	13.0	4.0
1	teaspoon baking powder	1.2	0
1/2	cup soy protein powder	0	32.2
	salt, trace	0	0
	Total	*62.9*	*90.2*

Preheat the oven to 350°F. For a layer cake, butter an 8-inch springform pan; for a sheet cake butter a 9-by-13-inch glass or similar size baking dish.

Melt the butter and the chocolate in the top of a double boiler over hot water kept at or below a simmer. Stir occasionally until the chocolate is melted and the mixture is smooth. Remove the melted chocolate from the heat. Allow it to cool.

You might want to prepare this recipe in an electric stand mixer. Put the eggs in the mixer bowl or other large bowl and beat until thick and creamy. Gradually add the sweeteners, about 1 tablespoon at a time. Beat well after each addition.

Stir in the vanilla extract and the melted chocolate mixture. Gently fold in the remaining ingredients.

Pour the batter into the springform pan and bake for about 35 minutes or until done. Do not overbake; this cake will not show much color change. If a knife inserted in the center comes out clean, then the cake is done. Allow the cake to cool in the pan. Remove the collar and transfer the cake carefully to a cake platter or leave it on the springform bottom. Slice the cake in two layers. Fill and frost with Mocha Crème Icing (page 181) or with another icing of your choice. Mocha Crème Icing adds about 3.5 grams of carb to a slice of cake. This cake keeps in the fridge for a few days. You can also freeze it.

Carrot Cake

Enjoy. You can bake this as a layer cake and frost it with Lemon Crème Icing (page 182) or the frosting of your choice. You can also bake it as a sheet cake and serve it with no more than a dollop of whipped cream—or all by itself.

PREPARATION TIME: 25 minutes. BAKING TIME: about 40 to 45 minutes.
SERVING SIZE: ⅒ of yield. AMOUNT PER SERVING: 7.5 grams of carb; 8.1 grams of protein. TOTAL YIELD: one 8-inch layer cake.

		CHO (g)	PRO (g)
4	eggs	1.8	18.0
8	tablespoons unsalted butter (1 stick), very soft	0	0
5	tablespoons xylitol	9.0	0
9	tablespoons Splenda	13.5	0
1½	teaspoons Stevia Plus (or equivalent)	0	0
2	teaspoons vanilla extract	1.0	0
2	cups raw carrots, finely grated	14.0	2.0
⅓	cup oat flour	17.3	5.0
1	cup whole almond meal	10.0	20.0
½	cup unprocessed wheat bran	6.0	4.0
½	cup soy protein powder	0	32.2
1	teaspoon ground cinnamon	0.7	0
1	teaspoon baking powder	1.2	0
	salt, trace (about ⅛ teaspoon)	0	0
	Total	*74.5*	*81.2*

Preheat the oven to 350°F. Butter an 8-inch springform pan or a 9-by-12-inch or similar size glass baking dish.

Combine the eggs, butter, sweeteners, and vanilla extract in a medium mixing bowl. Beat until light and creamy. Add the carrots.

Combine the dry ingredients in another mixing bowl and stir well. Add about half of this mix to the batter at a time and stir well. Spoon the batter into the pan and bake the cake for about 40 to 45 minutes or until done. If a knife inserted in the center comes out clean, then the cake is done. Cool slightly before removing the collar from the pan. You can leave the cake on the springform bottom or transfer it to a cake platter. Slice it in two layers and fill and frost as desired. (Icings begin on page 181.) A frosting adds about 3.0 grams of carb to a slice of cake. This cake keeps in the fridge for a few days. You can also freeze it.

Basic Cheesecake

Cheesecakes are great on the low-carb diet, managing to rise to their glamour without flour. Common flaws, such as sinking a bit or developing cracks on top, are just cosmetic problems that can be overcome by a cover-up such as sour cream. Enjoy.

PREPARATION TIME: 25 minutes. BAKING TIME: about 45 to 60 minutes.
SERVING SIZE: ⅒ of yield. AMOUNT PER SERVING: 6.8 grams of carb; 9.1 grams of protein. TOTAL YIELD: one 8-inch cake with crust.

		CHO (g)	PRO (g)
NUTTY PIE CRUST			
4	tablespoons unsalted butter (½ stick)	0	0
1½	cups whole almond meal	15.0	30.0
2	tablespoons Splenda	3.0	0
	salt	0	0
FILLING			
2	eggs, separated, room temperature	1.2	12.0
2	eight-ounce packets of cream cheese, very soft	12.8	33.6
5	tablespoons xylitol	9.0	0
9	tablespoons Splenda	13.5	0
1½	teaspoons Stevia Plus (or equivalent)	0	0
2	teaspoons vanilla extract	1.0	0
1	teaspoon lemon peel, grated	0.3	0
	salt, trace	0	0
2	whole eggs, room temperature	1.2	12.0
TOPPING (OPTIONAL)			
¾	cup sour cream	6.0	3.6
1	tablespoon xylitol	1.8	0
2	tablespoons Splenda	3.0	0
	Total	67.8	91.2

Preheat the oven to 350°F. Use an 8-inch springform pan. Use about ½ tablespoon of butter to rub the bottom and sides of the pan before adding the Nutty Pie Crust.

To make the crust, place the 4 tablespoons of butter in a small microwavable bowl and melt it in the microwave. Combine the almond meal, sweetener, and salt in a mixing bowl. Stir in the melted butter. Press the crust firmly into the springform bottom. Put the springform pan in the freezer while preparing the filling for the cheesecake. (You can also do this way ahead of time.) Freezing the butter in the pan helps the cheesecake stick less to the sides of the pan.

To prepare the filling, separate the eggs. Put the yolks in a large mixing bowl. In another bowl, beat the egg whites until they are quite firm but still hold soft peaks. Set aside.

Add the cream cheese, sweeteners, vanilla extract, lemon peel, and salt to the egg yolks. Beat the mixture until smooth and fluffy. Add the 2 whole eggs, one at a time, beating well after each addition. Fold in the beaten egg whites. Pour the batter into the prepared springform pan.

Bake the cheesecake until it turns a deep golden color, for about 45 to 60 minutes; do not let it get too dark. Allow the cake to cool in the oven, with the door kept slightly ajar, for about 1 hour. Set the pan on a cooling rack.

Add the optional sour cream topping next. Preheat the oven to 350°F. Mix together the sour cream and the sweeteners and spread the mixture over the top of the cheesecake. Return the cake to the oven for 5 to 6 minutes, then remove it to a cooling rack to cool. Slide a knife around the cheesecake before removing the collar. Leave the cake on the springform bottom unless you need it again soon. Otherwise, slide the cake carefully onto a cake platter. Instead of the sour cream topping, you can substitute the Whipped Cream Sauce on page 253. Strawberries or other fresh berries arranged on top add further eye appeal. Add the extra carb grams. This cheesecake will keep in the fridge for two or three days. You can also freeze it. If the cake is still on the springform bottom, loosen it with a knife but leave the cake in place. Once frozen, switch the cake to another tray and wrap it loosely in aluminum foil.

Variation: Amaretto Cheesecake

Follow the directions for Basic Cheesecake above. Make these changes: add 2 tablespoons of amaretto liqueur and 1 teaspoon of almond extract to the cream cheese mixture. This adds 1.4 grams of carb to a slice that is 1/10 of the cake.

Chocolate Cheesecake

Chocolate and cheesecake together—yum!

PREPARATION TIME: 25 minutes. BAKING TIME: about 45 to 60 minutes.
SERVING SIZE: ⅒ of yield. AMOUNT PER SERVING: 8.0 grams of carb,
9.8 grams of protein. TOTAL YIELD: one 8-inch cake with crust.

		CHO (g)	PRO (g)
NUTTY PIE CRUST			
4	tablespoons unsalted butter (½ stick)	0	0
1½	cups whole almond meal	15.0	30.0
2	tablespoons Splenda	3.0	0
	salt	0	0
FILLING			
1	ounce unsweetened baking chocolate	4.0	4.0
3	ounces sugar-free semisweet chocolate	8.1	3.0
4	tablespoons heavy cream	1.6	1.2
2	eggs, separated, room temperature	1.2	12.0
2	eight-ounce packets of cream cheese, very soft	12.8	33.6
5	tablespoons xylitol	9.0	0
9	tablespoons Splenda	13.5	0
1½	teaspoons Stevia Plus (or equivalent)	0	0
2	teaspoons vanilla extract	1.0	0
	salt, trace	0	0
2	whole eggs, room temperature	1.2	12.0
TOPPING (OPTIONAL)			
¾	cup sour cream	6.0	3.6
1	tablespoon xylitol	1.8	0
2	tablespoons Splenda	3.0	0
	Total	*79.9*	*98.2*

Preheat the oven to 350°F. Use an 8-inch springform pan. Use about ½ tablespoon of butter to rub the bottom and sides of the pan before adding the Nutty Pie Crust.

To make the crust, place the 4 tablespoons of butter in a small microwavable bowl and melt it in the microwave. Combine the almond meal, sweetener, and salt in a mixing bowl. Stir in the melted butter. Press the crust firmly into the springform bottom. Put the springform pan in the freezer while preparing the filling for the cheesecake. (You can also do this way ahead of time.) Freezing the butter in the pan helps the cheesecake stick less to the sides of the springform pan.

To prepare the filling, combine the chocolates and the heavy cream in the top of a double boiler over hot water kept at or below a simmer. Stir occasionally until the chocolate is smooth. Remove from the heat and let cool.

Separate the eggs. Put the yolks in a large mixing bowl. In another bowl, beat the egg whites until they are quite firm but still hold soft peaks. Set aside.

Add the cream cheese, sweeteners, vanilla extract, and salt to the egg yolks. Beat the mixture until smooth and fluffy. Add the 2 whole eggs, one at a time, beating well after each addition. Fold in the beaten egg whites. Stir in the chocolate mixture. Pour the batter into the prepared springform pan.

Bake the cheesecake for about 45 to 60 minutes; do not overbake. The cheesecake will darken slightly, but the color is harder to judge. Watch for evidence of drying; it will work from the outside in. Stop baking when most but not all of the cake surface appears to be dry. The cake will continue to mature when you turn off the heat. Allow the cake to cool in the oven, with the door kept slightly ajar, for about 1 hour. Set the pan on a cooling rack.

Add the optional sour cream topping next. Preheat the oven to 350°F. Mix together the sour cream and sweeteners and spread over the top of the cheesecake. Return the cheesecake to the oven and bake for 5 to 6 minutes, then remove it to a cooling rack. Let cool. Slide a knife around the cake before removing the collar. Leave the cake on the springform bottom unless you need it again soon. Otherwise, slide the cake carefully onto a cake platter. Instead of the sour cream topping, you can substitute the Whipped Cream Sauce on page 253. Strawberries or other fresh berries arranged on top add further eye appeal. Count the extra carb grams. This cheesecake will keep in the fridge for two or three days. You can also freeze it. If the cake is still on the springform bottom, loosen it with a knife but leave the cake in place. Once frozen, switch the cake to another tray and wrap it loosely in aluminum foil.

Mocha Swirl Cheesecake

If you like mocha flavor, you will love this scrumptious cheesecake.

PREPARATION TIME: 25 minutes. BAKING TIME: about 45 to 60 minutes.
SERVING SIZE: ⅒ of yield. AMOUNT PER SERVING: 7.9 grams of carb,
9.7 grams of protein. TOTAL YIELD: one 8-inch cake with crust.

		CHO (g)	PRO (g)
NUTTY PIE CRUST			
4	tablespoons unsalted butter (½ stick)	0	0
1½	cups whole almond meal	15.0	30.0
2	tablespoons Splenda	3.0	0
	salt	0	0
FILLING			
1	ounce unsweetened baking chocolate	4.0	4.0
3	ounces sugar-free semisweet chocolate	8.1	3.0
3	tablespoons heavy cream	1.2	0.9
2	tablespoons water	0	0
1	tablespoon instant coffee crystals	0	0
2	eggs, separated, room temperature	1.2	12.0
2	eight-ounce packets of cream cheese, very soft	12.8	33.6
5	tablespoons xylitol	9.0	0
9	tablespoons Splenda	13.5	0
1½	teaspoons Stevia Plus (or equivalent)	0	0
2	teaspoons vanilla extract	1.0	0
	salt, trace	0	0
2	whole eggs, room temperature	1.2	12.0
TOPPING (OPTIONAL)			
¾	cup sour cream	6.0	3.6
1	tablespoon xylitol	1.8	0
2	tablespoons Splenda	3.0	0
	Total	*79.5*	*97.1*

Preheat the oven to 350°F. Butter an 8-inch springform pan, using about ½ tablespoon of butter to rub the bottom and sides of the springform pan before adding the Nutty Pie Crust.

To make the crust, place the 4 tablespooons of butter in a microwavable bowl and melt it in the microwave. Combine the almond meal, Splenda, and salt in a mixing bowl. Stir in the melted butter. Press the crust firmly into the springform bottom. Put the springform pan in the freezer while preparing the filling for the cheesecake. (You can also do this way ahead of time.) Freezing the butter in the pan helps the cheesecake stick less to the sides of the pan.

To make the filling, combine the chocolates, heavy cream, water, and instant coffee crystals in the top of a double boiler over hot water kept at or below a simmer. Stir occasionally until all the chocolate is smooth. Remove from the heat and set aside.

Separate the eggs. Put the yolks in a large mixing bowl. In another bowl, beat the egg whites until they are quite firm but still hold soft peaks. Set aside.

Add the cream cheese, sweeteners, vanilla extract, and salt to the egg yolks. Beat the mixture until smooth and fluffy. Add the 2 whole eggs, one at a time, beating well after each addition. Fold in the beaten egg whites.

Add the mocha mixture to the cream cheese mixture; stir it in with very few strokes, leaving dark ribbons throughout the batter. Pour the batter into the prepared springform pan.

Bake the cheesecake until it turns a deep golden color, about 45 to 60 minutes; do not let it get too dark. Allow the cake to cool in the oven, with the door kept slightly ajar, for about 1 hour. Set the pan on a cooling rack.

Add the optional sour cream topping next. Preheat the oven to 350°F. Mix together the sour cream and the sweeteners and spread over the top of the cheesecake. Return the cheesecake to the oven and bake for 5 to 6 minutes, then remove it to a cooling rack. After cooling, slide a knife around the cake before removing the collar. Leave the cake on the springform bottom unless you need it again soon. Otherwise, slide the cake carefully onto a cake platter. Instead of the sour cream topping, you can use the Whipped Cream Sauce on page 253. Strawberries or other fresh berries arranged on top add further eye appeal. Add the extra carb grams for any topping that you use. This cheesecake will keep in the fridge for two or three days. You can also freeze it. If the cake is still on the springform bottom, loosen it with a knife but leave the cake in place. Once frozen, switch the cake to another tray or disposable pie pan and wrap loosely in aluminum foil.

Cranberry Cheesecake with Chocolate Chips

Tart cranberries and richly sweet chocolate make a sublime combination in this cheesecake.

PREPARATION TIME: 25 minutes. BAKING TIME: about 45 to 60 minutes.
SERVING SIZE: ⅒ of yield. AMOUNT PER SERVING: 8.6 grams of carb, 9.2 grams of protein. TOTAL YIELD: one 8-inch cake with crust.

		CHO (g)	PRO (g)
NUTTY PIE CRUST			
4	tablespoons unsalted butter (½ stick)	0	0
1½	cups whole almond meal	15.0	30.0
2	tablespoons Splenda	3.0	0
	salt	0	0
FILLING			
2	eggs, separated, room temperature	1.2	12.0
2	eight-ounce packets of cream cheese, very soft	12.8	33.6
5	tablespoons xylitol	9.0	0
9	tablespoons Splenda	13.5	0
1½	teaspoons Stevia Plus (or equivalent)	0	0
2	teaspoons vanilla extract	1.0	0
1	teaspoon lemon peel, grated	0.3	0
	salt, trace	0	0
2	whole eggs, room temperature	1.2	12.0
1	cup fresh cranberries, lightly crushed	8.0	0
1½	ounces sugar-free semisweet chocolate chips	4.0	1.0
1	tablespoon cornstarch	6.5	0
TOPPING (OPTIONAL)			
¾	cup sour cream	6.0	3.6
1	tablespoon xylitol	1.8	0
2	tablespoons Splenda	3.0	0
	Total	*86.3*	*92.2*

Preheat the oven to 350°F. Butter an 8-inch springform pan, using about ½ tablespoon of butter to rub the bottom and sides of the pan before adding the Nutty Pie Crust.

To make the crust, place the 4 tablespoons of butter in a microwavable bowl and melt in the microwave. Combine the almond meal,

Splenda, and salt in a mixing bowl. Stir in the melted butter. Press the crust firmly into the springform bottom. Put the springform pan in the freezer while preparing the filling for the cheesecake. (You can also do this way ahead of time.) Freezing the butter in the pan helps the cheesecake stick less to the sides of the pan.

To make the filling, separate the eggs. Put the yolks in a large mixing bowl. In another bowl, beat the egg whites until they are quite firm but still hold soft peaks. Set them aside.

Add the cream cheese, sweeteners, vanilla extract, lemon peel, and salt to the egg yolks. Beat the mixture until smooth and fluffy. Add the 2 remaining eggs, one at a time, beating well after each addition. Fold in the beaten egg whites.

Crush the cranberries lightly in a processor or a blender. Put the crushed berries in a mixing bowl. Add the chocolate chips and the cornstarch to the berries. Mix lightly and fold into the cheesecake batter. Pour the batter into the prepared springform pan.

Bake the cheesecake until it turns a golden color, about 45 to 60 minutes; do not let it get too dark. Allow the cake to cool in the oven, with the door kept slightly ajar, for about 1 hour. Set the pan on a cooling rack.

Add the optional sour cream topping next. Preheat the oven to 350°F. Mix together the sour cream and the sweeteners and spread it over the top of the cheesecake. Return the cheesecake to the oven and bake for 5 to 6 minutes, then remove it to a cooling rack. After cooling, slide a knife around the cake before removing the collar. Leave the cake on the springform bottom unless you need it again soon. Otherwise, slide the cake carefully onto a cake platter. Instead of the sour cream topping, you can substitute the Whipped Cream Sauce on page 253. Strawberries or other fresh berries arranged on top add further eye appeal. Add the extra carb grams for any topping that you use. This cheesecake will keep in the fridge for two or three days. You can also freeze it. If the cake is still on the springform bottom, loosen it with a knife but leave the cake in place. Once frozen, switch the cake to another tray or disposable pie pan and wrap it loosely in aluminum foil.

Orange Soufflé Cheesecake

This yummy version will remind you of an orange soufflé, but the creamy texture says all cheesecake.

PREPARATION TIME: 25 minutes. BAKING TIME: about 45 to 60 minutes.
SERVING SIZE: ⅒ of yield. AMOUNT PER SERVING: 7.5 grams of carb, 9.8 grams of protein. TOTAL YIELD: one 8-inch cake with crust.

		CHO (g)	PRO (g)
NUTTY PIE CRUST			
4	tablespoons unsalted butter (½ stick)	0	0
1½	cups whole almond meal	15.0	30.0
2	tablespoons Splenda	3.0	0
	salt	0	0
FILLING			
2	eggs, separated, room temperature	1.2	12.0
2	egg whites	0.6	7.0
8	tablespoons xylitol	14.4	0
2	eight-ounce packets of cream cheese, very soft	12.8	33.6
9	tablespoons Splenda	13.5	0
1½	teaspoons Stevia Plus (or equivalent)	0	0
2	teaspoons vanilla extract	1.0	0
1	teaspoon orange extract	1.0	0
1	tablespoon lemon peel, grated	0.8	0
1	tablespoon orange peel, grated	0.9	
	salt, trace	0	0
2	whole eggs, room temperature	1.2	12.0
TOPPING (OPTIONAL)			
¾	cup sour cream	6.0	3.6
1	tablespoon xylitol	1.8	0
2	tablespoons Splenda	3.0	0
	Total	*76.2*	*98.2*

Preheat the oven to 350°F. Butter an 8-inch springform pan, using about ½ tablespoon of butter to rub the bottom and sides of the springform pan before adding the Nutty Pie Crust.

To make the crust, place the 4 tablespoons of butter in a microwavable bowl and melt it in the microwave. Combine the almond meal, Splenda, and salt in a mixing bowl. Stir in the melted butter. Press the crust firmly into the springform bottom. Put the springform pan in the freezer while preparing the filling for the cheesecake. (You can also do this way ahead of time.) Freezing the butter in the pan helps the cheesecake stick less to the sides of the pan.

To make the filling, separate the eggs. Put the yolks in a large mixing bowl. In another bowl, beat the 4 egg whites until they are quite firm but still hold soft peaks. Gradually add 5 tablespoons of xylitol, beating well after each addition. Set the meringue aside.

Add the cream cheese, remaining sweeteners, vanilla extract, orange extract, lemon peel, orange peel, and salt to the egg yolks. Beat the mixture until smooth and fluffy. Add the 2 whole eggs, one at a time, beating well after each addition. Fold in the meringue. Pour the batter into the prepared springform pan.

Bake the cheesecake until it turns a golden color, about 45 to 60 minutes; do not let it get too dark. Allow the cake to cool in the oven, with the door kept slightly ajar, for about 1 hour. Set the pan on a cooling rack.

Add the optional sour cream topping next. Preheat the oven to 350°F. Mix together the sour cream and sweeteners and spread it over the top of the cheesecake. Return the cheesecake to the oven and bake for 5 to 6 minutes, then remove it to a cooling rack. After cooling, slide a knife around the cake before removing the collar. Leave the cake on the springform bottom unless you need it again soon. Otherwise, slide the cake carefully onto a cake platter. Instead of the sour cream topping, you can substitute the Whipped Cream Sauce on page 253. Orange slices or other fresh fruit arranged on top add further eye appeal. Add the extra carb grams for any topping that you use. This cheesecake will keep in the fridge for two or three days. You can also freeze it. If the cake is still on the springform bottom, loosen it with a knife but leave the cake in place. Once frozen, switch the cake to another tray or disposable pie pan and wrap it loosely in aluminum foil.

Refrigerator Cheesecake

If you are worried about tackling a baked cheesecake, though you needn't be, try this one. It is quite foolproof—and delicious.

PREPARATION TIME: 15 minutes (needs to be refrigerated for several hours). SERVING SIZE: 1/10 of yield. AMOUNT PER SERVING: 4.5 grams of carb, 6.2 grams of protein. TOTAL YIELD: one 8- or 9-inch cheesecake, filling only.

		CHO (g)	PRO (g)
1	prebaked crust (crust recipes begin on page 187)		

FILLING

		CHO (g)	PRO (g)
1	packet unflavored gelatin	0	6.0
¼	cup water	0	0
4	egg yolks	1.2	11.2
2	teaspoons vanilla extract	1.0	0.0
	salt, trace (about ⅛ teaspoon)	0	0
1	cup heavy cream	6.4	5.0
2	eight-ounce packets of cream cheese, very soft	12.8	33.6
5	tablespoons xylitol	9.0	0
9	tablespoons Splenda	13.5	0
1½	teaspoons Stevia Plus (or equivalent)	0	0
2	egg whites*	0.6	6.0
	Total	*44.5*	*61.8*

Have a springform pan ready with a baked crust inside or use a 9-inch pie pan with a prebaked crust. Add the gram counts of the crust to the count per slice.

Dissolve the gelatin in the water and set aside.

Put the egg yolks, vanilla extract, salt, and ¼ cup of the heavy cream in the top of a double boiler over simmering water. Beat this mixture until it thickens. Remove the pot from the heat. Add the gelatin and stir until it is soaked. Chill until ready to use.

In a large mixing bowl (an electric stand mixer is handy for this), beat the cream cheese and the sweeteners until thick and fluffy. In another bowl, whip the remaining heavy cream. You need a third mixing bowl to whip the egg whites until they form soft but firm peaks.

Combine all the ingredients. Beat the gelatin mixture into the cream cheese. Fold in the whipped cream, followed by the egg

*The egg whites in this cheesecake remain raw. If you want to be absolutely safe, use sterilized egg whites.

whites. Spoon the dessert into the pan of your choice. Refrigerate. The cheesecake needs to chill for 4 to 5 hours or overnight. It will be good for several days. Serve with fresh fruit or a dessert sauce. Add any extra carb grams.

Variation: Refrigerator Rum Cheesecake

Follow the directions for Refrigerator Cheesecake above. Make these changes: soak the gelatin in 1 tablespoon of water and 3 tablespoons of rum.

Vanilla Crème Icing

This lush, delicious icing turns any cake or dessert into a finger-lickin' delight.

PREPARATION TIME: less than 10 minutes (needs to be refrigerated for about 1 hour).

SERVING SIZE: ⅓ cup. AMOUNT PER SERVING: 2.8 grams of carb, 1.9 grams of protein. TOTAL YIELD: 2⅓ cups; icing for one 8- or 9-inch layer cake.

		CHO (g)	PRO (g)
6	ounces soft cream cheese	4.8	12.6
4	tablespoons unsalted butter (¾ stick), soft	0	0
3	tablespoons heavy cream	1.2	0.9
2	teaspoons vanilla extract	1.0	0
	salt, trace (about ⅛ teaspoon)	0	0
3	tablespoons xylitol	5.4	0
5	tablespoons Splenda	7.5	0
1½	teaspoons Stevia Plus (or equivalent)	0	0
	Total	*19.9*	*13.5*

This icing needs to be beaten until thick and fluffy; it takes a minute or two. Combine all the ingredients in a medium mixing bowl and beat until the icing has increased in volume and is silky soft and fluffy. Chill it for a few minutes. When you ice a cake, make a thin layer around the sides first. This will keep loose crumbs in place when you return for the final application. If the cake layers are uneven in height, put the bigger one on the bottom. For an extra touch, pipe some of the icing through a pastry bag for a decorative edge. This icing needs refrigeration. However, remove the cake from the fridge for at least a half hour before serving. Please note that the serving size is ⅓ cup. This is a good guide to keep in mind when counting carb grams whenever you use the icing for other purposes, such as a filling for cream puff shells or meringue shells.

Variation: Mocha Crème Icing

Follow the directions for Vanilla Crème Icing above. Make these changes: reduce the cream cheese by 1 ounce. Combine 3 tablespoons of espresso coffee (or mix 2 teaspoons of instant coffee crystals with 3 tablespoons of hot water) with 3 ounces of sugar-free semisweet chocolate in a microwavable bowl. Microwave for about 25 seconds or until the chocolate is melted. You can also do this in a double boiler over hot water kept at or below a simmer. Stir until smooth. Refrigerate the mixture for about 3 minutes and then stir it into the icing. This increases the total yield to approximately 2⅔ cups. A ⅓-cup serving of icing has 3.5 grams of carb.

Variation: Lemon Crème Icing

Follow the directions for Vanilla Crème Icing above. Make these changes: add 1 to 2 tablespoons of lemon juice to icing, depending on how lemony you want to make it. Add the juice slowly and taste the result. With 2 added tablespoons of lemon juice, a ⅓-cup serving of icing has 3.2 grams of carb.

Variation: Orange Crème Icing

Follow the directions for Vanilla Crème Icing above. Make these changes: add 1 tablespoon of finely grated orange peel and 2 teaspoons of finely grated lemon peel along with 1 or 2 teaspoons of orange extract. (Orange extract varies in strength. Add this slowly and check the flavor.) A ⅓-cup serving of icing has 3.2 grams of carb.

Variation: Chocolate Icing

Follow the directions for Vanilla Crème Icing above. Make these changes: reduce the cream cheese by 1 ounce. Combine 3 tablespoons of heavy cream with 4 ounces of sugar-free, semisweet chocolate in a microwavable bowl. Microwave for about 25 seconds or until the chocolate is melted. You can also do this in a double boiler over hot water kept at or below a simmer. Stir until smooth. Refrigerate the mixture for about 3 minutes and then stir it into the icing. Beat the icing until fluffy. This recipe yields about 3 cups. A ⅓-cup serving has about 3.3 grams of carb.

Variation: Peanut Butter Icing

Follow the directions for Vanilla Crème Icing above. Make these changes: add ⅓ cup of natural, smooth peanut butter to the icing as you begin whipping. This recipe yields 3 cups of icing. A ⅓-cup serving has 4.2 grams of carb and 3.0 grams of protein.

Variation: Butter Crème Icing

Follow the directions for Vanilla Crème Icing above. Make these changes: reduce the cream cheese to 5 ounces. Increase the butter to 8 tablespoons (1 stick). Increase the heavy cream by 3 tablespoons. Add 1 teaspoon of finely grated lemon peel. This yields 2⅔ cups of icing. A ⅓-cup serving has 2.6 grams of carb and less than 1.6 grams of protein.

7-Minute Icing

This is totally great. Note that only xylitol works well with this. Normally the icing asks for 1½ cups of sugar, but you get a pretty good icing with half that amount. Still, it is a lot of sugar alcohol, so eat sparingly.

PREPARATION TIME: 15 minutes.
SERVING SIZE: ¼ cup. AMOUNT PER SERVING: 2.8 grams of carb, negligible protein. TOTAL YIELD: about 2 cups of icing.

		CHO (g)	PRO (g)
2	egg whites	0.6	7.0
¾	cup xylitol	21.6	0
5	tablespoons water	0	0
¼	teaspoon cream of tartar	0	0
	salt, trace	0	0
1	teaspoon vanilla extract	0.5	0
	Total	22.7	7.0

This classic icing needs to be literally beaten for about 7 minutes or more. A portable electric mixer is ideal for this. Have a double boiler ready with simmering water. Put the egg whites, xylitol, water, cream of tartar, and salt in the top of the double boiler, but do not put it over the water yet. Beat this mix until well blended. After the mix is blended, place the double boiler over the simmering water. Set your timer. You will need 7 minutes over hot water. Take the frosting off the water and beat in the vanilla extract. You might improve the consistency a little if you beat the icing for another minute or two. This icing is ideal for a sheet cake.

Variation: Lemon 7-Minute Icing

Follow the directions for 7-Minute Icing above. Make these changes: replace some of the water with lemon juice; for a nice lemon flavor, use 2 tablespoons of lemon juice and 3 tablespoons of water. A ¼-cup serving of this icing has 3.2 grams of carb.

Meringue Topping

This is a wonderful, quick topping and is great on cream pies.

PREPARATION TIME: 5 minutes.

SERVING SIZE: ⅛ of yield. AMOUNT PER SERVING: 0.9 gram of carb, 1.3 grams of protein. TOTAL YIELD: topping for one 8- or 9-inch pie.

		CHO (g)	PRO (g)
3	egg whites	0.9	10.5
¼	teaspoon cream of tartar	0	0
	salt, trace	0	0
3	tablespoons xylitol	5.4	0
1	teaspoon vanilla extract	0.5	0
	Total	*6.8*	*10.5*

Beat the egg whites until they are just well mixed and frothy. Add the cream of tartar and salt (1 or 2 shakes). Beat until the whites are firm but still holding soft peaks. Gradually add the xylitol by the tablespoon. Do not overbeat. Add the vanilla extract last.

Spread the meringue over the pie you are baking, sealing all edges. Bake no longer than 10 to 15 minutes. The oven temperature should be set at 350°F or lower.

Chocolate Glaze

A great way to inspire awe in your creations. A smooth, lovely, shiny chocolate glaze looks delightful, tastes wonderful, and is very easy to make. While the recipe asks for semisweet chocolate, you can also substitute sugar-free milk or white chocolate.

PREPARATION TIME: 10 minutes.

SERVING SIZE: ⅛ of yield. AMOUNT PER SERVING: 1.8 grams of carb, negligible protein. TOTAL YIELD: Glaze for one 8-inch layer cake.

		CHO (g)	PRO (g)
5	ounces sugar-free, semisweet chocolate	13.5	5.0
3	tablespoons heavy cream*	0.9	0
	Total	*14.4*	*5.0*

Combine the chocolate and heavy cream in a microwavable bowl and microwave for about 35 seconds (depending on your microwave) until the chocolate is melted. Stir until completely smooth. You can do the same in a double boiler over hot water kept at or below a simmer. Cool the mixture for a few minutes. Unlike fluffy icings, the glaze shows every bump in a cake. Try to create a smooth surface if possible. Put the cake or pastry you want to glaze on a cooling rack with paper towels placed beneath it to catch any drips. Allow the glaze to harden completely. This may take several hours.

*You have some control over how thick or thin you want to make the glaze by increasing or reducing the amount of cream as desired.

Powdered Low-Carb Sugar Glaze

A powdered sugar glaze helps many a cookie achieve star billing. Now you can put this shiny, tasty glaze on any cookie or cookie bar you like by using xylitol powdered sugar. If you cannot find this product in a health food store near you, see Sources. This sugar looks, feels, and tastes like regular powdered sugar.

PREPARATION TIME: 3 minutes.

SERVING SIZE: About ½ teaspoon. AMOUNT PER SERVING: about 0.1 gram of carb, negligible protein. TOTAL YIELD: about 80 servings.

		CHO (g)	PRO (g)
6	tablespoons xylitol powdered sugar	6.2	5.0
4	teaspoons heavy cream	0.5	0.0
	Total	*6.7*	*5.0*

Mix the powdered xylitol with the cream and stir until smooth. You can add a little more cream for a thinner glaze if you like. You can apply the glaze with the tip of a knife or with a brush. You can also substitute lemon juice for the cream and create a lemon glaze. If you want to use real powdered (cane) sugar in place of the xylitol, ½ teaspoon of glaze will have about 0.7 gram of carb.

Hot Water Pastry Crust I

Hot water pastry crusts are practically foolproof to make; the pastry is rolled between sheets of wax paper. The result is a superb, flaky crust. The hot water pastry crusts (all three) have a fair amount of carbohydrates. It is best, therefore, to use the crusts as bottom crusts only; no pie in this book asks for a top crust. You can bake two pies or freeze one.

PREPARATION TIME: 15 minutes. BAKING TIME: about 20 to 25 minutes, crust only.

SERVING SIZE: 1/16 of yield. AMOUNT PER SERVING: 4.5 grams of carb, 2.0 grams of protein. TOTAL YIELD: two 8- or 9-inch pie crusts.

		CHO (g)	PRO (g)
4	tablespoons coconut oil	0	0
4	tablespoons unsalted butter (½ stick)	0	0
¼	cup hot (almost boiling) water	0	0
½	cup stone-ground whole wheat flour	36.2	8.0
¼	cup unbleached wheat (white) flour	23.0	3.0
¼	oat flour	13.0	0.0
⅓	cup soy protein powder	0	21.5
	salt to taste (less than ¼ teaspoon)	0	0
	Total	*72.2*	*32.5*

Preheat the oven to 350°F. Butter two 8- or 9-inch pie pans.

Put the coconut oil and butter into a medium mixing bowl or a quart jar. Add the hot water and stir or beat until fats are dissolved.

Combine and mix the dry ingredients thoroughly in a small bowl. Add them all at once to the fat-hot water mix and stir just until barely combined. With your hands (you may want to wear plastic gloves), form the dough into a ball. Handle as little as possible. Divide the dough in two equal pieces.

Cut or tear four sheets of wax paper, about 12 by 16 inches. Moisten the countertop with water. (If the countertop is not smooth, use a large cutting board; secure it against shifting by placing a wet kitchen towel beneath it.) Moisten the surface you will work on. Put a sheet of wax paper on top. Put half of the dough on the wax paper; flatten it with your hand as much as you can. Cover the dough with wax paper. With a rolling pin—and the dough wedged between the wax paper—roll out a sheet of dough as large and thin as possible, rolling in all directions. You do not need to make a perfect circle.

Pull off the top paper and discard. With both hands, pick up the bottom paper with the dough stuck to it; invert it and position it centrally above the pie pan. Drop the crust, with the paper still attached, into the pie pan. Carefully peel off the wax paper, leaving the crust behind in the pan. Cut off overhang and use for patches where needed. Flute the edge of the crust. Repeat with the other half of the dough.

Pierce the two crusts all over with a fork to avoid air bubbles. Bake the shells for 20 to 25 minutes or until the crusts turn light golden. Use these fully baked shells for cream pies and other desserts. Use partially baked shells for berry pies. For partially baked shells, bake them for about 12 to 15 minutes; remove them from the oven when they begin to show a hint of color.

Hot Water Pastry Crust II

This pastry crust has fewer carbohydrates. Otherwise it is like Hot Water Pastry Crust I.

SERVING SIZE: ⅟₁₆ of yield. AMOUNT PER SERVING: 4.0 grams of carb, 3.1 grams of protein. TOTAL YIELD: two 8- or 9-inch pie crusts.

		CHO (g)	PRO (g)
4	tablespoons coconut oil	0	0
4	tablespoons unsalted butter (½ stick)	0	0
¼	cup hot (almost boiling) water	0	0
¼	cup unbleached wheat (white) flour	23.0	3.0
⅓	cup stone-ground whole wheat flour	24.0	5.0
⅓	cup oat flour	17.3	0
⅔	cup soy protein powder	0	42.3
	salt, trace (less than ¼ teaspoon)	0	0
	Total	*64.3*	*50.3*

To make this crust, follow the directions for Hot Water Pastry Crust I on page 187.

Hot Water Pastry Crust III

This pastry crust is the most carb-friendly. Otherwise it is like Hot Water Pastry Crust I.

SERVING SIZE: ¹⁄₁₆ of yield. AMOUNT PER SERVING: 3.8 grams of carb, 2.8 grams of protein. TOTAL YIELD: two 8- or 9-inch pie crusts.

	CHO (g)	PRO (g)
4 tablespoons coconut oil	0	0
4 tablespoons unsalted butter (½ stick)	0	0
¼ cup hot (almost boiling) water	0	0
⅓ cup stone-ground whole wheat flour	24.0	5.0
⅓ cup unbleached wheat (white) flour	30.6	3.0
½ cup unprocessed wheat bran	6.0	4.0
½ cup soy protein powder	0	32.2
salt, trace (less than ¼ teaspoon)	0	0
Total	*60.6*	*44.2*

To make this crust, follow the directions for Hot Water Pastry Crust I on page 187.

Nutty Pie Crust

Great taste, quick to make, low in carbohydrates, ready to use.

PREPARATION TIME: 10 minutes. BAKING TIME: about 15 to 20 minutes, crust only.

SERVING SIZE: ⅛ of yield. AMOUNT PER SERVING: 2.3 grams of carb, 3.7 grams of protein. TOTAL YIELD: one 8-inch crust.

		CHO (g)	PRO (g)
4	tablespoons unsalted butter (½ stick)	0	0
1½	cups whole almond meal	15.0	30.0
2	tablespoons Splenda	3.0	0
	salt, trace	0	0
	Total	*18.0*	*30.0*

Preheat the oven to 325°F. Butter one 8-inch pie pan or a spring-form pan.

Place the 4 tablespoons of butter in a microwavable bowl and melt it in the microwave.

Combine the almond meal, Splenda, and salt in a small bowl and mix well. Add the melted butter and stir. Press the crust firmly into the pan of your choice. You can create a smooth crust by pressing a second pie pan firmly inside the pan holding the crust mixture. Pre-bake for about 15 to 20 minutes or until light golden. Adjust the gram counts per serving if you cut other than 8 slices.

Toasted Pecan Crust

Great pecan taste, quick to make. And low in carb count.

PREPARATION TIME: 10 minutes. BAKING TIME: about 15 to 20 minutes, crust only.

SERVING SIZE: ⅛ of yield. AMOUNT PER SERVING: 1.5 grams of carb, 1.6 grams of protein. TOTAL YIELD: one 8-inch crust.

		CHO (g)	PRO (g)
4	tablespoons unsalted butter (½ stick), melted	0	0
5	ounces toasted pecans, coarsely ground	9.0	13.0
2	tablespoons Splenda	3.0	0
	salt, trace	0	0
	Total	*12.0*	*13.0*

Preheat the oven to 325°F. Butter one 8-inch pie pan or a spring-form pan.

Combine the pecans, Splenda, and salt in a small bowl and mix well. Add the melted butter and stir. Press the crust firmly into the pan of your choice. You can create a smooth crust by pressing a second pie pan firmly inside the pan holding the crust mixture. Prebake for about 15 to 20 minutes or until golden.

Butterscotch Cream Pie

This velvety cream pie is a soothing palate pleaser. A small addition of white flour ensures that this tasty creation always comes through for you with flying colors. Quick and easy to make too.

PREPARATION TIME: 20 minutes. BAKING TIME: about 20 minutes (must be refrigerated for several hours or overnight).

SERVING SIZE: ⅛ of yield. AMOUNT PER SERVING: 5.2 grams of carb, 3.5 grams of protein. TOTAL YIELD: 1 cream pie, filling only.

		CHO (g)	PRO (g)
1	prebaked crust (crust recipes begin on page 187)		
FILLING			
4	egg yolks	1.2	11.2
1	egg	0.6	6.0
2	tablespoons wheat (white) flour	11.5	1.0
1	tablespoon unsalted butter (⅛ stick)	0	0
½	cup DiabetiSweet Brown Sugar Substitute	14.4	0
2	cups heavy cream	12.8	9.6
1	teaspoon vanilla extract	0.5	0
	salt, trace	0	0
	Total	*41.0*	*27.8*

Preheat the oven to 350°F. Prepare an 8- or 9-inch pie pan with the crust of your choice, fully baked. Add the gram counts to the total.

In a medium mixing bowl, beat the egg yolks and egg until well mixed. Set aside.

Put the flour, butter, brown sugar, and ¾ cup of heavy cream in the top of a double boiler. Keep the water at a simmer. Whisk the mixture until well combined. Stir occasionally until the cream begins to heat up, then whisk constantly until it begins to thicken. Remove from the heat.

Pour a small amount of the mixture, about 2 tablespoons, into the beaten eggs. Beat the eggs vigorously. Repeat this two or three times, beating well each time. Pour the egg mixture into the double boiler. Return it over the hot water and whisk continuously until the mixture thickens. Remove from the heat. Beat in the remaining cream, vanilla extract, and salt.

Put the pie shell you are using on a cookie sheet and carefully pour the cream filling into it. Put the cookie sheet with the pie on it in the oven and bake for about 20 minutes. Do not overbake. Remove the pie from the oven, keeping it on the cookie sheet.

If you would like to add a meringue (page 184), prepare it now. Leave the oven on and the pie on the cookie sheet. Spread the meringue over the pie and bake for an additional 10 to 15 minutes.

When the pie is done, remove it from the oven and allow it to sit at room temperature for about 45 minutes before chilling it. Wait several hours or overnight to serve. If you do not use meringue, serve with Whipped Cream Sauce (page 253) or with Toasted Pecan Topping (page 93) or with another topping of your choice. Add the gram counts for any topping to the total.

Chocolate Rum Cream Pie

Yo ho ho—chocolate, rum, and cream!

PREPARATION TIME: 20 minutes. BAKING TIME: about 20 minutes (must be
refrigerated for several hours or overnight).

SERVING SIZE: ⅛ of yield. AMOUNT PER SERVING: 5.4 grams of carb, 3.6
grams of protein. TOTAL YIELD: 1 cream pie, filling only.

		CHO (g)	PRO (g)
1	prebaked pie crust		
	(crust recipes begin on page 187)		
FILLING			
4	egg yolks	1.2	11.4
1	egg	0.6	6.0
2	tablespoons wheat (white) flour	11.5	1.0
1	tablespoon unsalted butter (⅛ stick)	0	0
3	tablespoons xylitol	5.4	0
5	tablespoons Splenda	7.5	0
2	cups heavy cream	12.8	9.6
1	teaspoon vanilla extract	0.5	0
3	tablespoons rum	0	0
	salt, trace	0	0
TOPPING			
1½	ounces sugar-free semisweet		
	chocolate, grated	4.0	1.0
	Total	*43.5*	*29.0*

Preheat the oven to 350°F. Prepare an 8- or 9-inch pie pan with the
crust of your choice, fully baked. Add the gram counts to the total.

In a medium mixing bowl, beat the egg yolks and egg until well
mixed. Set aside.

Put the flour, butter, sweeteners, and ¾ cup of heavy cream in the
top of a double boiler. Keep the water at a simmer. Whisk the mixture
until well combined. Stir occasionally as the cream begins to heat up,
then whisk constantly until it begins to thicken. Remove from the heat.

Pour a small amount, about 2 tablespoons, into the beaten eggs.
Beat the eggs vigorously. Repeat this two or three times, beating well
each time. Pour the egg mixture into the double boiler pan. Return it
over the hot water and whisk continuously until the mixture thickens.
Remove from the heat. Beat in the remaining cream, vanilla extract,
rum, and salt.

Put the pie crust you are using on a cookie sheet and carefully pour

the cream filling into it. Put the cookie sheet with the pie on it in the oven and bake for about 20 minutes. Do not overbake. Remove the pie from the oven, keeping it on the cookie sheet. Transfer it carefully to a cooling rack and let it sit at room temperature for about 45 minutes before chilling it. Wait several hours or overnight to serve. Before serving, sprinkle with grated chocolate. For an extra treat, you might want to cover the pie with Whipped Cream Sauce (page 253) and sprinkle the chocolate on top of it. Add the gram counts for the sauce to the total.

Banana Cream Pie

This is one of the most comforting of comfort foods. Enjoy as an occasional treat.

PREPARATION TIME: 20 minutes. BAKING TIME: about 20 minutes (must be refrigerated for several hours or overnight).

SERVING SIZE: ⅛ of yield. AMOUNT PER SERVING: 7.8 grams of carb, 3.6 grams of protein. TOTAL YIELD: 1 cream pie, filling only.

	CHO (g)	PRO (g)
1 prebaked pie crust (crust recipes begin on page 187)		
FILLING		
4 egg yolks	1.2	11.2
1 egg	0.6	6.0
2 tablespoons wheat (white) flour	11.5	1.0
1 tablespoon unsalted butter (⅛ stick)	0	0
3 tablespoons xylitol	5.4	0
5 tablespoons Splenda	7.5	0
2 cups heavy cream	12.8	9.6
¾ cup bananas, thinly sliced	23.1	1.0
1 teaspoon vanilla extract	0.5	0
salt, trace	0	0
Total	*62.6*	*28.8*

Preheat the oven to 350°F. Prepare an 8- or 9-inch pie pan with the crust of your choice, fully baked. Add the gram counts to the total.

In a medium mixing bowl, beat the egg yolks and egg until well mixed. Set aside.

Put the flour, butter, sweeteners, and ¾ cup of heavy cream in the top of a double boiler. Keep the water at a simmer. Whisk the mixture until well combined. Stir occasionally as the cream begins to heat up, then whisk constantly until it begins to thicken. Remove from the heat.

Pour a small amount, about 2 tablespoons, into the beaten eggs. Beat the eggs vigorously. Repeat this two or three times, beating well each time. Pour the egg mixture into the double boiler pan. Return it over the hot water and whisk continuously until the mixture thickens. Remove from the heat. Beat in the remaining cream, vanilla extract, and salt. Stir in the sliced bananas.

Put the pie crust you are using on a cookie sheet and carefully pour the cream filling into it. Put the cookie sheet with the pie on it in the oven and bake for about 20 minutes. Do not overbake. Remove the pie from the oven, keeping it on the cookie sheet.

If you would like to add a meringue (page 184), prepare it now. Leave the oven on and the pie on the cookie sheet. Spread the meringue over the pie and bake for an additional 10 to 15 minutes.

When the pie is done, remove it from the oven and allow it to sit at room temperature for about 45 minutes before chilling it. Wait several hours or overnight to serve. If you do not use meringue, serve with Whipped Cream Sauce (page 253) or with Toasted Pecan Topping (page 93) or with another topping of your choice. Add the gram counts for any topping to the total.

Mocha Cream Pie

It's a sophisticated and satisfying flavor. I think you'll love this pie.

PREPARATION TIME: 20 minutes. BAKING TIME: about 20 minutes (must be refrigerated for several hours or overnight).

SERVING SIZE: ⅛ of yield. AMOUNT PER SERVING: 5.8 grams of carb, 3.7 grams of protein. TOTAL YIELD: 1 cream pie, filling only.

	CHO (g)	PRO (g)
1 prebaked pie crust (crust recipes begin on page 187)		

FILLING

	CHO (g)	PRO (g)
2 ounces sugar-free semisweet chocolate	5.4	2.0
2 teaspoons instant coffee crystals	0	0
2 cups heavy cream	12.8	9.6
4 egg yolks	1.2	11.2
1 egg	0.6	6.0
2 tablespoons wheat (white) flour	11.5	1.0
1 tablespoon unsalted butter (⅛ stick)	0	0
3 tablespoons xylitol	5.4	0
5 tablespoons Splenda	7.5	0
½ teaspoon Stevia Plus (or equivalent)	0	0
1 teaspoon vanilla extract	0.5	0
salt, trace	0	0
Total	*44.9*	*23.8*

Preheat the oven to 350°F. Prepare an 8- or-9 inch pie pan with the crust of your choice, fully baked. Add the gram counts to the total.

Put the chocolate, coffee crystals, and 3 tablespoons of heavy cream in a microwavable bowl and microwave for about 30 seconds or until the chocolate is melted. You can do it in a double boiler over hot water too; keep the water at or below a simmer. Stir until smooth. Set aside.

In a medium mixing bowl, beat the egg yolks and egg until well mixed. Set aside.

Put the flour, butter, sweeteners, and ¾ cup of heavy cream in the top of a double boiler. Keep the water at a simmer. Whisk the mixture until well combined. Stir occasionally as the cream begins to heat up, then whisk constantly until it begins to thicken. Remove from the heat.

Pour a small amount, about 2 tablespoons, into the beaten eggs. Beat the eggs vigorously. Repeat this two or three times, beating well each time. Pour the egg mixture into the double boiler pan. Return it over the hot water and whisk continuously until the mixture thickens. Remove from the heat. Beat in the remaining cream, vanilla extract, and salt. Stir in the melted chocolate-coffee mix.

Put the pie crust you are using on a cookie sheet. and carefully pour the cream filling into it. Put the cookie sheet with the pie on it in the oven and bake for about 20 minutes. Do not overbake. Remove the pie from the oven, keeping it on the cookie sheet.

If you would like to add a meringue (page 184), prepare it now. Leave the oven on and the pie on the cookie sheet. Spread the meringue over the pie and bake it for an additional 10 to 15 minutes.

When the pie is done, remove it from the oven and allow it to sit at room temperature for about 45 minutes before chilling it. Wait several hours or overnight to serve. If you do not use meringue, serve with Whipped Cream Sauce (page 253) or with Toasted Pecan Topping (page 93) or with another topping of your choice. Add the gram counts for any topping to the total.

Coconut Cream Pie

Did you ever think you could have coconut cream pie again? This was my editor's favorite comfort food pie when he was a child. Now he's watching his carbs and can eat this again.

PREPARATION TIME: 20 minutes. BAKING TIME: about 20 minutes (must be refrigerated for several hours or overnight).

SERVING SIZE: ⅛ of yield. AMOUNT PER SERVING: 5.2 grams of carb, 3.8 grams of protein. TOTAL YIELD: 1 cream pie, filling only.

		CHO (g)	PRO (g)
1	prebaked pie crust (crust recipes begin on page 187)		
FILLING			
4	egg yolks	1.2	11.2
1	egg	0.6	6.0
2	tablespoons wheat (white) flour	11.5	1.0
1	tablespoon unsalted butter (⅛ stick)	0	0
3	tablespoons xylitol	5.4	0
5	tablespoons Splenda	7.5	0
½	teaspoon Stevia Plus (or equivalent)	0	0
1	cup coconut milk, canned	4.0	3.0
1	teaspoon vanilla extract	0.5	0
1	cup heavy cream	6.4	4.8
¾	cup finely grated, unsweetened coconut	4.5	4.5
	salt, trace	0	0
	Total	*41.6*	*30.5*

Preheat the oven to 350°F. Prepare an 8- or 9-inch pie pan with the crust of your choice, fully baked. Add the gram counts to the total.

In a medium mixing bowl, beat the egg yolks and egg until well mixed. Set aside.

Put the flour, butter, sweeteners, and coconut milk in the top of a double boiler. Keep the water at a simmer. Whisk the mixture until well combined. Stir occasionally as the milk begins to heat up, then whisk constantly until it begins to thicken. Remove from the heat.

Pour a small amount, about 2 tablespoons, into the beaten eggs. Beat the eggs vigorously. Repeat this two or three times, beating well each time. Pour the egg mixture into the double boiler pan. Return it over the hot water and whisk continuously until the mixture thickens. Remove from the heat. Beat in the vanilla extract, heavy cream, and salt. Stir in the grated coconut.

Put the pie crust you are using on a cookie sheet and carefully pour

the cream filling into it. Put the cookie sheet with the pie on it in the oven and bake for about 20 minutes. Do not overbake. Remove the pie from the oven, keeping it on the cookie sheet.

This pie calls for a meringue (page 184), so prepare it now. Leave the oven on and the pie on the cookie sheet. Spread the meringue over the pie and bake it for an additional 10 to 15 minutes. Add the gram counts for the meringue to the total.

When the pie is done, remove it from the oven and allow it to sit at room temperature for about 45 minutes before chilling it. Wait several hours or overnight to serve.

Pumpkin Cream Pie

Pumpkin surprise, creamy delight.

PREPARATION TIME: 20 minutes. BAKING TIME: about 20 minutes (must be refrigerated for several hours or overnight).

SERVING SIZE: ⅛ of yield. AMOUNT PER SERVING: 5.4 grams of carb, 3.6 grams of protein. TOTAL YIELD: 1 cream pie, filling only.

		CHO (g)	PRO (g)
1	prebaked pie crust		
	(crust recipes begin on page 187)		

FILLING

		CHO (g)	PRO (g)
4	egg yolks	1.2	11.2
1	egg	0.6	6.0
2	tablespoons wheat (white) flour	11.5	1.0
1	tablespoon unsalted butter (⅛ stick)	0	0
3	tablespoons xylitol	5.4	0
5	tablespoons Splenda	7.5	0
½	teaspoon Stevia Plus (or equivalent)	0	0
1¼	cups heavy cream	11.2	8.4
1	teaspoon vanilla extract	0.5	0
	salt, trace	0	0
½	cup canned pumpkin	4.0	2.0
1	teaspoon ground cinnamon	0.7	0
½	teaspoon ground cloves	0.5	0
	Total	*43.1*	*28.6*

Preheat the oven to 350°F. Prepare an 8- or 9- inch pie pan with the crust of your choice, fully baked. Add the gram counts to the total.

In a medium mixing bowl, beat the egg yolks and egg until well mixed. Set aside.

Put the flour, butter, sweeteners, and 1 cup of heavy cream in the top of a double boiler. Keep the water at a simmer. Whisk the mixture until well combined. Stir occasionally as the cream begins to heat up, then whisk constantly until it begins to thicken. Remove from the heat.

Pour a small amount, about 2 tablespoons, into the beaten eggs. Beat the eggs vigorously. Repeat this two or three times, beating well each time. Pour the egg mixture into the double boiler pan. Return it over the hot water and whisk continuously until the mixture thickens. Remove from the heat and beat in the remaining heavy cream, vanilla extract, and salt. Mix the pumpkin first with the two spices and then stir it in.

Put the pie crust you are using on a cookie sheet and carefully pour

the cream filling into it. Put the cookie sheet with the pie on it in the oven and bake for about 20 minutes. Do not overbake. Remove the pie from the oven, keeping it on the cookie sheet.

If you would like to add a meringue (page 184), prepare it now. Leave the oven on and the pie on the cookie sheet. Spread the meringue over the pie and bake it for an additional 10 to 15 minutes. Add the gram counts for the meringue to the total.

When the pie is done, remove it from the oven and allow it to sit at room temperature for about 45 minutes before chilling it. Wait several hours or overnight to serve. If you do not use meringue, serve with Whipped Cream Sauce (page 253) or with Toasted Pecan Topping (page 93) or with another topping of your choice. Add the gram counts for any topping to the total.

Lemon Cream Pie

The fabulous tartness of lemon merges wonderfully with the creamy sweetness of this terrific pie.

PREPARATION TIME: 20 minutes. BAKING TIME: about 20 minutes (must be refrigerated for several hours or overnight).

SERVING SIZE: ⅛ of yield. AMOUNT PER SERVING: 5.9 grams of carb, 3.0 grams of protein. TOTAL YIELD: 1 cream pie, filling only.

		CHO (g)	PRO (g)
1	prebaked pie crust (crust recipes begin on page 187)		

FILLING

		CHO (g)	PRO (g)
4	egg yolks	1.2	11.2
1	egg	0.6	6.0
2	tablespoons wheat (white) flour	11.5	1.0
1	tablespoon unsalted butter (⅛ stick)	0	0
4	tablespoons xylitol	7.2	0
5	tablespoons Splenda	7.5	0
½	teaspoon Stevia Plus (or equivalent)	0	0
1	tablespoon lemon peel, finely grated	1.0	0
1¾	cups heavy cream	11.2	8.4
1	teaspoon vanilla extract	0.5	0
	salt, trace	0	0
⅓	cup lemon juice	6.9	0
	Total	*47.6*	*26.6*

Preheat the oven to 350°F. Prepare an 8- or 9-inch pie pan with the crust of your choice, fully baked. Add the gram counts to the total.

In a medium mixing bowl, beat the egg yolks and the egg until well mixed. Set aside.

Put the flour, butter, sweeteners, lemon peel, and 1 cup of heavy cream in the top of a double boiler. Keep the water at a simmer. Whisk the mixture until well combined. Stir occasionally as the cream begins to heat up, then whisk constantly until it begins to thicken. Remove from the heat.

Pour a small amount, about 2 tablespoons, into the beaten eggs. Beat the eggs vigorously. Repeat this two or three times, beating well each time. Pour the egg mixture into the double boiler pan. Return it over the hot water and whisk continuously until the mixture thickens. Remove from the heat and beat in the remaining cream, vanilla extract, and salt. Stir in the lemon juice.

Put the pie crust you are using on a cookie sheet and carefully pour

the cream filling into it. Put the cookie sheet with the pie on it in the oven and bake for about 20 minutes. Do not overbake. Remove the pie from the oven, keeping it on the cookie sheet.

This pie calls for a meringue (page 184). Prepare it now. Leave the oven on and the pie on the cookie sheet. Spread the meringue over the pie and bake it for an additional 10 to 15 minutes. Add the gram counts for the meringue to the total.

Rhubarb Pie

The creamy egg mixture nicely tempers the tangy rhubarb, and the result is superb.

PREPARATION TIME: 25 minutes. BAKING TIME: about 50 minutes.

SERVING SIZE: ⅛ of yield. AMOUNT PER SERVING: 5.2 grams of carb, 3.5 grams of protein. TOTAL YIELD: one 8-inch pie, filling only.

		CHO (g)	PRO (g)
1	prebaked pie crust (crust recipes begin on page 187)		
RHUBARB FILLING			
4	cups crisp, fresh rhubarb	13.6	4.0
3	eggs	2.4	24.0
4	tablespoons xylitol	7.2	0
7	tablespoons Splenda	10.5	0
1½	teaspoons Stevia Plus (or equivalent)	0	0
1	teaspoon nutmeg (optional)	1.0	0
1	tablespoon ThickenThin not/Sugar thickener*	0	0
1	tablespoon cornstarch	7.0	0
	salt, trace	0	0
4	tablespoons unsalted butter (½ stick)	0	0
	Total	*41.7*	*28.0*

Preheat the oven to 350°F. Prepare the crust of your choice. If you use one of the Hot Water Pastry Crusts (beginning on page 187), pre-bake it for 10 to 15 minutes. Add the gram counts to the total.

Wash and dry the rhubarb, then cut it into ½-inch chunks. Put the pieces in a medium mixing bowl and set aside.

In a separate bowl, combine the eggs, sweeteners, nutmeg, ThickenThin thickener, cornstarch, and salt. Whisk together with a wire whisk just until thoroughly mixed; do not beat until thick and creamy.

Add the egg mixture to the rhubarb and mix well. Pour into the pie shell and dot with butter. Set the pie on a cookie sheet to catch any runs. Bake as directed or until the rhubarb is tender.

Variation: Creamy Rhubarb Dessert

Follow the directions for Rhubarb Pie above. Make these changes: omit the crust. Butter an 8-by-8-inch glass baking dish. Add an

---

*ThickenThin not/Sugar thickener is a fiber product by Expert Foods. See Sources or check the Internet if you cannot find it at your grocery store.

additional tablespoon of cornstarch to the egg-and-rhubarb mixture. Pour the mix in the baking dish. Dot with butter and bake at 350°F for about 45 to 50 minutes or until the rhubarb is soft. This recipe makes 8 servings. One serving has 6.0 grams of carb and 3.0 grams of protein.

Variation: **Blueberry Pie**

Follow the directions for Rhubarb Pie above. Make these changes: omit the rhubarb. Replace with 4 cups of fresh blueberries. Omit the nutmeg. Add 2 teaspoons of grated lemon peel to mixture. Each serving (⅛ of the pie) has 11.5 grams of carb.

Variation: **Cranberry-Blueberry Pie**

Follow the directions for Rhubarb Pie above. Make these changes: omit the rhubarb. Omit the nutmeg. Combine 2½ cups of fresh cranberries with 1½ cups of blueberries. Increase the xylitol by 1 tablespoon and the Splenda by 2 tablespoons. Each serving (⅛ of the pie) has 9.6 grams of carb.

Variation: **Strawberry-Rhubarb Pie**

Follow the directions for Rhubarb Pie above. Make these changes: reduce the rhubarb to 2 cups; add 2½ cups of sliced strawberries. Omit the nutmeg. Each serving (⅛ of the pie) has 7.7 grams of carb.

6

PUDDINGS, CUSTARDS, ICE CREAMS, JAMS, AND SAUCES

When you try to create small low-carb miracles, of all the food categories that you must shape, coax, and bend to the ways of low-carb cuisine, none is more obliging than the concoctions that follow. The wonderful secret they all share is that they are miles away from flour except for the occasional spoonful. It means that you do not have to put your energies into building elaborate make-believe facsimiles from scratch—as you must with every cookie, muffin, cake, or loaf of bread—you can work with the real thing. It is mainly the sweeteners that separate the high- from the low-carb world here. That problem is manageable. You should feel at home among the desserts in this chapter.

Cooking or mixing these desserts is usually neither elaborate nor time consuming, and the outcomes are pretty much reliable. Whenever I could shave time off a process, I have done so.

Some of these desserts are baked, many have a foolproof gelatin base, and many require the thickening of egg yolks either over hot water or in a saucepan over very low heat. Don't let this prospect discourage you. There are no mysteries. Do it a couple of times and you will probably wonder why you ever hesitated.

Often, I use lemon juice and lemon peel. You may find it practical to stock up on both ahead of time. Simply remove the peel or zest from a bunch of lemons before juicing them. Both can be frozen. If you put the lemon juice in small jars, you can have some available in the fridge at all times.

Most recipes will improve with—some even require—a relatively fine grind of "sugar"; remember it's helpful to process xylitol in a food processor before using. Keep the lid on the food processor while you grind the xylitol.

Many desserts contain chocolate, nearly always sugar-free chocolate, which is available in many forms and from many places.

You may have to experiment to find the flavor you like best, whether it's milk chocolate, semisweet chocolate, dark chocolate, or white chocolate. Sugar-free chocolates are expensive, mainly because sugar alcohol is expensive. Always check prices before you buy.

Cream Puff Shells

Quick and easy to make, the shells freeze well too. It is a perfect dessert to have on hand for instant retrieval.

PREPARATION TIME: 15 minutes. BAKING TIME: about 20 to 25 minutes.
SERVING SIZE: 1 cream puff shell. AMOUNT PER SERVING: 3.2 grams of carb, 4.4 grams of protein. TOTAL YIELD: 10 cream puff shells.

		CHO (g)	PRO (g)
5	tablespoons vital wheat gluten	7.5	29.0
¼	cup unbleached wheat (white) flour	23.0	3.0
	salt, trace	0	0
½	cup water	0	0
4	tablespoons unsalted butter (½ stick)	0	0
2	eggs, room temperature	1.2	12.0
	Total	*31.7*	*44.0*

Preheat the oven to 400°F. Prepare one large baking sheet with a silicone-coated liner.

Combine the wheat gluten, white flour, and salt in a small bowl and mix well. Set aside.

Combine the water and butter in a quart saucepan with a heavy bottom over medium heat. When the butter is melted and the liquid begins to bubble—and without removing the pan from the heat—add the flour mixture all at once. Stir vigorously with a wooden spoon until a smooth lump develops that follows the spoon around and leaves the sides of the pan. This takes a minute or less.

Remove the saucepan from the heat and put it on a heat-proof surface. Add one of the eggs, stirring with a sturdy whisk or wooden spoon, until the egg is blended into the dough. Repeat with the second egg. The dough should be smooth and hold soft peaks.

With 2 teaspoons, set mounds on the cookie sheet, allowing room for expansion. The cream puff shells will grow to about 3½ or 4 inches. If you want small shells, bake 12. You could even make very small cream puff shells, perhaps 20 or 25, to use as bite-size treats of any kind, even savory. (For savory fillings, see chapter 4 of *The Low-Carb Comfort Food Cookbook*.) Bake the shells for 20 to 25 minutes until golden. Check the smaller shells occasionally while baking. Put the shells on a cooling rack to cool. You can freeze them for future occasions.

Meringue Shells

You probably thought these were never to be revisited—after all, they are usually sugar, sugar, sugar with egg whites holding them together. Sugar alcohol does the trick here. The meringue ingredients are listed below. For directions to make the meringue, see page 132. Although the directions suggest that you can use either parchment or wax paper for baking—drying, really—the small meringue kisses described there can take the wax paper. Do not use it for meringue shells. They have to dry for many hours and the wax paper most likely will stick to them. It is hard to get off.

PREPARATION TIME: 20 minutes. BAKING TIME: several hours or overnight. SERVING SIZE: 1 meringue shell. AMOUNT PER SERVING: 3.8 grams of carb, 1.0 gram of protein. TOTAL YIELD: 6 large meringue shells.

		CHO (g)	PRO (g)
3	egg whites, room temperature	0.9	10.5
	salt, trace	0	0
¾	cup fine xylitol	21.6	0
1	teaspoon vanilla extract	0.5	0
	Total	*23.0*	*10.5*

To make the meringue shells, put 6 large, circular mounds on the parchment paper. Shape them a little with a spoon and make a depression in the center. For a more elegant look, squeeze the meringue through a pastry bag. A fairly large amount of the mixture will be lost in the process; be prepared for a rather sticky business. The shells will look lovely, though.

Tiramisu

This deliciously creamy cake is usually interlaced with ladyfingers soaked in espresso and a touch of coffee liqueur. The classic basic ingredient is a cheese called mascarpone, a special kind of cream cheese. It is not easy to find. If you do locate it, and wish to use it, omit the cream cheese, sour cream, and ¼ cup of the heavy cream that make up for it here. I use Vanilla Cookies (page 100), Macadamia Nut Biscotti or Almond Biscotti (pages 105 and 106), or small chunks of Best Yellow Cake (page 145) in place of the ladyfingers.

PREPARATION TIME: 30 minutes.

SERVING SIZE: ¹⁄₁₅ of yield. AMOUNT PER SERVING: 5.8 grams of carb, 5.5 grams of protein. TOTAL YIELD: one 9-by-13-inch cake.

		CHO (g)	PRO (g)
FILLING			
40	Vanilla Cookies (page 100)*	28.0	40.0
½	cup espresso or double-strength coffee, cool	0	0
3	tablespoons Kahlúa liqueur	20.0	0
CAKE			
1¼	cup heavy cream	8.0	6.0
1	8-ounce packet of cream cheese, very soft	6.4	16.8
¼	cup sour cream	2.0	1.2
2	teaspoons vanilla extract	1.0	0
	salt, trace	0	0
6	egg yolks	1.8	16.8
4	tablespoons xylitol	7.2	0
7	tablespoons Splenda	10.5	0
TOPPING			
1½	ounces sugar-free semisweet chocolate, grated	4.0	1.0
	Total	*88.9*	*81.8*

Butter a 9-by-13-inch glass baking dish (or one of a similar size).

Spread the cookies in the bottom of a large pan (not the one for the cake). Avoid extensive overlapping. Combine the espresso and the

---

*Instead of Vanilla Cookies, you can use about 30 biscotti. Macadamia Nut Biscotti is on page 105. Break the biscotti in half. You can also use Best Yellow Cake (page 145). Slice a loaf (10 slices to a loaf) and cut each slice in approximately 1-inch squares.

Kahlúa. Drizzle this cool liquid almost by the drop over the assembled cookies to make sure all get moistened (if the cookies get mushy, they are difficult to move later). Set aside.

Combine ¼ cup of the heavy cream, cream cheese, sour cream, vanilla extract, and salt in the bowl of an electric stand mixer or a large mixing bowl. Beat the cream cheese mix until fluffy and until it increases considerably in volume. Do not underbeat.

Combine the egg yolks, sweeteners, and ¼ cup of heavy cream in the top of a double boiler (off heat); beat well. Set the pot over hot water kept at a simmer. With a balloon whisk or portable electric beater, whisk the mixture, slowly at first, but whisk continuously as it begins to heat up. When the mixture is thick and creamy, remove it from the heat. Cool the mixture for about 5 minutes in the fridge. Stir or beat it briefly before adding it, slowly, to the cream cheese mixture. Mix well. In a separate bowl, beat the remaining cream until quite firm but still slightly soft. Fold the whipped cream into the cream cheese mixture.

Assemble the tiramisu. Carefully, using a small spatula, place 20 of the cookies on the bottom of the baking dish, spreading them out evenly. Follow this with about ⅓ of the batter, and repeat the cookie process. Cover with the rest of the batter, forming a level surface. Sprinkle with the grated chocolate. Cover. Chill the dessert for several hours or overnight. This cake keeps well in the fridge for two or three days and can also be frozen.

Chocolate Swirl Tiramisu

Perhaps an unorthodox variation of tiramisu but a tasty one, if you love chocolate.

PREPARATION TIME: 30 minutes.
SERVING SIZE: ⅟₁₅ of yield. AMOUNT PER SERVING: 6.4 grams of carb, 4.8 grams of protein. TOTAL YIELD: one 9-by-13-inch cake.

		CHO (g)	PRO (g)
FILLING			
40	Chocolate Cookies (page 101)*	28.0	40.0
⅔	cup espresso or double-strength coffee, cool	0	0
1	tablespoon Kahlúa liqueur	7.0	0
CAKE			
1½	cups heavy cream	9.6	7.2
1	8-ounce packet of cream cheese, very soft	6.4	16.8
2	teaspoons vanilla extract	1.0	0
	salt, trace	0	0
4	tablespoons xylitol	7.2	0
7	tablespoons Splenda	10.5	0
8	ounces sugar-free semisweet or milk chocolate	21.6	8.0
TOPPING			
1½	ounce sugar-free semisweet chocolate, grated	4.0	1.0
	Total	*95.3*	*73.0*

Butter a 9-by-13-inch glass baking dish (or a dish of similar size).

Spread the cookies in the bottom of a large pan (not the cake pan). Avoid extensive overlapping. Combine the espresso and the Kahlúa. Drizzle this cool liquid almost by the drop over the assembled cookies to make sure all get moistened (if the cookies get mushy, they are difficult to move later). Set aside.

Combine ⅓ cup of the heavy cream, cream cheese, vanilla extract, salt, and sweeteners in the bowl of an electric stand mixer or a large mixing bowl. Beat the cream cheese mix until very fluffy and until

---

*Instead of Chocolate Cookies, you can use about 30 biscotti. Macadamia Nut Biscotti is on page 105. Break the biscotti in half. You can also use Best Yellow Cake (page 145). Slice a loaf (10 slices to a loaf) and cut each slice in approximately 1-inch squares.

it increases considerably in volume. This takes a while. Do not underbeat.

While the cream cheese is being mixed, or once this has been done, combine the chocolate of your choice with 3 tablespoons of the heavy cream in a microwavable bowl and microwave for about 40 seconds or until the chocolate is melted. You can also do this in a double boiler over hot water; keep the water at or below a simmer. Stir the mixture until completely smooth. Remove from the heat and refrigerate for about 3 minutes.

In a separate bowl, beat the remaining cream until quite firm but still slightly soft. Fold the cream into the cream cheese mixture. Mix well.

Add the chocolate mixture to the cream cheese mixture and stir just enough to get a good distribution of chocolate swirls throughout.

Assemble the tiramisu. Carefully, using a small spatula, put 20 of the cookies on the bottom of the baking dish, spreading them out evenly. Follow this with about ⅓ of the tiramisu mixture, and repeat the cookie process. Cover with the rest of the batter, forming a level surface. Sprinkle this with the grated chocolate. Cover. Chill for several hours or overnight. Cut into 15 pieces (about 2 by 3 inches) or whatever size you want.

This cake keeps well in the fridge for two or three days and can also be frozen.

Marshmallow Fluff

This will be much in demand, especially with kids. Luckily, it is a cinch to make. Please note that xylitol is the best sugar to use here.

PREPARATION TIME: 15 minutes (needs chilling).
SERVING SIZE: ⅛ of yield. AMOUNT PER SERVING: 3.3 grams of carb, 4.3 grams of protein. TOTAL YIELD: about 8 servings, ½ cup each.

		CHO (g)	PRO (g)
1	packet gelatin	0	6.0
½	cup water	0	0
1½	cups heavy cream	9.6	7.2
2	teaspoons vanilla extract	1.0	0
	salt, trace	0	0
4	egg whites*	1.2	14.0
7	tablespoons xylitol	10.8	0
	Total	*22.6*	*27.2*

Soak the gelatin in the water and set aside.

In a quart saucepan with a heavy bottom, scald the cream over low heat until the cream comes to a boil; stir often. Remove the pan from the heat. Stir in the vanilla extract, salt, and gelatin. Stir until the gelatin is completely dissolved. Chill this mixture. Wait until it begins to thicken slightly, like soup. This takes approximately 60 to 75 minutes. Stir occasionally to prevent a skin from forming.

Once the cream begins to thicken, put the egg whites in a medium mixing bowl and beat until fairly stiff while maintaining soft peaks. Gradually add the xylitol, no more than a tablespoon at a time, beating thoroughly after each addition.

Slowly stir the gelatin mixture into the egg whites in about 3 portions, stirring lightly with a small balloon whisk after each addition. Pour into dessert glasses or a dessert bowl. It is delicious topped with a handful of fresh berries (raspberries, strawberries, blueberries) or a flavorful sauce. Sauce recipes begin on page 250. Add the gram counts for any additions.

---

*These egg whites are not cooked. To be entirely safe you might want to use pasteurized egg whites or powdered egg whites, available at most grocery stores.

Rich Vanilla Pudding

Lush and velvety smooth.

PREPARATION TIME: 15 minutes (needs chilling).
SERVING SIZE: ⅛ of yield. AMOUNT PER SERVING: 3.3 grams of carb,
4.7 grams of protein. TOTAL YIELD: about 4 cups, eight ½ cup servings.

		CHO (g)	PRO (g)
1	packet gelatin	0	6.0
½	cup water	0	0
4	egg yolks	1.2	11.2
1¼	cups heavy cream	8.0	6.0
3	teaspoons vanilla extract	1.5	0
2	tablespoons Splenda	3.0	0
7	tablespoons xylitol	10.8	0
	salt, trace	0	0
4	egg whites*	1.2	14.0
	Total	*25.7*	*37.2*

Soak the gelatin in the water and set aside.

Combine the egg yolks and the heavy cream in a double boiler over
hot, simmering water. Beat the mixture vigorously to combine. Stir
occasionally until it begins to warm up, then beat continuously until the
mixture thickens. Remove from the heat. Stir in the gelatin until dissolved.

Add the vanilla extract, sweeteners, and salt. Chill this mixture.
Wait until it begins to thicken slightly, like soup. This takes approximately 45 to 60 minutes. Stir occasionally to prevent a skin from
forming.

Put the egg whites in a medium mixing bowl and beat until quite
stiff but maintaining soft peaks.

Slowly stir the gelatin mixture into the egg whites, stirring lightly
with a small balloon whisk. Pour the pudding into dessert glasses or a
dessert bowl. Serve with fresh berries (raspberries, strawberries, blueberries) or a flavorful sauce. Sauce recipes begin on page 250. Add
the gram counts for any additions.

*These egg whites are not cooked. To be entirely safe you might want to use pasteurized egg
whites or powdered egg whites, available at most grocery stores.

Lemon Cloud Pudding

Airy, light, with a lively lemon flavor. Although a pudding, this can become a pie if you put it in a prebaked pie shell (page 187).

PREPARATION TIME: 15 minutes (needs chilling).
SERVING SIZE: ⅛ of yield. AMOUNT PER SERVING: 4.5 grams of carb, 3.0 grams of protein. TOTAL YIELD: about 4 cups.

		CHO (g)	PRO (g)
1½	teaspoons of gelatin (½ packet)	0	3.0
¼	cup water	0	0
4	egg yolks	1.2	11.2
3	tablespoons xylitol	5.4	0
5	tablespoons Splenda	7.5	0
1	teaspoon Stevia Plus (or equivalent)	0	0
	salt, trace	0	0
½	cup fresh lemon juice	10.4	0
2	teaspoons vanilla extract	1.0	0
1½	cups heavy cream	9.6	7.2
2	egg whites* (optional)	0.6	7.0
	Total	*35.7*	*28.4*

Soak the gelatin in the ¼ cup of water. Set aside.

Put the egg yolks, sweeteners, salt, and lemon juice in the top of a double boiler or in a heavy-bottomed 1- or 1½-quart saucepan and whisk together (off heat).

Put the double boiler over hot, simmering water; use a low heat setting if you use the stove top. Use a balloon whisk and stir frequently at first. As the mixture heats up, beat continuously until it thickens. Remove from the heat. Stir in the vanilla extract and the gelatin. Stir until the gelatin is dissolved. Chill the mixture until it begins to thicken slightly; this takes about 40 to 60 minutes. Stir occasionally.

Beat the heavy cream in a medium mixing bowl until it is thick but not stiff. In a separate bowl, whip the egg whites until firm but not stiff. Slowly fold the lemon-egg mixture into the whipped cream. Mix until smooth. Fold in the egg whites last.

Pour the lemon pudding into dessert glasses or a dessert bowl. Chill for a few hours or overnight. If you like, serve with a dollop of whipped cream. Count any extra carb grams.

---

*The egg whites are not cooked. To be entirely safe, use pasteurized egg whites or powdered egg whites instead, available at most grocery stores.

Peanut Butter Fudge Pudding

Rich and sublime. If you like peanut butter and fudge, this may become your all-time favorite dessert.

PREPARATION TIME: 15 minutes.

SERVING SIZE: ⅛ of yield. AMOUNT PER SERVING: 5.5 grams of carb, 4.7 grams of protein. TOTAL YIELD: 8 servings, about ½ cup each.

		CHO (g)	PRO (g)
10	tablespoons heavy cream	4.0	3.0
4	ounces cream cheese, soft	3.2	18.4
3	tablespoons unsalted butter (⅜ stick), soft	0	0
2	teaspoons vanilla extract	1.0	0
	salt, trace	0	0
2	tablespoons xylitol	3.6	0
4	tablespoons Splenda	6.0	0
1	teaspoon Stevia Plus (or equivalent)	0	0
¼	cup natural peanut butter	10.0	14.0
2	ounces sugar-free milk chocolate (or semisweet chocolate)	5.4	2.0
	Total	*33.2*	*37.4*

Reserve 2 tablespoons of the cream. Whip the rest until firm but not stiff and chill until ready to use.

In a medium mixing bowl, combine the cream cheese, butter, vanilla extract, salt, and sweeteners. Beat these ingredients until they are thick and fluffy; they should increase considerably in volume. Do not underbeat. Add the peanut butter and beat again to increase volume. Add the chilled whipped cream into the mix. Stir well.

Put the reserved cream and the chocolate in a small microwavable bowl and microwave for about 25 seconds or until the chocolate is melted. Stir until smooth. You can do this over hot water too; keep the water at or below a simmer. Cool the chocolate for about 3 or 4 minutes. Carefully add the chocolate mixture to the dessert. Stir just enough to create dark ribbons throughout the dessert. Spoon into dessert glasses or a dessert bowl. This dessert is ready to eat almost immediately and will keep well for several days. Remove from the fridge about 30 minutes before serving.

Double Chocolate Pudding

As decadent as it sounds. But oh so good!

PREPARATION TIME: 20 minutes.

SERVING SIZE: ⅛ of yield. AMOUNT PER SERVING: 3.4 grams of carb, 2.0 grams of protein. TOTAL YIELD: 8 servings, about ½ cup each.

		CHO (g)	PRO (g)
¾	cup heavy cream	4.8	3.6
5	ounces soft cream cheese	4.0	10.5
4	tablespoons unsalted butter (½ stick), soft	0	0
2	teaspoons vanilla extract	1.0	0
	salt, trace	0	0
2	tablespoons xylitol	3.6	0
4	tablespoons Splenda	6.0	0
1	teaspoon Stevia Plus (or equivalent)	0	0
1½	ounces sugar-free milk chocolate	4.0	1.0
1½	ounces sugar-free semisweet chocolate	4.0	1.0
	Total	*27.4*	*16.1*

Reserve 4 tablespoons of the cream. Whip the rest until firm but not stiff, and chill until ready to use.

In a medium mixing bowl, combine the cream cheese, butter, vanilla extract, salt, and sweeteners. Beat these ingredients until they are thick and fluffy; they should increase considerably in volume. Do not underbeat. Fold in the whipped cream and stir well.

Combine 2 tablespoons of the reserved cream with each of the 2 chocolates in separate microwavable bowls and microwave each for about 20 seconds or until the chocolate is melted. You can do this in a double boiler over hot water too; keep the water at or below a simmer. Stir until smooth. Cool for 5 minutes.

Remove one half of the cream cheese mixture and put it into another bowl. Stir the semisweet chocolate into one container, the milk chocolate into the other. To combine them, alternate the mixtures in dessert glasses, starting with one layer and finishing with the other. You can also intermix the two colors, stirring only enough to create different shades throughout. Refrigerate.

This dessert is ready within an hour. It will keep well for several days. Remove from the fridge about 30 minutes before serving.

Chocolate Soufflé

It is easy to make and—in case making a soufflé worries you—should turn out just fine. Timing is of the essence, though. Serve this promptly; soufflés do not stay up long.

PREPARATION TIME: 35 minutes. BAKING TIME: about 35 to 45 minutes.
SERVING SIZE: ⅛ of yield. AMOUNT PER SERVING: 5.5 grams of carb, 4.5 grams of protein. TOTAL YIELD: 1 casserole.

		CHO (g)	PRO (g)
3	tablespoons unsalted butter (⅜ stick)	0	0
1	cup heavy cream	6.4	4.8
1	ounce unsweetened baking chocolate (square)	4.0	4.0
2	ounces sugar-free semisweet chocolate	5.4	2.0
3	tablespoons xylitol	5.4	0
5	tablespoons Splenda	7.5	0
2	tablespoons Wondra flour	11.5	1.0
2	teaspoons vanilla extract	1.0	0
4	eggs, separated, room temperature	2.4	24.0
	Total	*43.6*	*35.8*

About 35 minutes before you plan to bake the soufflé, put it together. Preheat the oven to 350°F. Butter a straight-sided casserole dish.

Combine 1 tablespoon of the butter, 2 tablespoons of heavy cream (reserve the rest), chocolates, and sweeteners in the top of a double boiler. Stir over hot water that is kept at or below a simmer. Stir frequently until the chocolate is melted. Remove from the heat and set aside.

In a medium, heavy-bottomed saucepan, heat the remaining cream with the remaining butter. Before the cream reaches a boiling point, stir in the flour, 1 tablespoon at a time. Sprinkle the flour on top of the cream and whisk in. Stir continuously after that until the cream thickens. Remove the pan from the heat. Add the vanilla extract.

Put the egg yolks in a small mixing bowl and beat until well mixed. Add about 2 tablespoons of the hot cream mixture to the eggs, beating well; repeat. Add the yolks to the cream in the saucepan. Stir well. Add the melted chocolate and stir well again.

Beat the egg whites until quite stiff. Fold them into the creamy mixture. Pour the mixture into the casserole. Bake for about 35 to 45 minutes or until the soufflé is nicely puffed up. Serve immediately. Sauce recipes begin on page 250.

Strawberry Soufflé

Strawberry sweetness, soufflé creaminess—aaah.

PREPARATION TIME: 30 minutes. BAKING TIME: about 35 to 45 minutes.
SERVING SIZE: ⅛ of yield. AMOUNT PER SERVING: 6.7 grams of carb,
4.3 grams of protein. TOTAL YIELD: 1 casserole.

		CHO (g)	PRO (g)
2	cups fresh, ripe strawberries	15.6	2.0
1	tablespoon lemon juice	1.3	0
⅓	cup cognac or brandy	0	0
3	tablespoons xylitol	5.4	0
5	tablespoons Splenda	7.5	0
3	tablespoons unsalted butter (⅜ stick)	0	0
1½	cups heavy cream	9.6	7.2
2	tablespoons Wondra flour	11.5	1.0
4	eggs, separated, room temperature	2.4	24.0
	Total	*53.3*	*34.2*

Use clean strawberries without blemishes. Slice and put them in a medium mixing bowl. Add the lemon juice and the cognac or brandy. Add the sweeteners but reserve 1 tablespoon of Splenda. Stir well. Set aside, stirring them occasionally. You can also do this quite early in the day for a delicious flavor. In that case, keep the strawberries refrigerated.

About 30 minutes before you plan to bake the soufflé, put it together. Preheat the oven to 350°F. Butter a straight-sided casserole dish.

Combine the butter and 1 cup of the heavy cream in a saucepan and heat over low heat. Use a balloon whisk to stir occasionally. When the cream heats up, but well before it boils, sprinkle 1 tablespoon of Wondra flour on top and whisk it into the cream; repeat with the second tablespoon. Stir continuously until the cream thickens. Remove the pan from the heat.

Put the egg yolks in a small mixing bowl and beat until well mixed. Add about 2 tablespoons of the hot cream mixture to the egg yolks and beat vigorously. Add more of the cream mixture in small amounts, about ½ cup in all, beating after each addition. Return the egg mixture to the remaining cream in the saucepan. Set aside.

Whip the egg whites until they form firm but soft peaks and fold them into the sauce.

Put the strawberries in the bottom of the casserole. Do not transfer the marinating juice that has accumulated in the bowl; save it. Pour the hot egg sauce over the strawberries and bake the casserole for about 35 to 45 minutes or until puffed up high and golden brown.

While the soufflé is baking, whip the remaining ½ cup of cream until firm but still soft. Add the reserved tablespoon of Splenda. Pour dollops of the cream over the soufflé when it comes from the oven. Heat and drizzle the strawberry juice over it as well. Serve the soufflé right away.

Peach Soufflé

A little high in carb count—it's just for that occasional splurge. There is something special about peaches.

PREPARATION TIME: 35 minutes. BAKING TIME: about 35 to 45 minutes. SERVING SIZE: ⅛ of yield. AMOUNT PER SERVING: 8.4 grams of carb, 4.3 grams of protein. TOTAL YIELD: 1 casserole.

		CHO (g)	PRO (g)
2	cups fresh, ripe peaches, peeled and sliced	30.8	2.0
⅓	cup cognac or brandy	0	0
3	tablespoons xylitol	5.4	0
5	tablespoons Splenda	7.5	0
3	tablespoons unsalted butter (⅜ stick)	0	0
1½	cups heavy cream	9.6	7.2
2	tablespoons Wondra flour	11.5	1.0
4	eggs, separated, room temperature	2.4	24.0
	Total	*67.2*	*34.2*

You need perfect peaches for this one—ripe and with tons of flavor. Put them in a medium mixing bowl. Add the cognac or brandy and the sweeteners. Reserve 1 tablespoon of Splenda. Stir well. Stir the peaches occasionally while you prepare the soufflé. You can also get the peaches ready earlier in the day for a more concentrated flavor. If you do that, keep them refrigerated.

About 35 minutes before you plan to bake the soufflé, put it together. Preheat the oven to 350°F. Butter a straight-sided casserole dish.

Combine the butter and 1 cup of the heavy cream in a medium saucepan and heat over low heat. Use a balloon whisk and stir occasionally. When the cream heats up, but well before it boils, sprinkle 1 tablespoon of flour on top and whisk it into the cream; repeat with the second tablespoon. Stir continuously until the cream thickens. Remove the pan from the heat.

Put the egg yolks in a small mixing bowl and beat until well mixed. Add about 2 tablespoons of the hot cream mixture to the egg yolks and beat vigorously. Add more cream in small amounts, about ½ cup in all, beating after each addition. Return the egg mixture to the remaining cream in the saucepan. Set aside.

Whip the egg whites until they form firm but soft peaks and fold them into the sauce.

Put the peaches in the bottom of the casserole. Do not transfer any marinating juice that has accumulated in the bowl; save it. Pour the hot egg sauce over the peaches and bake the casserole for about 35 to 45 minutes or until puffed up high and golden brown.

While the soufflé is baking, whip the remaining ½ cup of cream until firm but still soft. Add the reserved tablespoon of Splenda. Pour dollops of the cream over the soufflé when it comes from the oven. Heat and drizzle the peach juice over it as well. Serve the soufflé right away.

Vanilla Custard

An old favorite, with all the comforting goodness of vanilla.

PREPARATION TIME: 15 minutes. BAKING TIME: about 30 to 45 minutes.
SERVING SIZE: ⅙ of yield. AMOUNT PER SERVING: 5.3 grams of carbs, 4.7 grams of protein. TOTAL YIELD: 6 custard cups.

		CHO (g)	PRO (g)
2	egg yolks	0.6	5.6
2	eggs	1.2	12.0
3	tablespoons xylitol	5.4	0
5	tablespoons Splenda	7.5	0
1	teaspoon Stevia Plus (or equivalent)	0	0
	salt, trace	0	0
¼	teaspoon ground nutmeg (optional)	0.3	0
2	cups heavy cream	12.8	9.6
2	teaspoons vanilla extract	1.0	0

TOPPING

		CHO (g)	PRO (g)
1	ounce sugar-free semisweet chocolate, grated	2.7	1.0
	Total	*31.5*	*28.2*

Preheat the oven to 325°F. You will need 6 lightly buttered custard cups or ramekins.

Put the egg yolks, eggs, sweeteners, salt, optional nutmeg, and 1 cup of heavy cream in the top of a double boiler or in a heavy-bottomed 1- or 1½-quart saucepan. Whisk together (off heat).

Put the pot over hot, simmering water; if you use the stove top, do it on a low heat setting. Beat the mixture occasionally. When it heats up, whisk it continuously until it thickens. Remove from the heat. Beat in the vanilla extract and the remaining heavy cream. If you want to strain the custard, do it now.

Pour the custard into the ramekins. Set them inside a shallow baking pan and put it in the oven. Pour warm water in the bottom of the baking pan. Bake the custard for about 30 to 45 minutes. When done, the surface should lose its gloss and the custard should shake like jelly if touched lightly. It should not brown. Cool the custard for 20 minutes at room temperature; then refrigerate for a few hours. To prevent a skin from forming, cover the tops with rounds of wax paper cut to fit.

Before serving, sprinkle the custard with the grated chocolate. A dollop of whipped cream goes well with this (for Whipped Cream Sauce, see page 253), or sprinkle a spoonful of Praline (page 280) over the top. Add the extra carb grams.

Mocha Custard

Yum—mocha goodness throughout.

PREPARATION TIME: 15 minutes. BAKING TIME: about 30 to 45 minutes.
SERVING SIZE: ⅙ of yield. AMOUNT PER SERVING: 5.6 grams of carb, 4.6 grams of protein. TOTAL YIELD: 6 custard cups.

		CHO (g)	PRO (g)
2	ounces sugar-free semisweet chocolate	5.4	2.0
1½	cups heavy cream	9.6	7.2
½	cup espresso or double-strength coffee	0	0
2	egg yolks	0.6	5.6
2	eggs	1.2	12.0
3	tablespoons xylitol	5.4	0
5	tablespoons Splenda	7.5	0
	salt, trace	0	0
2	teaspoons vanilla extract	1.0	0

TOPPING

1	ounce sugar-free semisweet chocolate, grated	2.7	1.0
	Total	*33.4*	*27.8*

Preheat the oven to 325°F. You will need 6 lightly buttered custard cups or ramekins.

Put the chocolate and 2 tablespoons of the heavy cream in a microwavable bowl and microwave for about 20 seconds or until the chocolate is melted. Stir until smooth. Set aside.

Combine the egg yolks, eggs, sweeteners, salt, and 1 cup of the heavy cream in the top of a double boiler or in a heavy-bottomed medium saucepan. Whisk together (off heat).

Put the pot over hot, simmering water; if you use the stove top, do it on a low heat setting. Beat the mixture occasionally as it heats up; once it is hot, whisk continuously until it thickens. Remove from the heat. Beat in the chocolate, remaining cream, and vanilla extract. If you want to strain the custard, do it now.

Pour the custard into the ramekins. Set them inside a shallow baking pan and put them in the oven. Pour some warm water in the bottom of the baking pan. Bake the custard for about 30 to 45 minutes. When done, the surface should lose its gloss and the custard should shake like jelly if touched lightly. It should not brown. Allow the custard to cool at room temperature for 20 minutes; then refrigerate for a few hours. To prevent a skin from forming, cover the tops with rounds of wax paper cut to fit.

Before serving, sprinkle the custard with grated chocolate. A dollop of whipped cream goes well with this (for Whipped Cream Sauce, see page 253). Add the extra carb grams.

Wine Custard

Sounds a touch odd? Just try it—I think you'll love it.

PREPARATION TIME: 15 minutes. BAKING TIME: about 30 to 45 minutes.
SERVING SIZE: ⅙ of yield. AMOUNT PER SERVING: 5.9 grams of carb, 3.6 grams
of protein. TOTAL YIELD: 6 custard cups.

		CHO (g)	PRO (g)
6	egg yolks	1.8	16.8
4	tablespoons xylitol	7.2	0.0
7	tablespoons Splenda	10.5	0
1	teaspoon Stevia Plus (or equivalent)	0	0
	salt, trace	0	0
1¼	cups dry white wine	10.0	0
¾	cup heavy cream	4.8	3.6

TOPPING

1	ounce sugar-free semisweet chocolate, grated	2.7	1.0
	Total	*37.0*	*21.4*

Preheat the oven to 325°F. You will need 6 lightly buttered custard
cups or whatever number you prefer.

In a medium mixing bowl, beat the egg yolks, sweeteners, and salt
until thick and creamy. Set aside.

Heat the wine in the top of a double boiler or in a heavy-bottomed
medium saucepan. When the wine is hot, pour it slowly, almost drop
by drop, into the beaten egg yolks, beating the eggs as you do this.

Return the egg-wine mix to the double boiler. Keep water at a simmer; if you use the stove top, use a low setting. Whisk the mixture
continuously until it thickens. Beat in the heavy cream and remove
the pot from the heat. If you want to strain the custard, do it now.

Pour the custard into the baking cups. Set them inside a shallow
baking pan and put them in the oven. Pour some warm water in the
bottom of the baking pan. Bake the custard for about 30 to 45 minutes. When done, the surface should lose its gloss and the custard
should shake like jelly if touched lightly. It should not brown. Allow
the custard to cool at room temperature for 20 minutes; then refrigerate for a few hours. To prevent a skin from forming, cover the tops
with rounds of wax paper cut to fit.

Before serving the custard, sprinkle with grated chocolate. You can
also add a dollop of whipped cream and sprinkle the chocolate on top
of it. For Whipped Cream Sauce, see page 253. Add the extra carb
grams.

Raspberry Dream

For when you're dreaming of raspberries . . .

PREPARATION TIME: 10 minutes (if Basic Custard Sauce, page 250, is available).

SERVING SIZE: ⅛ of yield. AMOUNT PER SERVING: 5.4 grams of carb, 2.0 grams of protein. TOTAL YIELD: approximately eight to nine ½ cup servings.

		CHO (g)	PRO (g)
3	cups fresh raspberries	17.0	2.0
3	tablespoons xylitol	5.4	0
5	tablespoons Splenda	7.5	0
½	cup heavy cream	3.2	2.4
1	cup Basic Custard Sauce (page 250)	9.8	9.0

TOPPING

		CHO (g)	PRO (g)
2	ounces sugar-free semisweet grated chocolate	5.4	2.0
	Total	*48.3*	*15.4*

Put the 3 cups of fresh raspberries in a medium mixing bowl. Mix with the sweeteners.

Whip the heavy cream until firm but not stiff and combine with the Basic Custard Sauce. Fold this mixture into the raspberries. Pour into dessert glasses or a serving bowl. Sprinkle with the grated chocolate. This dessert should be eaten the day it is made.

Bavarian Cream

The old familiar, now made low-carb. Gelatin based, this is virtually foolproof.

PREPARATION TIME: 15 minutes (requires some chilling time).
SERVING SIZE: ⅛ of yield. AMOUNT PER SERVING: 2.9 grams of carb, 3.8 grams of protein. TOTAL YIELD: about 8 individual servings.

		CHO (g)	PRO (g)
1	packet gelatin	0	6.0
½	cup water	0	0
4	egg yolks	1.2	11.2
3	tablespoons xylitol	5.4	0
5	tablespoons Splenda	7.5	0
1½	teaspoons Stevia Plus (or equivalent)	0	0
1½	cups heavy cream	8.0	6.0
	salt, trace	0	0
2	teaspoons vanilla extract	1.0	0
2	egg whites* (optional)	0.6	7.0
	Total	*23.7*	*30.2*

Soak the gelatin in the water. Set aside.

Beat the egg yolks and sweeteners in a small bowl until thick and creamy.

Heat ½ cup of the heavy cream in the top of a double boiler or in a heavy-bottomed medium saucepan. Put the double boiler over simmering water; use a low heat setting if you're using the stove top.

When the cream is hot, beat it almost drop by drop into the beaten egg yolks. Beat well. Return all to the double boiler and beat until the mixture thickens. Remove from the heat. Stir in the gelatin until it is dissolved. Stir in the salt and the vanilla extract. If you want to strain the mixture, do it now. Chill the mixture for about 5 minutes.

Whip the remaining cream until thick but not stiff. Set aside. Whip the egg whites, if used, until quite firm but with soft peaks. Gently fold the egg whites into the egg-yolk mixture, followed by the whipped cream. Pour the dessert in a serving bowl or dessert glasses. Chill for several hours or overnight.

Great topped with fresh berries such as strawberries, raspberries, or blueberries. If desired, add a touch of Splenda to the berries. You can also use a dessert sauce; sauce recipes begin on page 250. Count any extra carb grams for toppings and sauces.

---

*The egg whites are used raw. If you prefer, use pasteurized egg whites, available at most grocery stores.

Chocolate Bavarian Cream

A popular dessert, good all year round.

PREPARATION TIME: 15 minutes (requires some chilling time).
SERVING SIZE: ⅛ of yield. AMOUNT PER SERVING: 4.5 grams of carb, 4.5 grams of protein. TOTAL YIELD: about 8 individual servings.

		CHO (g)	PRO (g)
1	packet gelatin	0	6.0
½	cup cold water	0	0
1¾	cups heavy cream	11.2	8.4
1	ounce unsweetened baking chocolate (1 square)	4.0	4.0
2	ounces sugar-free semisweet chocolate	5.4	2.0
4	egg yolks	1.2	11.2
3	tablespoons xylitol	5.4	0
5	tablespoons Splenda	7.5	0
1	teaspoon Stevia Plus (or equivalent)	0	0
2	teaspoons vanilla extract	1.0	0
	salt, trace	0	0
2	egg whites* (optional)	0.6	7.0
	Total	*36.3*	*38.6*

Soak the gelatin in the water. Set aside.

Combine 3 tablespoons of the heavy cream (reserve the rest) and the chocolates in the top of a double boiler. Stir over hot water kept at or below a simmer. Stir frequently until the chocolate is melted. Remove from the heat and set aside.

Beat the egg yolks and the sweeteners in a small bowl until thick and creamy. Heat ½ cup of the heavy cream in the top of a double boiler or in a heavy-bottomed medium saucepan. Put the double boiler over simmering water. Use a low heat setting if you use the stove top.

When the cream is hot, beat it slowly, almost drop by drop, into the beaten egg yolks. Return all to the double boiler and beat until the mixture thickens. Remove from the heat and stir in the gelatin until it is dissolved. Stir in the melted chocolate, vanilla extract, and salt. If you want to strain the mixture, do it now. Chill the mixture for about 10 minutes.

Whip the remaining cream until thick but not stiff. Set aside. Whip

---

*The egg whites are used raw. If you prefer, use pasteurized egg whites, available in most grocery stores.

the egg whites, if used, until they are firm with soft peaks. Gently fold the egg whites into the egg-yolk mixture, followed by the whipped cream. Pour the dessert into a serving bowl or dessert glasses. Chill for several hours or overnight. Top with Whipped Cream Sauce on page 253. Add the extra carb grams.

Strawberry Bavarian Cream

This cooling indulgence really improves a hot day.

PREPARATION TIME: 15 minutes (requires some chilling time).
SERVING SIZE: ⅛ of yield. AMOUNT PER SERVING: 6.9 grams of carb, 2.3 grams of protein. TOTAL YIELD: 8 to 10 servings.

		CHO (g)	PRO (g)
1½	packets gelatin	0	6.0
¼	cup water	0	0
1	tablespoon lemon juice	1.3	0
4	cups fresh, ripe strawberries	31.2	2.0
3	tablespoons xylitol sugar	5.4	0
5	tablespoons Splenda	7.5	0
1	teaspoon Stevia Plus (or equivalent)	0	0
	salt, trace	0	0
1½	cups heavy cream	9.6	7.2
	Total	*55.0*	*15.2*

Soak the gelatin in the water and the lemon juice. Set aside.

Clean the strawberries and mash lightly. Put them in a medium mixing bowl. Mix the sweeteners and the salt. Stir into the strawberries and mix well. Set aside.

In a small saucepan over low heat, warm the gelatin mixture until the gelatin is completely dissolved. Pour this over the strawberries and mix well. Put the strawberries in the fridge and allow to thicken slightly (about 45 minutes). Check on them and stir occasionally.

Beat the cream until it is thick and firm, but not stiff, and mix it into the thickened strawberries. Spoon the strawberries into dessert glasses or a dessert bowl. Chill until set.

Cranberry Bavarian Cream

Crisp and zesty, a new twist on an old favorite.

PREPARATION TIME: 15 minutes (requires some chilling time).

SERVING SIZE: ⅛ of yield. AMOUNT PER SERVING: 6.5 grams of carb, 1.9 grams of protein. TOTAL YIELD: 8 to 10 servings.

		CHO (g)	PRO (g)
1	packet gelatin	0	6.0
¾	cup water	0	0
1	tablespoon lemon juice	1.3	0
3	cups cranberries	24.0	2.0
4	tablespoons xylitol	7.2	0
7	tablespoons Splenda	10.5	0
1	teaspoon Stevia Plus (or equivalent)	0	0
	salt, trace	0	0
1½	cup heavy cream	9.6	7.2
	Total	*52.6*	*15.2*

Soak the gelatin in ¼ cup of the water and the lemon juice. Set aside.

Put the cranberries in a saucepan with the remaining ½ cup of water, sweeteners, and salt. With the heat kept low, simmer the cranberries briefly until barely soft. Remove the pan from the heat; add the gelatin and stir until it is dissolved. Cool slightly.

Transfer the berries to a food processor and puree. Put them in a medium mixing bowl; chill the berries until they begin to thicken.

Beat the cream until it is thick, firm, but not stiff and mix this into the cranberries. Spoon the cranberries into dessert glasses or a dessert bowl. Chill until set. Decorate with dollops of whipped cream if you like. For Whipped Cream Sauce, see page 253. Add gram counts as needed.

Dessert Crepes

A delicious dessert you can whip up in minutes and use in many winning ways. If you like these, you might also want to try making the very thin breakfast crepes with delicious fillings found in the Low-Carb Comfort Food Cookbook. *Some of those fillings would also go well with these crepes.*

PREPARATION TIME: 12 minutes.

SERVING SIZE: 1 crepe. AMOUNT PER SERVING: 2.1 grams of carb, 8.3 grams of protein. TOTAL YIELD: about 4 crepes.

		CHO (g)	PRO (g)
3	eggs	1.8	18.0
2	egg whites	0.6	6.0
¼	cup sour cream	2.0	1.2
2	tablespoons Splenda	3.0	0
2	tablespoons soy protein powder	0	8.0
1	teaspoon vanilla extract	0.5	0
½	teaspoon baking powder	0.6	0
	salt, trace	0	0
	unsalted butter, as needed, for cooking crepes	0	0
	Total	*8.5*	*33.2*

Put all the ingredients in a food processor or blender and process just until well combined, about 15 seconds.

Heat a 10-inch crepe skillet over medium heat. Add about 1 teaspoon of butter to the skillet. The butter should sizzle slightly, but it should not turn brown; if it does, promptly lower the heat. Pour approximately ¼ cup of the batter into the skillet and swirl it to cover the whole bottom. As soon as the edge of the crepe begins to look a little dry or takes on a faint coloring—within about a minute—gently flip the crepe. Put it back into the skillet for 5 seconds, just long enough to dry off on that side. The crepe is finished.

For an instant dessert, fill each crepe with ⅓ cup of raspberries, strawberries, blueberries, or small chunks of honeydew melons. Place the fruits along the center of the crepe. Sprinkle a package of Splenda on top and cover the fruit, or the crepe when it is rolled up, with sweetened whipped cream (see Whipped Cream Sauce on page 253). Add the extra carb grams. Berry carb counts for ⅓ cup are: raspberries, 1.4; strawberries, 1.6; blueberries, 5.3; honeydew melon, 4.8.

Raspberry Bread Pudding

A delicious treat and high in protein.

PREPARATION TIME: 30 minutes (if crepes are available). BAKING TIME: 30 to 35 minutes.

SERVING SIZE: ⅙ of yield. AMOUNT PER SERVING: 5.6 grams of carb, 9.0 grams of protein. TOTAL YIELD: about 6 servings.

		CHO (g)	PRO (g)
1	recipe Dessert Crepes (page 239)	8.5	33.2
1	cup raspberries	5.9	1.0
3	eggs, separated	1.8	18.0
½	cup heavy cream	3.2	2.0
2	tablespoons xylitol	3.6	0
3	tablespoons Splenda	4.5	0
1	tablespoon Wondra flour	5.7	0
1	teaspoon vanilla extract	0.5	0
	salt, trace	0	0
	Total	*33.7*	*54.2*

Preheat the oven to 350°F. Butter a 1- or 1½-quart casserole.

Pile up the crepes on top of one another and cut them into half-inch strips in one direction and then the same in the opposite direction. Put the pieces of crepes in the baking dish. Put the raspberries on top of the crepes.

In a 1-quart saucepan, whisk together the egg yolks, heavy cream, sweeteners, and flour over low heat until the mixture thickens. Remove from the heat. Add the vanilla extract and the salt.

Beat the egg whites until stiff but still holding soft peaks. Fold them into the egg mixture. Spoon this mixture over the crepes and the berries. Bake the casserole for about 30 to 35 minutes or until the pudding is lightly browned. Serve hot. A touch of ice cream goes well with this. Add the extra carb grams.

Variation: Peanut Butter Bread Pudding

Follow the directions for Raspberry Bread Pudding above. Make these changes: omit the raspberries. Add 4 tablespoons of natural peanut butter and 1 ounce of sugar-free chocolate chips to the egg mixture before beating in the egg whites. Spoon over the crepes. The carb gram count per serving increases by 2.0 grams; protein increases by 2.7 grams.

Frozen Yogurt Ice Cream

Homemade frozen desserts that are churned in an ice cream machine are hard to beat. The ice cream tastes best when freshly made, though, and does not keep as well as commercial ice creams. Plan on making small portions and doing it often. The chore is fairly minimal. Make the ice cream mix a few hours ahead of time. Any cooked ingredients need to be chilled thoroughly.

PREPARATION TIME: 15 minutes (plus 15 to 25 minutes for churning). Requires refrigeration.

SERVING SIZE: ⅐ of yield. AMOUNT PER SERVING: 4.6 grams of carb, 3.5 gram of protein. TOTAL YIELD: 7 servings, about ½ cup each.

		CHO (g)	PRO (g)
3	egg yolks	0.9	9.0
2	tablespoons xylitol	3.6	0
4	tablespoons Splenda	6.0	0
1	cup heavy cream	6.4	4.8
1	8-ounce cup of plain (full-fat) yogurt	14.0	11.0
2	teaspoons vanilla extract	1.0	0
	Total	*31.9*	*24.8*

In the top of a double boiler (off heat) combine the egg yolks and the sweeteners. Beat until thick. Beat in the heavy cream and set the pot over simmering water. With a balloon whisk, beat the mixture occasionally at first. Beat continuously once the mixture is heating up and until it thickens. Remove from heat. Add the yogurt and the vanilla extract; beat until well mixed.

Cover and refrigerate this mixture for several hours until chilled. Stir occasionally to prevent a skin from forming. About an hour before serving time, make the ice cream, following the manufacturer's instructions. Churning takes from 15 to 25 minutes. Serve soon afterward.

Coconut Ice Cream

Perfect for a hot summer day.

PREPARATION TIME: 15 minutes (plus 15 to 25 minutes for churning). Requires refrigeration.

SERVING SIZE: ⅐ of yield. AMOUNT PER SERVING: 3.6 grams of carb, 3.1 grams of protein. TOTAL YIELD: 7 servings, about ½ cup each.

	CHO (g)	PRO (g)
½ cup toasted coconut, finely grated	3.0	3.0
4 egg yolks	1.2	11.2
2 tablespoons xylitol	3.6	0
4 tablespoons Splenda	6.0	0
1 cup heavy cream	6.4	4.8
2 teaspoons vanilla extract	1.0	0
1 cup coconut milk, canned	4.0	3.0
Total	*25.2*	*22.0*

Toast the grated coconut. Heat a heavy, small skillet over medium heat and put the coconut in it when the skillet is hot. Stir constantly. This takes but minutes. Remove the skillet from the heat as soon as the coconut turns color and quickly empty it into another container. Set aside.

In the top of a double boiler (off heat), combine the egg yolks and sweeteners. Beat until thick. Beat in the heavy cream and set the pot over simmering water. Beat occasionally at first. As soon as the mixture begins to heat up and steam rises, beat continuously until it thickens. A balloon whisk works well for this. Remove from the heat. Add the vanilla extract and the coconut milk and beat for a moment longer.

Cover and refrigerate for several hours until chilled. Stir occasionally to prevent a skin from forming. About one hour before serving time, make the ice cream, following the manufacturer's instructions. Churning takes from 15 to 25 minutes. Serve soon afterward.

Strawberry Sherbet

This is delicious and soothing.

PREPARATION TIME: 15 minutes (plus 15 to 25 minutes for churning). Requires refrigeration.

SERVING SIZE: ⅐ of yield. AMOUNT PER SERVING: 5.6 grams of carb, less than 1.0 gram of protein. TOTAL YIELD: 7 servings, about ½ cup each.

		CHO (g)	PRO (g)
2	cups fresh, ripe strawberries	15.6	1.0
4	tablespoons xylitol	7.2	0
7	tablespoons Splenda	10.5	0
1	tablespoon lemon juice	1.3	0
¾	cup heavy cream (optional)	4.8	3.6
	Total	*39.4*	*4.6*

Use only clean strawberries without blemishes. Put them in a food processor or a blender and puree; transfer to a mixing bowl.

Add the sweeteners and the lemon juice. Stir well. Refrigerate the strawberries until they are thoroughly chilled.

If you want to use the cream—it makes a cross between ice cream and sherbet but is delicious—add this when you are ready to put the mixture in the ice cream machine. Make the sherbet about an hour before serving time, following the manufacturer's instructions. Churning takes from 15 to 25 minutes. Serve promptly.

Peach Ice Cream

Simply scrumptious.

PREPARATION TIME: 15 minutes (plus 15 to 25 minutes for churning). Requires refrigeration.

SERVING SIZE: ⅛ of yield. AMOUNT PER SERVING: 6.8 grams of carb, 3.1 grams of protein. TOTAL YIELD: 7 to 8 servings, about ½ cup each.

		CHO (g)	PRO (g)
1	cup fresh, ripe peaches	17.0	1.0
4	egg yolks	1.2	11.2
3	tablespoons xylitol	5.4	0
5	tablespoons Splenda	7.5	0
1	cup heavy cream	6.4	4.8
¾	cup half-and-half	7.8	5.0
	Total	*45.3*	*22.0*

Peel, slice, and cut the peaches into small chunks. Crush lightly. Set aside.

In the top of a double boiler (off heat), combine the egg yolks and sweeteners. Beat until thick. Beat in the heavy cream and set the pot over simmering water. With a balloon whisk, beat the mixture occasionally as it heats up. Keep a close eye on it. As soon as steam begins to escape, beat continuously until the mixture becomes thick. Stir in the half-and-half and the peaches.

Cover and refrigerate this mixture for several hours until chilled. About one hour before serving time, put the ice cream mixture in the ice cream machine, following manufacturer's instructions. Serve soon after the ice cream is ready (churning usually takes 15 to 25 minutes).

Peanut Butter Swirl Ice Cream

Comfort food at its best.

PREPARATION TIME: 15 minutes (plus 15 to 25 minutes for churning). Requires refrigeration.

SERVING SIZE: ⅛ of yield. AMOUNT PER SERVING: 6.9 grams of carb, 5.7 grams of protein. TOTAL YIELD: 7 to 8 servings, about ½ cup each.

		CHO (g)	PRO (g)
4	egg yolks	1.2	11.2
4	tablespoons xylitol	7.2	0
7	tablespoons Splenda	10.5	0
1	cup heavy cream	6.4	4.8
¾	cup half-and-half	7.8	5.0
2	teaspoons vanilla extract	1.0	0
⅓	cup natural peanut butter	13.3	19.0
	Total	*47.4*	*40.0*

Put the egg yolks and the sweeteners in the top of a double boiler (off heat) and beat until creamy. Beat in the heavy cream. Put the pot over simmering water and beat the mixture with a balloon whisk. Beat it occasionally at first, but once the mixture heats up and steam begins to escape, beat it continuously until it thickens. Remove from the heat. Add the half-and-half and the vanilla extract. Stir well.

Cover and refrigerate this mixture for several hours until chilled. About an hour before serving time make the ice cream, following the manufacturer's instructions. Serve soon after the ice cream is ready (churning usually takes 15 to 25 minutes).

When the ice cream is ready, put it in a mixing bowl. Stir the peanut butter carefully into the ice cream, creating swirls and ribbons. Return the ice cream to the freezer. Serve promptly.

Easy Freezer Vanilla Ice Cream

Still-frozen ice cream, while not as spectacular as the ice cream that comes out of the ice cream machine, is truly excellent and enjoyable; it also keeps fairly well in the freezer for a month or so.

PREPARATION TIME: 15 minutes. Requires chilling during preparation.
SERVING SIZE: ⅛ of yield. AMOUNT PER SERVING: 3.8 grams of carb, 1.9 grams of protein. TOTAL YIELD: 7 to 8 servings, about ½ cup each.

		CHO (g)	PRO (g)
2	teaspoons gelatin	0	4.0
¼	cup cold water	0	0
½	cup half-and-half	5.2	4.0
1¼	cups heavy cream	8.0	6.0
3	tablespoons xylitol	5.4	0
5	tablespoons Splenda	7.5	0
2	teaspoons vanilla extract	1.0	0
	salt, trace	0	0
	Total	*27.1*	*13.0*

Soak the gelatin in the cold water.

Combine the half-and-half, ¼ cup of heavy cream, and sweeteners in a heavy-bottomed medium saucepan over low heat. Stir occasionally, increasing as the cream heats up. When bubbles begin to form—bring to a near boil—remove it from the heat and stir in the gelatin. Stir in the vanilla extract and the salt.

Refrigerate the mixture until it begins to thicken, about 60 minutes or so. Whisk it once or twice to prevent a skin from forming.

In a medium mixing bowl, beat the remaining heavy cream until it is firm but still soft. Gradually add the cooled, slightly thickened gelatin mixture to the whipped cream.

Set the bowl in the freezer compartment of the fridge. It will take several hours for the ice cream to freeze. During that time, take it out once or twice and beat it again with a sturdy balloon whisk or use a fork to fluff it up if it has become too hard to beat. Transfer to a storage container. This ice cream keeps fairly well. The trick to getting perfect ice cream every time is to take it out of the freezer about 30 to 40 minutes before you want to use it. Allow it to soften. Beat it briefly with a sturdy small balloon whisk and return to the freezer until serving time. This ice cream is also great to use in milk shakes, whey smoothies, and other frosty treats.

Easy Freezer Lemon Ice Cream

This is a deliciously tangy and refreshing ice cream.

PREPARATION TIME: 15 minutes. Requires chilling during preparation.
SERVING SIZE: ⅛ of yield. AMOUNT PER SERVING: 5.3 grams of carb, 1.4
grams of protein. TOTAL YIELD: 7 to 8 servings, about ½ cup each.

		CHO (g)	PRO (g)
2	teaspoons gelatin	0	4.0
¼	cup cold water	0	0
¼	cup half-and-half	2.6	2.0
½	cup fresh lemon juice	10.4	0
1	cup heavy cream	6.4	4.8
4	tablespoons xylitol	7.2	0
7	tablespoons Splenda	10.5	0
	salt, trace	0	0
	Total	*37.1*	*10.8*

Soak the gelatin in the cold water.

Combine the half-and-half, lemon juice, ¼ cup of heavy cream, sweeteners, and salt in a heavy-bottomed medium saucepan over low heat. Stir occasionally. When the mixture heats up and bubbles begin to form—bring to a near boil—remove it from the heat and stir in the gelatin.

Refrigerate the mixture until it begins to thicken, about 60 minutes or so. Whisk it once or twice to prevent a skin from forming.

In a medium mixing bowl, beat the remaining heavy cream until it is firm but still soft. Gradually add the gelatin mixture to the whipped cream. Set the bowl in the freezer compartment of the fridge. It will take several hours for the ice cream to freeze. During that time, take it out once or twice and beat it again with a sturdy balloon whisk or use a fork to fluff it up if it has become too hard to beat. Transfer it to a storage container. This ice cream keeps fairly well. The trick to getting perfect ice cream every time is to take it out of the freezer about 30 to 40 minutes before you want to use it. Allow it to soften. Beat it briefly with a sturdy small balloon whisk and return to the freezer until serving time. This ice cream is also great to use in milk shakes, whey smoothies, and other frosty treats.

Easy Freezer Chocolate Ice Cream

An easy-to-make version of a rich old favorite.

PREPARATION TIME: 15 minutes. Requires chilling during preparation.
SERVING SIZE: ⅐ of yield. AMOUNT PER SERVING: 4.9 grams of carb, 2.5 grams of protein. TOTAL YIELD: 7 to 8 servings, about ½ cup each.

		CHO (g)	PRO (g)
2	teaspoons gelatin	0	4.0
¼	cup cold water	0	0
1¼	cups heavy cream	6.4	4.8
1	ounce unsweetened baking chocolate (1 square)	4.0	4.0
2	ounces sugar-free semisweet chocolate	5.4	2.0
½	cup half-and-half	5.2	4.0
3	tablespoons xylitol	5.4	0
5	tablespoons Splenda	7.5	0
2	teaspoons vanilla extract	1.0	0
	salt, trace	0	0
	Total	*34.9*	*18.8*

Soak the gelatin in the cold water.

Combine ¼ cup of the heavy cream (reserve the rest) and the chocolates in the top of a double boiler. Stir over hot water kept at or below a simmer. Stir and check frequently until the chocolate is melted. Remove the mixture from the heat and set aside.

Combine the half-and-half, ¼ cup of the heavy cream, sweeteners, vanilla extract, and salt in a heavy-bottomed medium saucepan over low heat. Stir occasionally and more often as the cream heats up. When it is hot, remove from the heat. Stir in the gelatin until it is dissolved. Add the melted chocolate.

Refrigerate the mixture until it begins to thicken, about 60 minutes. Whisk it once or twice to prevent a skin from forming.

In a medium mixing bowl, beat the remaining heavy cream until it is firm but still soft. Gradually add the cooled, slightly thickened gelatin mixture to the whipped cream.

Set the bowl in the freezer compartment of the fridge. It will take several hours for the ice cream to freeze. During that time, take it out once or twice and beat it again with a sturdy balloon whisk or use a fork to fluff it up if it has become too hard to beat. Transfer it to a storage container. This ice cream keeps fairly well. The trick to getting perfect ice cream every time is to take it out of the freezer about 30 to 40 minutes before you want to use it. Allow it to soften. Beat it briefly with a sturdy small balloon whisk and return to the freezer until serving time. This ice cream is also great to use in milk shakes, whey smoothies, and other frozen treats.

Basic Custard Sauce

A velvety sauce that is easy to make. A little of this will improve many desserts. Stevia sweetener has been left out of this recipe to make sure no aftertaste is present. If you wish, though, feel free to add it. Serve hot or cold.

PREPARATION TIME: 15 minutes.

SERVING SIZE: ¼ cup. AMOUNT PER SERVING: 2.4 grams of carb, 2.6 grams of protein. TOTAL YIELD: approximately 9 servings.

		CHO (g)	PRO (g)
1½	cups heavy cream	9.6	7.2
½	cup water	0	0
6	egg yolks	1.8	16.8
2	tablespoons xylitol	3.6	0
4	tablespoons Splenda	6.0	0
	salt, trace	0	0
2	teaspoons vanilla extract	1.0	0
	Total	22.0	24.0

Slowly heat ½ cup of the heavy cream and the water in a double boiler set over hot water kept at or below a simmer.

Meanwhile, put the egg yolks, sweeteners, and salt in a mixing bowl and beat until thick and fluffy. Once the cream is hot, add about 2 tablespoons of the hot liquid to the egg yolks, beating as you do. Repeat this two more times, beating well after each addition. Add the yolks to the double boiler and beat the mixture continuously until it thickens. Add the vanilla extract and remove from the heat. Add the remaining cream and beat well. Strain this sauce if you wish. Refrigerate. You can serve the sauce cold or hot. To serve it hot, warm it in the microwave.

Variation: Lemon Custard Sauce

Follow the directions for Basic Custard Sauce above. Make these changes: replace the water with ⅓ cup of fresh lemon juice. One serving (¼ cup) increases by 0.8 gram of carbohydrate.

Variation: Orange Custard Sauce

Follow the directions for Basic Custard Sauce above. Make these changes: replace the water with ½ cup of fresh orange juice. One serving (¼ cup) increases by 0.9 gram of carbohydrate.

Chocolate Custard Sauce

Quick and easy to make. A little of this will go well with many desserts. Add stevia if you wish. Serve hot or cold.

PREPARATION TIME: 15 minutes.

SERVING SIZE: ¼ cup. AMOUNT PER SERVING: 2.7 grams of carb, 3.0 grams of protein. TOTAL YIELD: approximately 10 to 11 servings.

		CHO (g)	PRO (g)
1½	cups heavy cream	9.6	7.2
1	ounce unsweetened baking chocolate (1 square)	4.0	4.0
2	ounces sugar-free semisweet chocolate	5.4	2.0
½	cup water	0	0
6	egg yolks	1.8	16.8
2	tablespoons xylitol	3.6	0
4	tablespoons Splenda	6.0	0
	salt, trace	0	0
2	teaspoons vanilla extract	1.0	0
	Total	*27.4*	*30.0*

Combine ¼ cup of the heavy cream (reserve the rest) and the chocolates in the top of a double boiler. Stir over hot water kept at or below a simmer. Stir and check frequently until the chocolate is melted. Remove from the heat and set aside.

Slowly heat ½ cup of the heavy cream and the water in a double boiler set over hot water kept at or below a simmer.

Meanwhile, put the egg yolks, sweeteners, and salt in a mixing bowl and beat until thick and fluffy. Once the cream is hot, add about 2 tablespoons of the hot liquid to the egg yolks, beating as you do. Repeat this two more times, beating well after each addition. Add the yolks to the double boiler and beat the mixture continuously until it thickens. Add the vanilla extract and remove from the heat. Add the remaining cream and the melted chocolate. Beat well. Strain the sauce if you wish. Refrigerate. You can serve the sauce cold or hot. To serve it hot, warm it in the microwave.

Mocha Custard Sauce

Quick and easy to make, with all that mocha goodness. Add stevia if you wish. Serve hot or cold.

PREPARATION TIME: 15 minutes.

SERVING SIZE: ¼ cup. AMOUNT PER SERVING: 3.1 grams of carb, 3.0 grams of protein. TOTAL YIELD: approximately 10 to 11 servings.

		CHO (g)	PRO (g)
1½	cups heavy cream	9.6	7.2
1	ounce unsweetened baking chocolate (1 square)	4.0	4.0
2	ounces sugar-free semisweet chocolate	5.4	2.0
½	cup espresso or double-strength coffee	0	0
6	egg yolks	1.8	16.8
2	tablespoons xylitol	3.6	0
4	tablespoons Splenda	6.0	0
	salt, trace	0	0
2	teaspoons vanilla extract	1.0	0
	Total	*31.4*	*30.0*

Combine ¼ cup of the heavy cream (reserve the rest) and the chocolates in the top of a double boiler. Stir over hot water kept at or below a simmer. Stir and check frequently until the chocolate is melted. Remove from the heat and set aside.

Slowly heat ½ cup of the heavy cream and the espresso in a double boiler set over hot water kept at or below a simmer.

Meanwhile, put the egg yolks, sweeteners, and salt in a mixing bowl and beat until thick and fluffy. Once the cream is hot, add about 2 tablespoons of the hot liquid to the egg yolks, beating as you do. Repeat this two more times, beating well after each addition. Add the yolks to the double boiler and beat the mixture continuously until it thickens. Add the vanilla extract and remove from the heat. Add the remaining cream and the melted chocolate. Beat well. Strain the sauce if you wish. Refrigerate. You can serve the sauce cold or hot. To serve it hot, warm it in the microwave.

Whipped Cream Sauce

This one enhances any dessert in an instant.

PREPARATION TIME: 3 minutes.

SERVING SIZE: ⅙ of yield. AMOUNT PER SERVING: 2.2 grams of carb, 0.8 gram of protein. TOTAL YIELD: approximately 6 servings.

	CHO (g)	PRO (g)
1 cup heavy cream	6.4	4.8
4 tablespoons Splenda	6.0	0
1 tablespoon sour cream (optional)	0.5	0.3
Total	*12.9*	*5.1*

Whip the heavy cream until it is quite firm but still soft. Avoid overbeating. Add the sugar and the sour cream (if using). This will keep for a while in the fridge.

Blueberry Jam

Great stuff to replace all those hugely high-carb jams.

PREPARATION TIME: 10 minutes.

SERVING SIZE: 1 tablespoon. AMOUNT PER SERVING: 1.4 grams of carb, negligible protein. TOTAL YIELD: approximately 32 servings.

		CHO (g)	PRO (g)
2	cups fresh blueberries	32.0	1.0
1	tablespoon lemon juice	1.3	0
1	cup water		
5	teaspoons ThickenThin not/Sugar thickener*	0	0
3	tablespoons xylitol	5.4	0
5	tablespoons Splenda	7.5	0
2	teaspoons Stevia Plus (or equivalent)	0	0
	Total	*46.2*	*1.0*

Put the blueberries, lemon juice, and water in a medium saucepan and cook over very low heat for a few minutes; the blueberries should stay intact and soften only slightly. Put the berries in a food processor or a blender and puree lightly. Measure the amount to make sure it is 2 cups. Add water if necessary to make 2 full cups. Return the berries to the pan; reheat. Add the thickener before adding the sweeteners. Add these gradually, and taste the jam as you do. Do not use more sweeteners than needed to satisfy you. It is best to put the jam in small jars and freeze all but one.

Variation: Raspberry Jam

Follow the directions for Blueberry Jam above. Make these changes: combine 3 cups of raspberries with ¾ cup of water and 1 tablespoon of lemon juice. Put the mixture immediately in a food processor and puree. Measure the amount to make sure it is 2 cups. Add water if needed to make 2 full cups. Put the mixture in a saucepan and heat it briefly to add the thickener and the sweeteners. Remove from the heat and store in jars. One tablespoon of raspberry jam has 1.0 gram of carb.

*ThickenThin not/Sugar thickener from Expert Foods is available on the Internet. See also Sources.

7

CHOCOLATES
AND CANDIES

Most of these sweet treats take advantage of that wonderful creation, sugar-free chocolate sweetened with sugar alcohol. As you know, these are not entirely sugar-free and also can have unpleasant side effects if eaten in excess. Candies that do not use chocolate often also rely heavily on sugar alcohol because there is no other way to create them as deliciously. Unlike the other recipes in this book, with the exception of cookies, where you generally find diverse sweeteners and where you have the option of changing them if you like, the recipes in this chapter are a bit more restricted. However, when a recipe that calls for sugar-free chocolate requires an additional sweetener, only Splenda is used to reduce the amount of sugar alcohol. In those instances, you can also try substituting stevia for Splenda, if you like.

These days you can find much sugar-free chocolate on the market, in many flavors: semisweet, milk chocolate, dark chocolate, white chocolate. They are all expensive, mainly because sugar alcohol is expensive. You may want to experiment to see which chocolates you like best. Always check prices. Sugar-free chocolates are available from many sources on the Internet, although be aware that most vendors suspend shipping during the summer months. One vendor who ships year round is listed in the Sources. Some sugar-free chocolates are sold as thick blocks that you have to crack when you want to use them. I find that chocolates that are sold as small disks, for example, are more convenient to use. Chocolate chips are also good for melting. You will often have leftover chocolate from melting, and usually you can reheat it carefully to use again.

Many of the candies in this chapter are filled with nuts, seeds, coconut, peanut butter, and such, which help stretch the sugar-free chocolate and dilute the impact of the sugar alcohol.

The process of making these sweet treats is simple. Most of the time you are just required to melt ingredients. The exceptions are toffee-related candies, which require the sugar to be cooked for a while. However, all you do is time the process. No candy thermometer is needed.

If you find that you make candies quite a bit, you will want one piece of equipment that I have come to see as virtually indispensable—a marble slab. It is especially useful if chilled before using it, though the marble usually stays cool on its own. Either way, the slab speeds up the process of hardening the chocolate. In its absence use oiled ceramic or porcelain plates. You might want to wear disposable plastic gloves for all candy-making.

Look at these candies as special, delightful little treasures that will help you stay away from the high-carb world of empty calories and insulin spikes. It won't be hard—you will find your taste buds happily satisfied with the gems you find here. Not to mention that many are healthier and nutritious as well.

The recipes in this chapter are incredibly delicious—they will completely stop your longing to march into even the best chocolate store. It happened to me, and I think it will happen to you too. I also find that the sizes most often suggested as a serving size here, either ½ or ⅓ ounce, are just right, just sufficient for enjoyment, even if you take a second helping. Somehow it works out better to have two ½-ounce pieces than one 1-ounce piece. It is especially important to use a scale, certainly when you're first starting to make candy. After a while, you will get a good feel for these weights, right down to 10 or 11 grams, for example. The sizes are approximately like small and medium grapes, or ¾-inch squares. Enjoy these jewels—eat them sparingly and always take small bites!

Pecan Spread

You will find this spread to be irresistible. You can use it on low-carb toast , on ice cream, as a topping for custards. It is also great on waffles and crepes, both of which you can find in The Low-Carb Comfort Food Cookbook.

PREPARATION TIME: 15 minutes.

SERVING SIZE: 1 tablespoon. AMOUNT PER SERVING: 1.2 grams of carb, 0.7 gram of protein. TOTAL YIELD: about 2 cups.

		CHO (g)	PRO (g)
6	ounces toasted pecans, finely ground	10.8	15.6
4	ounces sugar-free milk chocolate	10.8	4.0
4	tablespoons unsalted butter (½ stick)	0	0
⅔	cup heavy cream	4.3	3.2
6	tablespoons Splenda	9.0	0
1	teaspoon Stevia Plus (or equivalent)	0	0
2	teaspoons vanilla extract	1.0	0
	salt, trace	0	0
	Total	*35.9*	*22.8*

For this recipe, it is best to grind your own toasted pecans as finely as you can; you need to watch them because they tend to get oily in a hurry. Don't let them get sticky, but some oiliness is okay.

Put all the other ingredients in a medium microwavable bowl; microwave for about 30 to 35 seconds or until the chocolate is melted. You can also do this in a double boiler over hot water; keep the water at or below a simmer. Stir until smooth.

Stir in the pecans. Cool slightly. The spread will be liquid at this time. It stays fresh for about 8 days in the fridge. You might consider dividing it into three portions and freezing two of them for later.

Once refrigerated it will become like butter. To turn it into a sauce, simply dilute a ¼ cup of Pecan Spread with 3 tablespoons of heavy cream and 1 tablespoon of water; add 1 tablespoon of Splenda. Each tablespoon has 1.0 gram of carb.

White Walnut Fudge

A delicious fudge that is easy to throw together. High in protein, it is made with white chocolate. Keep it refrigerated. This fudge keeps for several weeks and can be frozen.

PREPARATION TIME: 15 minutes (needs cooling during preparation).
SERVING SIZE: ½ ounce piece (14 grams). AMOUNT PER SERVING: 1.0 gram of carb, 2.7 grams of protein. TOTAL YIELD: about 15 ounces, 30 pieces.

	CHO (g)	PRO (g)
4 ounces sugar-free white chocolate	10.8	4.0
3 tablespoons unsalted butter (⅜ stick)	0	0
½ cup heavy cream	3.2	2.4
6 tablespoons Splenda	9.0	0
1 teaspoon Stevia Plus (or equivalent)	0	0
2 teaspoons vanilla extract	1.0	0
salt, trace	0	0
½ cup whey protein powder (natural, zero-carb)	0	40.0
5 ounces walnuts, coarsely chopped*	5.0	34.0
Total	*29.0*	*80.4*

Put all the ingredients, except for the whey protein powder and the walnuts, in a medium-size microwavable bowl. Microwave until the chocolate is melted, or about 30 seconds. You can also do this in a double boiler over hot water. Keep the water at or below a simmer. Stir vigorously until smooth.

Allow the mix to cool for a few minutes. Stir in the whey protein powder and the walnuts. Spread the fudge in a buttered 9-by-9-inch glass baking dish or one of a similar size. Level the fudge and allow it to harden. When it is hardened, cut it into small squares equal to half-ounce pieces. Best wrapped in foil candy wrappers, this fudge keeps for several weeks in the fridge.

*You can substitute 6 ounces of toasted, chopped pecans for the walnuts.

Hazelnut Squares

A delicious chocolatey/nutty treat.

PREPARATION TIME: 15 minutes (needs cooling during preparation).
SERVING SIZE: one ⅓-ounce serving (9.3 to 10 grams). AMOUNT PER SERVING: 1.0 gram of carb, less than 1.0 gram of protein. TOTAL YIELD: about 30 pieces.

	CHO (g)	PRO (g)
5 ounces sugar-free semisweet or milk chocolate	13.5	5.0
2 tablespoons heavy cream	0.8	0.6
4 tablespoons Splenda	6.0	0
1 teaspoon Stevia Plus (or equivalent)	0	0
1 teaspoon vanilla extract	0.5	0
salt, trace	0	0
4 ounces toasted hazelnuts, coarsely chopped	7.6	16.0
Total	*28.4*	*21.6*

Put all the ingredients except the hazelnuts in a medium microwavable bowl and microwave for about 35 to 40 seconds or until the chocolate is melted. You can do this in a double boiler over hot water; just keep the water at or below a simmer. Stir the mixture until it is smooth.

Stir in the hazelnuts. Allow the mixture to cool down and become quite firm but soft enough to shape. If you cool the mixture in the fridge, stir it occasionally to ensure uniform hardening. Shape the mixture into small squares, about ¾ inch and about 10 grams each, and set out on a cooling rack to dry some more. After 36 to 48 hours, wrap the candy in candy foil. You can keep it at normal room temperature for about a week; after that, store it in the fridge.

Smooth Fudge

Great, velvety stuff. As good as you remember from childhood.

PREPARATION TIME: 15 minutes (needs cooling during preparation).
SERVING SIZE: About ⅓ ounce (9.3 to 10.0 grams). AMOUNT PER SERVING:
1.2 grams of carb, less than 1.0 gram of protein. TOTAL YIELD: 30 pieces
(about 11 ounces).

		CHO (g)	PRO (g)
4	ounces sugar-free milk chocolate	10.8	4.0
4	ounces sugar-free semisweet chocolate	10.8	4.0
2	tablespoons unsalted butter (½ stick)	0	0
3	tablespoons heavy cream	1.2	0.9
2	tablespoons Splenda	3.0	0
1	teaspoon vanilla extract	1.0	8.9
	Total	*26.8*	*17.8*

Combine all ingredients in a medium microwavable bowl.
Microwave until the chocolate is melted, about 35 to 40 seconds. You
can also do this in a double boiler over hot water; keep the water at or
below a simmer. Stir the mixture until it is completely smooth; use a
small balloon whisk.

Spread the mixture in a buttered 7-by-7-inch glass baking dish or
one of a similar size. When it has solidified, cut it into small squares
(about ¾ inch and 10 grams each). Cover and store in the fridge, or cut
and wrap the pieces in candy foil.

Macadamia Nut or Pecan Fudge

Toasted nuts in a fudgy landscape—what could be bad?

PREPARATION TIME: 20 minutes (needs cooling during preparation).

SERVING SIZE: ½ ounce (14.0 grams). AMOUNT PER SERVING: 1.4 grams of carb, less than 1.0 gram of protein. TOTAL YIELD: 32 pieces (about 16 ounces).

		CHO (g)	PRO (g)
4	ounces sugar-free milk chocolate	10.8	4.0
4	ounces sugar-free semisweet chocolate	10.8	4.0
2	tablespoons unsalted butter (¼ stick)	0	0
4	tablespoons heavy cream	1.6	1.0
8	tablespoons Splenda	12.0	0
1	teaspoon vanilla extract	1.0	0
6	ounces toasted macadamia nuts or pecans, chopped	10.2	13.8
	Total	*46.4*	*22.8*

Combine all the ingredients except the nuts in a medium microwavable bowl. Microwave until the chocolate is melted, about 35 to 40 seconds. You can also do this in a double boiler over hot water; just keep the water at or below a simmer. Stir the mixture until it is completely smooth.

Add the chopped macadamia nuts or the pecans (the gram values are very close). Spread the mixture in a buttered 8-by-8 inch glass baking dish or one of a similar size. When the fudge has solidified, cut it into squares equal to 14 grams. Cover and store in the fridge, or cut and wrap the pieces in candy foil.

Date Coconut Balls

These taste as good as they sound.

PREPARATION TIME: 25 minutes (needs cooling during preparation).
SERVING SIZE: ⅓ ounce. AMOUNT PER SERVING: 1.5 grams of carb, negligible
amount of protein. TOTAL YIELD: thirty-three ⅓-ounce pieces, about 11
ounces.

	CHO (g)	PRO (g)
4 ounces sugar-free milk chocolate	10.8	4.0
2 tablespoons unsalted butter (¼ stick)	0	0
4 tablespoons heavy cream	1.6	1.2
4 tablespoons Splenda	6.0	0
1 teaspoon vanilla extract	1.0	0
1 teaspoon lemon juice	0.9	0
5 soft, pitted dates, chopped	25.0	2.0
1 cup unsweetened coconut, finely grated	6.0	6.0
Total	*51.3*	*13.2*

Combine all the ingredients except for the dates and the coconut in
a medium microwavable bowl. Microwave until the chocolate is
melted, about 25 seconds. You can also do this in a double boiler over
hot water; keep the water at or below a simmer. Stir the mixture until
it is completely smooth.

Cool the mixture slightly. Chop the dates into tiny pieces. Add
them along with the coconut to the chocolate mixture. Wait until the
candy is cool and firm enough to shape. If you cool it in the fridge,
stir the mixture occasionally to let it harden uniformly. When solid
enough to handle, shape it into balls the size of medium grapes (9.3 to
10 grams each).

Allow the candies to sit at room temperature for about 24 to 48
hours. After that, wrap them in candy foil. They can stay at room temperature for a few days. For longer periods, it is best to refrigerate the
candy.

Pecan Date Chews

These confections stay deliciously soft and are slightly chewy. The combination of dates, toasted pecans, chocolate, and a touch of lemon makes for a wonderful flavor. The dates boost carb counts, though.

PREPARATION TIME: 20 minutes (needs cooling during preparation).
SERVING SIZE: ⅓ ounce. AMOUNT PER SERVING: 1.9 grams of carb, less than 1.0 gram of protein. TOTAL YIELD: 36 pieces (12 ounces).

		CHO (g)	PRO (g)
4	ounces sugar-free milk chocolate	10.8	4.0
3	tablespoons heavy cream	1.2	0
3	tablespoons Splenda	4.5	0.9
1	teaspoons vanilla	1.0	0
1	teaspoon lemon juice	0.9	0
8	soft, pitted dates, chopped	40.0	2.0
5	ounces toasted pecans, chopped	9.0	15.0
	Total	*67.4*	*21.9*

Combine all the ingredients except the dates and the pecans in a medium microwavable bowl. Microwave until chocolate is melted, about 30 seconds. You can also do this in a double boiler over hot water; just keep the water at or below a simmer. Stir the mixture until it is completely smooth.

Cool the mixture slightly. Chop the dates into tiny pieces. Add them along with the pecans to the chocolate mixture. Wait until the candy is firm enough to shape. If you cool the candy down in the fridge, stir the mixture occasionally to let it harden uniformly. When solid enough to handle, shape it into small bars (about 10 grams and 1-by-¾-inch each).

Allow the candies to sit at room temperature for about 24 to 36 hours. After that, wrap them in candy foil. For longer periods, it is best to refrigerate the candy.

Variation: Orange-Flavored Pecan Date Chews

Follow the directions for Pecan Date Chews above. Make these changes: when you melt the chocolate and other ingredients, add 3 teaspoons of finely grated orange peel and 1 teaspoon of orange extract (more, if desired) to the mixture. This does not increase the carb count significantly.

Nutty Hi-Pro Mini Bars

It does not get better than this for a low-carb, high-protein treat.

PREPARATION TIME: 25 minutes (needs cooling during preparation).
SERVING SIZE: two ½-ounce bars. AMOUNT PER SERVING: 2.3 grams of carb,
  7.0 grams of protein. TOTAL YIELD: about fifteen 1-ounce pieces.

		CHO (g)	PRO (g)
4	tablespoons unsalted butter (½ stick)	0	0
5	ounces sugar-free white chocolate	13.5	5.0
2	teaspoons vanilla extract	1.0	0
4	tablespoons heavy cream	1.6	1.2
8	tablespoons Splenda	12.0	0
1	teaspoon Stevia Plus (or equivalent)	0	0
	salt, trace	0	0
¾	cup whey protein powder (natural, zero-carb)	0	60.0
6	ounces walnuts (about 1½ cups), finely chopped*	6.0	40.8
	Total	*34.1*	*107.0*

In a medium microwavable bowl, combine the butter, white chocolate, vanilla extract, heavy cream, sweeteners, and salt. Microwave
for about 35 to 40 seconds or until the chocolate is melted. You can do
the same in a double boiler; just keep the water at or below a simmer.
Remove from the heat as soon as the chocolate is melted. Stir well
until smooth.

Cool the mixture so you can work it with your hands. It takes just
2 minutes or so. Work in the whey protein powder and follow with the
finely chopped walnuts. (You can pulse the nuts in a food processor
once or twice, but do not grind them to a meal.) If the mixture is too
soft, add a bit more whey protein powder. If it is too dry, add a tablespoon of cream.

You can shape the mixture right away, but it is easier if you wait an
hour or two. Shape the mixture into small, ½-ounce bars (14 grams)—
that's about 1¼ inches long, ½ inch wide, and about the same height.

Put the bars on a cooling rack; this allows air to circulate underneath. The bars need to dry a little but should not dry out completely.
Wrap them individually in candy foil within 48 hours. Store the
candy in the fridge or the freezer.

---

*You can replace the walnuts with 6 ounces of toasted, finely chopped pecans. Changes in
gram counts are negligible for carb; protein drops by 3 grams per serving.

Pumpkin Seed Power Bars

You may be surprised to see how tasty pumpkin seeds can be in this high-protein treat.

PREPARATION TIME: 25 minutes (needs cooling during preparation).
SERVING SIZE: two ½-ounce bars. AMOUNT PER SERVING: 2.2 grams of carb,
  4.5 grams of protein. TOTAL YIELD: about sixteen 1-ounce pieces.

		CHO (g)	PRO (g)
4	tablespoons unsalted butter (½ stick)	0	0
5	ounces sugar-free milk chocolate	13.5	5.0
2	teaspoons vanilla extract	1.0	0
4	tablespoons heavy cream	1.6	1.2
8	tablespoons Splenda	12.0	0
1	teaspoon Stevia Plus (or equivalent)	0	0
	salt, trace	0	0
½	cup natural whey protein powder (natural, zero-carb)	0	40.0
¼	cup toasted sunflower seeds, chopped	2.3	6.3
½	cup toasted pumpkin seeds, coarsely chopped	5.0	18.8
	Total	*35.4*	*71.3*

In a medium microwavable bowl, combine the butter, chocolate, vanilla extract, heavy cream, sweeteners, and salt. Microwave for about 35 seconds or until the chocolate is melted. You can do the same in a double boiler; just keep the water at or below a simmer. Remove from the heat as soon as the chocolate is melted. Stir well and beat until smooth.

Cool the mixture for a few minutes so you can work it with your hands. Work in the whey protein powder and add the sunflower and pumpkin seeds. (You can pulse the seeds in a food processor once or twice; keep them coarse, though.) If the mixture is too soft, add a bit more whey protein powder. If it is not soft enough to shape, add a tablespoon of cream.

It is best to wait an hour or two to shape the bars. The firmer the dough, the neater the bars will look. Shape the mixture into small, ½-ounce bars (14 grams)—that's about 1½ inches long, ¾ inch wide, and about ½ inch thick.

Put them on a cooling rack; this allows air to circulate underneath. The bars need to dry for about 48 hours or longer. Wrap them individually in candy foil within a day. Store the bars in the fridge.

Peanut Sesame Power Bars

Great favorites, high protein.

PREPARATION TIME: 20 minutes (needs cooling during preparation).
SERVING SIZE: two ½-ounce bars. AMOUNT PER SERVING: 3.2 grams of carb,
   7.0 grams of protein. TOTAL YIELD: about fifteen 1-ounce pieces.

		CHO (g)	PRO (g)
4	ounces sugar-free white or milk chocolate	10.8	4.0
2	teaspoons vanilla extract	1.0	0
2	tablespoons heavy cream	0.8	0.6
8	tablespoons Splenda	12.0	0
1	teaspoon Stevia Plus (or equivalent)	0	0
	salt, trace	0	0
½	cup natural peanut butter	20.0	28.0
¾	cup whey protein powder (natural, zero-carb)	0	60.0
½	cup sesame seeds	6.0	14.0
	Total	*50.6*	*106.6*

In a medium microwavable bowl, combine the chocolate, vanilla extract, heavy cream, sweeteners, and salt. Microwave for about 30 seconds or until the chocolate is melted. You can do this in a double boiler over hot water too; just keep the water at or below a simmer. Remove from the heat as soon as the chocolate is melted. Stir well until smooth.

Stir in the peanut butter. Cool the mixture for a few minutes so you can work it with your hands. Work in the whey protein powder and add the sesame seeds. If the mixture is too soft to shape, add a bit more whey protein powder; if it is not soft enough, add a tablespoon of cream.

Wait an hour or two before shaping the bars. Shape into small, ½-ounce bars (14 grams)—that's about 1¼ inches long, ½ inch wide, and about ½ inch thick.

Put the bars on a cooling rack; this allows air to circulate underneath. The bars need to dry a little but should not dry out completely. Wrap them individually in candy foil within two to four days. Store the bars in the fridge or the freezer.

Coconut Bites

A big treat if you like coconut. Try them with a chocolate glaze; they are lower-carb without.

PREPARATION TIME: 20 minutes (needs cooling during preparation).

SERVING SIZE: two ½-ounce pieces (14.0 grams). AMOUNT PER SERVING: 2.8 grams of carb, 3.4 grams of protein. TOTAL YIELD: 34 pieces; about 17 ounces.

		CHO (g)	PRO (g)
5	tablespoons unsalted butter (⅝ stick)	0	0
4	ounces sugar-free white chocolate	10.8	4.0
4	tablespoons heavy cream	1.6	1.2
6	tablespoons Splenda	9.0	0
1	teaspoon Stevia Plus (or equivalent)	0	0
2	teaspoons vanilla extract	1.0	0
	salt, trace	0	0
1½	cups unsweetened coconut, finely grated	9.0	9.0
½	cup natural whey protein powder (instant, zero-carb)	0	40.0

CHOCOLATE GLAZE

5	ounces sugar-free semisweet or milk chocolate	13.5	4.0
5	tablespoons heavy cream	1.6	1.2
	Total	*46.2*	*59.4*

In a medium microwavable bowl combine the butter, white chocolate, heavy cream, sweeteners, vanilla extract, and salt. Microwave for about 35 seconds or until the chocolate is melted. You can do the same in a double boiler over hot water; just keep the water at or below a simmer. Stir the mixture well until smooth.

Cool the mixture for a couple of minutes and mix in the coconut flakes. Add the whey protein powder. If needed, add a little more whey protein powder for shaping. If the mixture is dry, add another tablespoon of heavy cream.

Wait for an hour or two before shaping the bars. It is easier to do when the mixture is firm. Shape into small, ½-ounce bars (14 grams)—that's about 1½ inches long, ¾ inch wide, and about ¾ inch thick. Put them on a cooling rack. Apply the glaze a few hours later or the next day.

To make the glaze, combine the chocolate with the heavy cream and microwave it in a small bowl until the chocolate is melted, about

35 seconds. Stir until completely smooth. Dip and coat the bars. A fork works well for this. Drain well and put the candies on an oiled marble slab or two oiled china plates. Allow them to harden completely, at least 48 hours or longer. Avoid humid conditions when the candy is hardening. The candy will keep well at room temperature for about a week. Otherwise, wrap the bars in candy foil and store in the fridge.

Low-Carb Marzipan
with Chocolate Glaze

Quick and easy; a dream come true for marzipan lovers. This confection is made partly with real almond paste, which is essential for the flavor. The paste does contain real sugar, but this is greatly diluted with help from the other ingredients, especially the whey protein powder, which helps maintain the special marzipan texture and adds nutritional value.

PREPARATION TIME: 30 minutes (needs cooling during preparation).
SERVING SIZE: 1 piece (⅓ ounce). AMOUNT PER SERVING: 1.3 grams of carb,
   1.5 grams of protein. TOTAL YIELD: 80 pieces.

		CHO (g)	PRO (g)
5	ounces sugar-free white chocolate	13.5	5.0
3½	ounces pure almond paste	60.6	10.0
6	tablespoons Splenda	9.0	0
2	tablespoons unsalted butter (¼ stick)	0	0
3	tablespoons heavy cream	1.2	0.9
2	teaspoons vanilla extract	1.0	0
1	teaspoon almond extract		
	(or as desired)	1.0	0
1	teaspoon lemon juice	0.4	0
	salt, trace	0	0
1¼	cup whey protein powder		
	(natural, zero-carb)	0	100.0

CHOCOLATE GLAZE

		CHO (g)	PRO (g)
5	ounces semisweet chocolate	13.5	5.0
4	tablespoons heavy cream	1.6	1.2
	Total	*101.8*	*122.1*

In a medium microwavable bowl, combine all the ingredients except for the whey protein powder. The almond paste should be cut or shaved into pieces about the size of small peas. Microwave this mixture until the chocolate is melted and the almond paste is soft, about 45 to 50 seconds. You can also do this in a double boiler over hot water; just keep the water at or below a simmer. Stir until the mixture is completely smooth; a small balloon whisk can be helpful here.

Cool the mixture slightly, for about 5 minutes. Mix in the whey protein powder with your hands (you may want to use plastic gloves) once the mixture is comfortable to handle. Create a smooth paste. Shape into balls the size of grapes, about 9 grams each. Put the balls on a cookie sheet or a tray to dry for several hours. If the balls sink slightly when you put them on the cookie sheet, add a touch more whey protein powder. Chill the balls for a couple of hours or overnight before glazing.

You are not limited to creating balls. Create any shape you like and paint the objects with vegetable colors. If you do, though, you have to store the marzipan in a closed container and refrigerate.

To make the chocolate glaze, combine the chocolate and the heavy cream in a small microwavable bowl. Microwave until the chocolate is melted, about 30 to 35 seconds. You can also do this in a double boiler over hot water; just keep the water at or below a simmer. Stir until completely smooth.

Coat the balls with chocolate, drain well (a fork works well for this), and put them on an oiled marble slab or oiled china plates. The chocolate will dry to the touch within hours and harden usually within 24 to 36 hours. Avoid humid conditions when the candy is hardening. The candy will not dry out for up to two weeks if kept at room temperature. If you plan to keep the candy for a longer time, wrap the pieces in candy foil and refrigerate.

Marzipan Toffee Confections

Your friends may not believe it's low-carb or that you made it.

PREPARATION TIME: 30 minutes (needs cooling during preparation).
SERVING SIZE: A ⅓-ounce piece (9 to 10 grams). AMOUNT PER SERVING:
1.3 grams of carb, 0.69 gram of protein. TOTAL YIELD: 58 pieces.

	CHO (g)	PRO (g)
3 ounces sugar-free white chocolate	8.1	3.0
2 ounces pure almond paste	32.0	2.0
1 tablespoon unsalted butter (⅛ stick)	0	0
2 tablespoons heavy cream	0.8	0
2 teaspoons vanilla extract	1.0	0
salt, trace	0	0
½ cup whey protein powder		
(natural, zero-carb)	0	40.0
2 ounces Pecan Toffee Crunch (page 278)	4.4	1.0
CHOCOLATE GLAZE		
5 ounces sugar-free semisweet chocolate	13.5	2.0
5 tablespoons heavy cream	1.6	1.2
Total	*61.4*	*49.2*

In a medium microwavable bowl, combine the white chocolate and all the other ingredients except for the whey protein powder and the Pecan Toffee Crunch. Cut or shave the almond paste into pieces about the size of small peas. Microwave the mixture until the chocolate is melted and the almond paste is soft, about 30 seconds. You can also do this in a double boiler over hot water; just keep the water at or below a simmer. Stir until the mixture is completely smooth; a small balloon whisk can be helpful.

Cool the mixture briefly until you can handle it comfortably and work in the whey protein powder. Create a smooth paste. Cool the paste until it is about room temperature. Put the Pecan Toffee Crunch in a small plastic bag and crush it into crumbs with a mallet or similar tool. Work the crushed pieces into the cooled paste. Shape the marzipan into balls the size of small grapes. Put them on a tray and refrigerate the balls for several hours or overnight.

To make the chocolate glaze, combine the chocolate and the heavy cream in a small microwavable bowl and microwave until the chocolate is melted, about 30 to 35 seconds. You can also do this in a double boiler over hot water; just keep the water at or below a simmer. Stir until completely smooth.

Coat the balls with chocolate, drain well (a fork works well for this), and put them on an oiled marble slab or oiled china plates. The chocolate will dry to the touch within hours and harden usually within 24 to 36 hours. Avoid humid conditions when the candy is hardening. The candy will keep well for up to two weeks at room temperature. If you plan to keep the candy for a longer time, wrap the pieces in candy foil and refrigerate.

Chocolate Marzipan

This is another way to make marzipan accessible without going to high-carb excesses. This is delicious—so eat sparingly.

PREPARATION TIME: 15 minutes (needs cooling during preparation).
SERVING SIZE: One ⅓-ounce piece. AMOUNT PER SERVING: 1.8 grams of carb, negligible protein. TOTAL YIELD: 33 pieces.

		CHO (g)	PRO (g)
8	ounces sugar-free semisweet or milk chocolate	20.8	8.0
3	tablespoons heavy cream	1.2	0.9
2	teaspoons vanilla extract	1.0	0
	salt, trace		
2	ounces pure almond paste	32.0	5.0
	Total	*55.0*	*13.9*

In a medium microwavable bowl combine all the ingredients except the almond paste. Microwave until the chocolate is melted, about 40 seconds. You can also do this over hot water kept at or below a simmer. Stir until the mixture is smooth. Set aside.

Cut the almond paste in small ¼-inch cubes or as small as possible. Allow the chocolate to thicken and cool to room temperature before stirring in the almond paste chunks (if the chocolate is too warm, the paste will soften and melt). Once the marzipan is mixed into the chocolate, allow the candy to harden further so you can shape it by hand. It is easier to shape a fairly firm mixture.

Shape the mixture into small squares (about 10 grams each). Set them on a tray or a cookie sheet to harden. Wrap the pieces in candy foil. They will keep for a few days at room temperature. Otherwise refrigerate.

Mocha Truffles

Melt-in your-mouth truffles with a chocolate glaze. The recipe makes a small portion. Double it if you like.

PREPARATION TIME: 20 minutes (needs cooling during preparation).
SERVING SIZE: one ⅓-ounce truffle. AMOUNT PER SERVING: 1.0 gram of carb, negligible protein. TOTAL YIELD: 18 pieces.

	CHO (g)	PRO (g)
3 ounces sugar-free semisweet chocolate	8.1	3.0
2 tablespoons Splenda	3.0	0
4 teaspoons heavy cream	0.5	0.3
1 teaspoon vanilla extract	0.5	0
4 teaspoons espresso or double-strength coffee	0	0
salt, trace	0	0
CHOCOLATE GLAZE		
2 ounces sugar-free semisweet chocolate or milk chocolate	5.4	2.0
2 tablespoons heavy cream	0.8	0.6
Total	*18.3*	*5.9*

In a small microwavable bowl, combine all the ingredients except for the glaze. Microwave until the chocolate is melted, about 20 seconds. You can also do this in a double boiler over hot water; just keep the water at or below a simmer. Stir the mixture until it is smooth.

Cool the mixture until it is firm enough to be shaped. If you chill it in the fridge, stir occasionally to ensure uniform thickening. Roll the truffles into balls the size of small grapes. Put them on a plate and chill them thoroughly, either for several hours or overnight.

To make the glaze, combine the chocolate and the heavy cream in a microwavable bowl. Microwave until the chocolate is melted, about 20 seconds. You can do this in a double boiler over hot water; keep the water at or below a simmer. Stir until smooth. Coat the chilled truffles with the chocolate. Drain well and put the truffles on an oiled marble slab or an oiled china plate (a fork works well for this). Allow the glaze to harden. It takes about 24 hours; the truffles will cease to be sticky much sooner, though, for you to taste them.

Within a day or two, wrap the truffles in candy foil and refrigerate.

Praline Truffles

These are impressively scrumptious but need a little more work than other truffles.

PREPARATION TIME: 25 minutes (needs cooling during preparation).
SERVING SIZE: one ⅓-ounce truffle. AMOUNT PER SERVING: 1.3 grams of carb, negligible protein. TOTAL YIELD: 18 pieces.

	CHO (g)	PRO (g)
3 ounces sugar-free semisweet or milk chocolate	8.1	3.0
2 tablespoons Splenda	3.0	0
3 teaspoons heavy cream	0.4	0
1 teaspoon vanilla extract	0.5	0
3 teaspoons espresso or double-strength coffee	0	0
salt, trace	0	0
2 ounces Praline (page 280)	4.4	1.0
CHOCOLATE GLAZE		
2 ounces sugar-free semisweet or milk chocolate	5.4	2.0
2 tablespoons heavy cream	0.8	0.6
Total	*22.6*	*6.9*

In a small microwavable bowl, combine all the ingredients except the praline. Microwave the mixture until the chocolate is melted, about 20 seconds. You can also do this in a double boiler over hot water; keep the water at or below a simmer. Stir the mixture until it is smooth.

It is best to cool this mixture in the fridge. Stir occasionally to ensure uniform thickening. When the mixture is cooled to room temperature, stir in the praline. Shape into balls the size of small grapes. Put them on a plate and chill them before glazing. Chill for several hours or overnight.

To make the glaze, combine the chocolate and the heavy cream in a microwavable bowl. Microwave until the chocolate is melted, about 20 seconds. You can do this in a double boiler over hot water; keep the water at or below a simmer. Stir until smooth. Coat the chilled truffles with the chocolate. Drain well and put the truffles quickly on an oiled marble slab or an oiled china plate. Allow the glaze to harden. It takes about 24 hours; the truffles will cease to be sticky much sooner, though, for you to taste them.

Within a day or two, wrap the truffles in candy foil and refrigerate.

Pecan Toffee Crunch

Candy heaven—perhaps the best single reason to get a marble slab. This recipe requires DiabetiSweet Brown Sugar Substitute and contains a fairly large amount of sugar alcohol.

PREPARATION TIME: 20 minutes.

SERVING SIZE: one ½-ounce piece. AMOUNT PER SERVING: 1.0 gram of carb, less than 1.0 gram of protein. TOTAL YIELD: twenty-four ½-ounce pieces.

		CHO (g)	PRO (g)
8	ounces toasted pecan halves or pieces	10.8	15.6
½	cup DiabetiSweet Brown Sugar Substitute	14.4	0
4	tablespoons unsalted butter (½ stick), soft	0	0
1	tablespoon water	0	0
1	teaspoon vanilla extract	0.5	0
	salt, trace	0	0
	Total	*25.2*	*15.6*

Coat a marble slab with oil or use two oiled china plates. Measure the pecans and put them aside.

Put all the ingredients, except the pecans, in a heavy-bottomed medium saucepan. Use medium-low heat to begin with; lower the heat once the mixture bubbles. Stir the mixture continuously and vigorously for 8 minutes. A wooden spoon works well for this. It will be thick, hot, and foamy when ready.

Remove the pan from the heat and stir in the pecans. Make sure that all the nuts are well coated. Put the mixture on the oiled marble slab or distribute on two oiled china plates. With a spoon or a fork, flatten the mixture so that the nuts are spread out in a single layer. You can increase or decrease the number of nuts. Within about 24 hours—depending on the humidity (avoid a humid day to do this)—the nuts will look gloriously glossy and be dry to the touch. Allow the nuts to dry completely, then store in a covered container. Some chewiness may remain for many days. The candy will become hard and brittle eventually. Do not store the candy until it does.

Variation: Macadamia Toffee Crunch

Follow the directions for Pecan Toffee Crunch above. Make these changes: substitute 1½ cups of toasted chopped macadamia nuts for the pecans. The carb gram count remains very close to the original recipe.

Peanut Brittle

You did not really believe you could have this, did you? In the interest of keeping the ratio of sugar to nuts low, this brittle has lots of peanuts. You can reduce the number of peanuts if you like.

PREPARATION TIME: 15 minutes.
SERVING SIZE: one ½-ounce piece. AMOUNT PER SERVING: 1.8 grams of carb, 2.3 gram protein. TOTAL YIELD: thirty-six ½-ounce pieces.

		CHO (g)	PRO (g)
1	12-ounce can of peanuts, lightly salted	36.0	84.0
⅔	cup DiabetiSweet Brown Sugar Substitute	28.8	0
5	tablespoons unsalted butter (⅝ stick), soft	0	0
1	tablespoon water	0	0
1	teaspoon vanilla extract	0.5	0
	salt, trace	0	0
	Total	*65.3*	*84.0*

Rub a marble slab with oil or use two oiled china plates. Open the can of peanuts and put them in a strainer to shake out all the loose salt. Measure the peanuts and put them aside.

Put all the ingredients, except the peanuts, in a heavy-bottomed medium saucepan. Use medium-low heat to begin with; lower the heat once the mixture bubbles. Stir the mixture continuously and vigorously for 8 minutes. A wooden spoon works well for this. It will be thick, hot, and foamy when ready.

Remove the pan from the heat and stir in the peanuts. Make sure that all the nuts are well coated. Put the mixture on the oiled marble slab or distribute on two oiled china plates. With a spoon or a fork, flatten the mixture so that the nuts are spread out in a single layer. Within about 24 hours—depending on the humidity (avoid a humid day to do this)—the nuts will look gloriously glossy and be dry to the touch. Allow to dry completely, then store in a covered container. Some chewiness may remain for many days, but the peanut brittle will become hard eventually. Do not store the brittle until it does.

Praline

This is a wonderful invention made from crushed candied nuts that can add sizzle and sparkle to many a dessert or candy. You can sprinkle it on ice cream, on tiramisu, on crème brûlée (for which you can successfully and deliciously use it instead of broiled sugar). Best of all, this is a cinch to make. There is no reason not to have it on hand.

PREPARATION TIME: 5 minutes (if Pecan Toffee Crunch or Peanut Brittle is available).

SERVING SIZE: 2 tablespoons. AMOUNT PER SERVING: 2.4 grams of carb, less than 1.0 gram of protein. TOTAL YIELD: 8 tablespoons (4 servings).

	CHO (g)	PRO (g)
4 ounces Pecan Toffee Crunch (page 278) or Peanut Brittle (page 279)* or Macadamia Toffee Crunch (page 278)	9.6	7.0
Total	*9.4*	*7.0*

Put the nuts of your choice in a small plastic bag and use a mallet or other utensil to crush them. Keep the nuts in a closed container until ready to serve. Avoid a humid environment. At serving time, sprinkle the crushed nuts over your dessert as desired.

*If you use Peanut Brittle, add 4.0 grams of carb to the total.

Macadamia Chocolate Clusters

As always, the quality of the chocolate is very important here. So enjoy!

PREPARATION TIME: 15 minutes plus toasting time for the nuts.
SERVING SIZE: ½ ounce. AMOUNT PER SERVING: 1.0 gram of carb, less than
  1.0 gram of protein. TOTAL YIELD: eighteen ½-ounce pieces.

	CHO (g)	PRO (g)
5 ounces toasted macadamia nuts, whole or halves	7.5	10.0
4 ounces sugar-free semisweet or milk chocolate	10.8	0
1 tablespoon heavy cream	0.4	0
Total	*18.7*	*10.0*

Rub a marble slab with oil or use one or two oiled china plates. Measure the macadamia nuts and set aside.

Melt the chocolate and the heavy cream in a microwave until the chocolate is melted, about 30 seconds. You can do this in a double boiler over hot water; keep the water at or below a simmer.

Stir until perfectly smooth. Pour the chocolate over the nuts. Wait until the chocolate begins to harden and set small clusters on the slab or plates. Allow the clusters to harden. They are edible within hours but need a couple of days or so to harden. Avoid a humid environment.

Variation: Pecan Chocolate Clusters

Follow the directions for Macadamia Chocolate Clusters above. Substitute the macadamia nuts with 5 ounces of toasted pecan halves. Use whole or lightly chopped nuts. There is an insignificant change in carb gram counts.

Candy Macaroons (Nut-Free)

It is hard to say which is the best candy in this chapter, but whichever it is, these macaroons must come close. Crunchy exterior, chewy interior. Heaven. Wait until you hear the raves.

PREPARATION TIME: 20 minutes. BAKING TIME: 30 to 34 minutes (requires two cookie sheets).

SERVING SIZE: one ⅓-ounce macaroon. AMOUNT PER SERVING: 0.8 gram of carb, less than 1.0 gram of protein. TOTAL YIELD: forty-eight ½-ounce pieces.

		CHO (g)	PRO (g)
½	cup DiabetiSweet Brown Sugar Substitute	14.4	0
10	tablespoons unsalted butter (1¼ stick), soft	0	0
2	tablespoons water	0	0
1	teaspoon vanilla extract	0.5	0
	salt, trace	0	0
3	cups unsweetened coconut, finely grated	18.0	18.0
3	egg whites	0.9	10.5
	Total	*33.8*	*28.0*

Preheat the oven to 325°F. Use two large cookie sheets with silicone-coated liners.

Put the sugar, 8 tablespoons of butter (reserve 2 tablespoons), water, vanilla extract, and salt in a heavy-bottomed medium saucepan. Use medium-low heat to begin with and stir continuously for 5 minutes (a wooden spoon works well for this). Reduce the heat when the mixture begins to bubble. Remove the pan from the heat.

Stir in the remaining butter. Wait about 10 minutes and stir in the coconut. In a medium mixing bowl, beat the egg whites until they are totally stiff. Fold the coconut mixture into the egg whites. Set small mounds on the cookie sheets. The cookies will flatten out slightly as they bake.

Bake the cookies for about 15 to 17 minutes per batch until they are golden brown all over. Transfer them to a cooling rack. Avoid a humid environment. These cookies will keep well for a few days and can be frozen. They can also be left out if you like crunchy cookies.

SOURCES

All of the items you may need for your low-carb pantry and kitchen can be found here. Check out their Web sites. However, with interest in the low-carb diet growing, so is the number of suppliers. You may want to investigate on your own and compare prices.

FOODS

Bob's Red Mill Natural Foods, Inc.
5209 S.E. International Way
Milwaukie, OR 97222
Phone: (toll-free) 800-349-2173; fax: 503-653-1339
E-mail: www.bobsredmill.com
Although Bob's Red Mill offers a broad range of products, its chief interest is whole grain. The Mill sells flaxseed meal; this meal is also available in many grocery stores.

Buy Gourmet Foods
www.buygourmetfoods.com
E-mail: info@gourmetfoods.com
Source of hazelnut meal.

Diabetic Friendly LLC
806 Morrison Road
Gahanna, OH 43230
Phone: 614-530-4058
www.diabeticfriendly.com
E-mail: info@diabeticfriendly.com
This company specializes in sugar-free foods and sweets and sells a variety of chocolates that are good for candy making. They ship chocolates year-round with no extra charge for insulated packaging. They also sell DiabetiSweet Brown Sugar Substitute, which is featured in many recipes. The sugar is made by Hi-Tech Pharmacal Co. Inc., Diabetes Care Division; www.diabeticprod-ucts.com. This sugar is also available elsewhere on the Internet. Diabetic

Friendly also sells Thicken Thin/not Starch thickener and Thicken Thin/not Sugar thickener, which are made by Expert Foods.

Global Sweet Polyols, LLC
125 Tremont Street
Rehoboth, MA 02769
Phone: (toll-free) 800-601-0688; fax: 800-778-2357
www.globalsweet.com
This company sells xylitol powdered sugar. Other vendors may sell this product too.

Lucy's Kitchen Shop, Inc.
930 Sixteenth Street
Bellingham, WA 98225
Phone: (toll-free) 888-484-2126
www.scdkitchen.com
Lucy's Kitchen Shop is a specialty store catering to people with colitis and other intestinal disorders. However, and it is the only reason it is listed here, this store sells a super-fine type of blanched almond meal. It is made by Campos Brothers (www.camposbrothers.com), a wholesale company that has developed a special way to process almonds. Prices for this meal are competitive with other blanched almond meals. The minimum order is 5 pounds. Regular blanched almond meal does work very well too. I have used it for years. This super-fine meal is very good, though. You might try both kinds and see which you like best.

MannaHarvest.Net
192 West 1480 South
Orem, UT 84058
Phone: (toll-free) 866-436-1390
www.mannaharvest.net
E-mail: support@mannaharvest.net
This company offers a broad selection of supplies and also carries xylitol. They sell many nut flours, including macadamia nut meal, defatted macadamia nut flour (finer than the meal), walnut meal and pecan meal, and also whole nuts.

TrueFoods Market
517 West 100 North
Providence, UT 84332
Phone: (toll-free) 800-758-8245
www.truefoodsmarket.com
E-mail: support@truefoodsmarket.com
This company offers a broad selection of supplies and also carries xylitol. They sell many nut flours, including macadamia nut meal, defatted macadamia nut flour (finer than the meal), walnut meal and pecan meal, and also whole nuts.

Vitamin Cottage—Natural Food Markets
12612 Alameda Parkway
Lakewood, CO 80228
Phone: (toll-free) 877-986-4600, ext. 129; fax: 303-986-1891
E-mail: mailorder@vitamincottage.com
Vitamin Cottage sells a broad selection of supplies. They are a source of natural, zero-carb whey protein powder, xylitol, and many stevia products too, as well as whole nuts. Vitamin Cottage also sells *The Low-Carb Baking and Dessert Cookbook* and the *Low-Carb Comfort Food Cookbook.* On orders over $100 they pay for shipping (unless the items are very heavy).

Nutty Guys
P.O. Box 1011
American Fork, UT 84003
Phone: 801-974-0633
Fax: 801-973-6734
www.nuttyguys.com
E-mail: nuttyguys@yahoo.com
Nutty Guys has a great selection of whole nuts and nut meals, including hazelnut meal, at very reasonable prices.

KITCHEN SUPPLIES AND EQUIPMENT

These suppliers carry just about all the kitchen stuff you might need, including scales and exopat (silicone-coated) cookie sheet liners. Silicone-coated mats, also known as Exopat mats and Silpat mats, are available in many housewares stores or department stores, including Macy's, Chef's, Sur La Table, and Williams-Sonoma. All will send catalogs upon request.

Chef's
P.O. Box 620048
Dallas, TX 75262-0048
Phone: (toll-free) 800-338-3232; fax: 800-967-3291
E-mail: www.chefscatalog.com
Chef's offers a broad range of kitchen supplies and equipment.

Med-Express
P.O. Box 1192
Arden, NC 28704
Phone: (toll-free) 800-447-0495
E-mail: www.med-express.com
Med-Express sells inexpensive disposable latex and vinyl gloves. The minimum order is four boxes.

Sur La Table
1765 Sixth Avenue South
Seattle, WA 98134
www.surlatable.com
customerservice@surlatable.com
Phone: (toll-free) 866-328-5416 (customer service)
800-243-0852 (to place an order)
Sur La Table offers a broad range of kitchen supplies and tools.

Williams-Sonoma
Phone: (toll-free) 877-812-6235
www.williams-sonoma.com
Williams-Sonoma offers a broad range of kitchen supplies and tools, including heavy-duty springform pans in various sizes.

BOOKS

The Low-Carb Comfort Food Cookbook
By Michael R. Eades, M.D., Mary Dan Eades, M.D., and Ursula Solom
From John Wiley & Sons
ISBN 0-471-26757-0 (hardcover)

30-Day Low-Carb Diet Solution
By Michael R. Eades, M.D., and Mary Dan Eades, M.D.
From John Wiley & Sons
ISBN 0-471-43050-1 (hardcover)
ISBN 0-471-45415-X (paperback)

INDEX